C000068550

Deer Women and Elk Men

THE LAKOTA NARRATIVES OF ELLA DELORIA

Deer Women and Elk Men

THE LAKOTA NARRATIVES OF ELLA DELORIA

Julian Rice

UNIVERSITY OF NEW MEXICO PRESS
ALBUQUERQUE

Library of Congress Cataloging-in-Publication Data

Deloria, Ella Cara.
    Deer women and elk men : the Lakota narratives of Ella Deloria /
Julian Rice.
        p.   cm.
    Includes index.
    ISBN 0-8263-1362-0
    1. Dakota Indians—Folklore. 2. Dakota Indians—Sexual behavior.
3. Lakota dialect—Grammar. 4. Lakota dialect—Social aspects.
5. Deloria, Ella Cara. I. Rice, Julian, 1940- . II. Title.
E99.D1D37   1992
398.2'089975—dc20   91-46077
                                                              CIP

Parts of chapter 7 appeared in "Ella Deloria's *Waterlily*,"
North Dakota Quarterly 56.4 (Fall 1988): 39–44.

© 1992 by the University of New Mexico Press
All rights reserved.
First edition

For Carol

Contents

Acknowledgments

The audiotape of Pete Catches referred to in the introduction was obtained at the Oglala Lakota College archives with the assistance of its director, Ted Hamilton, and his assistant, Belva Hollow Horn.

Vine Deloria, Jr. granted permission to quote from several unpublished manuscripts by Ella Deloria: Correspondence with Franz Boas (1927–1934), *Dakota Autobiographies, Dakota Commentary on Walker's Texts, Dakota Tales in Colloquial Style,* and *Teton Myths* (the George Bushotter collection). All are housed in the Boas Collection of the American Philosophical Society in Philadelphia.

The South Dakota Historical Society granted permission to quote from the unpublished book, *Camp Circle Society* by Ella Deloria. Marvene Riis, archivist, facilitated access to the manuscript.

Two of the songs referred to in chapter 2 were collected by Kevin Locke, the foremost living practitioner of the Lakota courting flute. One song was recorded on "Lakota Wiikijo Olowan: Lakota Flute Music by Kevin Locke" (Pipestone, Minnesota: Featherstone, 1983). The other was sung by an elderly man on a personally owned tape that Mr. Locke permitted me to hear.

Parts of chapter 7 appeared in "Ella Deloria's *Waterlily,*" *North Dakota Quarterly* 56.4 (Fall 1988): 39–44.

1
Introduction

ELLA DELORIA'S ACHIEVEMENT in linguistics and ethnology has long
been known and admired. In 1988 her posthumous novel, *Waterlily*,
was enthusiastically received by an international readership. Since
Waterlily is in English, many of its readers may not know that Deloria
wrote thousands of narrative pages in the Santee, Yankton, and Lakota
dialects of her own Dakota language. Like Walker, Wissler, and Boas
before here, Deloria used "Dakota" in preference to "Sioux" to ge-
nerically designate several tribal groups living primarily in Minnesota
and South Dakota. Their band divisions, dialects, and the word "Sioux"
as a French corruption of the Ojibway word for "snake," have been
explained in almost every published study of the tribe (see the sum-
maries in Powers, *Oglala Religion* 3–14 and Nurge xii–xv). For present
purposes it is sufficient to say that the Minnesota and western "Sioux"
have mutually intelligible languages, diverging most noticeably in the
replacement of *d* with *l* by the western Lakota, as they call themselves.
A third dialect spoken by a smaller group in south-central South
Dakota uses *n* where their eastern and western relatives use *d* or *l*.
They are Nakota.

   The Lakota are the largest and most historically prominent group,
the Teton Sioux of Red Cloud, Spotted Tail, Sitting Bull, and Crazy
Horse. Even the Lakota names of the four principal bands have be-

come universally familiar: Oglala, Siċaṅġu (Brulé), Huṅkpapa, and Mnikowoju. Whether she acknowledged this interest, found more Lakota-speaking storytellers, or assumed that greater Teton numbers enhanced linguistic survival, Deloria wrote more pages in Lakota than anyone else before or since. This is the first of three volumes intended to introduce her creation of a unique form of fiction adapted from the oral tradition and set down for the first time as a Lakota language literature, respecting but not deferring to its oral source.

Ella's father, the Reverend Philip Deloria, born in 1858, spent his childhood in a traditional Yankton camp circle and was one of the first Dakota (eastern, central, or western) to receive a college education and to be ordained in the Episcopal Church. Ella's mother was also a Yankton, but since Philip Deloria was assigned to St. Elizabeth's Mission on the Standing Rock Reservation one year after Ella was born, her childhood and most of her adolescence were spent among Sitting Bull's people, the Huṅkpapa, who spoke Lakota. During this time the advanced English spoken by both of her parents did not prevent Nakota from being the "primary language in the Deloria home" (Picotte, "Biographical Sketch" in *Waterlily* 230; brief biographies also appear in the 1983 edition of *Dakota Texts*, *Speaking of Indians*, and Murray).

Her formal education nourished this bicultural beginning. As a 1915 graduate of Columbia University, she worked under Franz Boas and Ruth Benedict and was a contemporary of Margaret Mead and Ruth Bunzel. Her published writings comprise a small percentage of her scholarship in linguistics, ethnology, and folklore, most of which is now housed in manuscript at the American Philosophical Society in Philadelphia. It seems clear in retrospect that much of the writing was not published because Deloria never received the financial support she needed to carry it through. After her mother's death in 1916 she assumed the care of her adolescent brother and sister, and this responsibility continued for about ten years after her graduation from Columbia. Even when she began to work seriously again under Boas in 1929, the care of her aging father forced her to delay and otherwise restrict her research: "I like the work and hope always to come back, but I have been unable to. I know white people leave their parents and go off, but we are not trained that way, and I can't bring myself to do it till I have things arranged as I plan, and am working on" (letter to Boas, 4 October 1929).

Even then, however, Deloria was forced to spend more time than scholars like Mead or Benedict in seeking the financial support she rarely got. In 1935 she suggested to Boas that institutional funds were not forthcoming because she "did not have a degree after my name," and she regretted that she "did not think of that in time" (letter to Boas, 5 December 1935). Boas provided intermittent paid assignments, but one wonders how Deloria would be regarded today if she had obtained the requisite academic keys. Although she was respected at Columbia, she was forced to work as an informant rather than a colleague, conducting research for Boas rather than for herself. In 1935 she wrote to Eleanor Roosevelt, seeking a research or educational appointment on any Dakota reservation. The federal government usually filled such positions with non-Indians, and President Roosevelt's wife sent no reply, personal or official.

In 1936 she had to refuse Boas's recommendation that she come to Columbia to rework the many texts she had collected during the previous seven years. In a letter from Martin, South Dakota, she reports that blizzard conditions, thirty-two-below-zero temperatures, and blocked roads have stopped her from collecting stories, and that she cannot return to New York because she must "provide the roof" for her sister, nieces, and nephews: "To leave them would not be right; besides we have no home at all. I live in my car, virtually; all our things are in it. And if I go anywhere, I find it cheapest to go in my car; and take my sister with me. I love her, I can not do otherwise than give her a home of sorts" (letter to Boas, 7 February 1936). After a lengthy explanation of her responsibilities, she tells Boas that his offer of financial assistance has been appreciated but is simply insufficient.

At this time Deloria was forty-seven years old, as advanced in linguistic and ethnological skill as Margaret Mead but still having to live on a research assistant's wage. She closes her letter with an ironic reflection on competitive scholarship, monetary necessity, and the continuing social invisibility of Indian people, even those who had bought the assimilationist promise of prosperity and prestige in return for education and effort:

If I might be able to collect material for say another two or three months; and then stop, by then I could better myself, I am quite sure. I used to be satisfied to go from year to year, taking a chance; but I guess I have grown up at last. I see everyone else trying to better themselves; and I think I should too. And I do not think it safe to try returning to New York for one hundred dollars a month, with all I have on my mind to do. Isn't it too bad Mrs. Roosevelt never even acknowledged my letter? If she had, it would all have been so nice, for I do love working with you on Dakota. . . (letter to Boas, 7 February 1936)

At least Margaret Mead recognized Deloria's scholarship and, in particular, her literary skill. In introducing her long, still unpublished ethnographic volume, entitled variously *Camp Circle Society*, *Dakota Family Life*, and *The Dakota Way of Life* (1954), Mead praises her for being a better writer than most ethnographers. Deloria's linguistic work was already known, especially through *Dakota Grammar* (1941), coauthored with Boas, and the three-dialect dictionary, then in manuscript (and soon to be published in an augmented form by Agnes Picotte). The introduction refers to Deloria's "disciplined scientific inquiry," but Mead's strongest advocacy resembles literary criticism: "Miss Deloria has produced a volume which supplements, in cadence and image, the formal descriptions with the introspective reality" (Mead, intro. to *Camp Circle Society*, qtd. in Murray 213). Novels are often described in such terms.

Like the most recent American Nobel prize winner, Isaac Bashevis Singer, Deloria preferred to write in a language other than English, and like Singer, her works are likely to be known to more readers in their English translations than in the Dakota dialects of her initial versions. Her native language texts and translations, derived from personal audition, range from reminiscences of elderly Dakota, to dramatized conversations on many topics between several elders, to political meetings, to the myths and legends she is most known for. The Deloria papers in the Boas collection include her translations and emendations of texts recorded by earlier ethnographers such as James O. Dorsey's 1894 collection of the George Bushotter writings (see Jahner's description in Walker, *Lakota Myth* 36–37). Deloria began her work under Boas in 1927 by editing and rewriting the

Bushotter documents in an improved orthography with extensive explanatory notes, both linguistic and ethnological. In 1941 she was to similarly rework the 1839 papers of Samuel and Gideon Pond in the Santee-Dakota dialect. But her most creative achievement is based on her own direct collections from Dakota (mostly Teton or Lakota) informants during the 1930s.

Working without a tape recorder or short hand notes, Deloria simply listened to stories without direct notation of any kind. She later wrote the stories as she remembered them, first in Lakota, then in English. One story, given in 1937 by the noted Makula ("Breast," also known as "Left Heron") runs to seventy-seven pages in the Lakota version alone. Makula had also given long stories to James R. Walker twenty years earlier, but Walker depended on an interpreter and set them down in his own Victorian prose (see Jahner, intro. to Walker, *Lakota Myth* 11–14). Deloria made a sincere effort to retain the flavor of each narrative, but ultimately she herself was the author of the stories in the sense that any writer transforms what he or she reads in the act of what recent criticism calls re-vision. Certainly the "polyphony" emphasized in dialogic (Bakhtinian) literary criticism, and the interpretive anthropology exemplified by James Clifford, coalesces in a unique way in Deloria's texts. Most interviewers from Walker through John Neihardt to Thomas Mails have worked through interpreters. Richard Erdoes's subjects, John Fire Lame Deer and Mary Crow Dog, speak in English. Only Deloria was fully bilingual.

Her father, the Reverend Philip Deloria, was old enough to have known prereservation Dakota culture and acculturated enough to rely heavily and fondly on Shakespeare in writing his sermons (Murray 89). Her formal higher education included study at Oberlin and the University of Chicago before receiving her B.S. from Columbia. A polyvocal confluence of cultural voices cohered in her rather than in the usual "space between" informant and recorder. By writing in Lakota Deloria achieved her position as the first, so far the only, American Indian writer to produce an extensive *oeuvre* in her own language. It is true that Deloria heard the stories told by traditional storytellers and tried to remain true to their meanings, even their tones of voice, but she could deliver them only through her own memory, imagination, and vocabulary.

Deloria's work may set a precedent for new multilingual literatures of the United States. Singer was her partner in this effort though she was his chronological precursor. While he is internationally known through the English translations he helped to make, he always wrote first in Yiddish, even though he lived in the United States since 1931. One of his translators, Ruth Whitman, comments that "a tremendous percentage of meaning and aroma is usually lost in the English" (Whitman 46). Nevertheless, Singer published much of his work in Yiddish against the apparent odds: "Yiddish is a sick language because the young people don't speak it. And many consider it a dead language. But in our history between being sick and dying is a long way" (Andersen 425). The same can be said for the Lakota language. Although the number of Lakota speakers has declined in the last generation, young people are now learning the language from texts as well as through the oral tradition. By 1992 Oglala Lakota College expects 80 percent of its faculty to be Lakota speakers (*Visions: 1992* 6).

At present, however, Singer and Deloria, like their languages, are "out of place in modern or American times and terms" (Buchen 198). As Singer was "not familiar with the works of so-called Jewish-American writers," so Deloria preceded the advent of the recognized English language leaders—Momaday, Silko, and Welch. Singer's definition of the Jewish writer, if analogously applied to most Native American writers of today, would not be welcomed by believers in a racial unconscious (see Krupat on Momaday, *The Voice in the Margin* 13). According to Singer, a Jewish writer must know both Yiddish and Hebrew, be saturated in Jewish history and traditions, and be familiar with both the Torah and the commentaries" (Buchen 218n). In 1987 an attorney, collecting statements by elders for the Bear Butte litigation, was taken aback by holy man Pete Catches's condemnation of the American Indian Movement (AIM). She wondered how they could correct the caricatures of ritual and custom he had described: "What is the first step?" she asked. "Learn the language! . . . is the first step," he conclusively replied (1987 Catches interview, Oglala Lakota College archives).

For the literary study of American Indian oral tradition, no tribe has been more enriched by the work of a single individual than the Lakota have been by Ella Deloria. Her work must be read in Lakota to be appreciated as the equal of Silko and Welch. Deloria writes her own translations, but they were obviously intended to assist the reading of the Lakota texts, not to exist as literature in and of themselves. Even Singer, who worked phrase by phrase with his translators to ensure the best possible translation, philosophically accepted its limitations: "It is true that in every translation the author loses—you do not gain in translation. Once in awhile you may gain in one sentence, but as a rule you keep on losing, this is true in all translations, because all writers lose a lot and some lose less" (Breger and Barnhart 34). Between her Lakota texts and her English translations, Deloria loses a great deal, but she intended her English translations to convey only the objective meanings of any text. While Silko, Welch, and even Singer to a lesser extent, want their English to convey the feeling and symbolic dimensions of their stories, Deloria felt it necessary to add extensive annotations on the subtleties of the Lakota language texture, including the cultural implications of idioms and symbols, even the subtle tones of voice conveyed by accents and glottal stops.

This extreme nurturance of every phrase, word, and particle anticipates an audience as interested in reading and writing Lakota as in speaking it. The many intricate surface details help retain the underlying spirit and feeling. Like Singer, she protects in her own consciousness and writing the atmosphere of a culture and way of regarding the world that was sick but far from dead. While Singer accepted the dominance of English to enlarge his readership, he used a 1967 National Arts Council grant of ten thousand dollars to publish his works in Yiddish (Malin 47).

To fulfill Deloria's initiatory promise of a Lakota language literature, certain fixed approaches to oral narratives must be unfixed (see Krupat, "Post-Structuralism" 124–25): that they are to be studied primarily to classify intra- and intertribal motifs; that they are scores for linguistic analysis and rearrangement; that they are primarily valued as performed events and that texts should be near facsimiles thereof. The last assumption is currently encumbered by the weightiest scholarly dogma (see Mattina 129–37). No matter how deferentially and reverentially scholars approach the original narrator, a story in any variety of print is never a performance. For those without access to a storytelling session, videotapes are now available (Evers, *Words and Place.* For an analysis of a Hopi story taped by Evers, see Wiget 297–336).

Dennis Tedlock has attempted to speak to the literate eye by presenting stories in verse with breaks after each natural pause: "the flow of the voice is paced with pauses that segment its sounds into what I have chosen to call lines" (Tedlock 55). The lines are ornamented in an ingenious array of sound-evoking punctuations and print irregularities. The exit of a prose that "never breathes" (Tedlock 48) precedes the entrance of a "dramatic poetry" (51) that means to approximate performance. But do we hear Tedlock any better in the following demonstration of his method?

> Now
> I'll
> tell you one of those Zuni stories.
> (*opening a book*) My apologies for
> relying on the
> SCRIPT
> this is the story of the Shumeekuli.
> Shumeekuli
> is something like a kachina, one of these
> beings who wears a mask whenever you see him—
> when they're among themselves they don't wear masks; when
>   they come to visit people they do. (*Tedlock 23*)

Tedlock's capitalization of SCRIPT represents increased volume, though that particular word "sounds" odd when the speaker HITS it arbitrarily.

Readers of English language literature have certain reading expectations. One of these is that prose conveys the sound of all but the most formal speech. An intensification or raising of the imagined voice often accompanies the shifts of mood and meaning inherent in the plot. The "acting" is intrinsic to the fictive situation and does not have to be spelled out in stage directions or superfluous description. From Shakespeare to Mark Twain to Toni Cade Bambara, writers have trusted prose to convey authentic speech, while assuming that writing does not need to justify its difference from speech. If a reader has never heard contemporary black urban speech, he or she will not hear the language of Toni Cade Bambara. Mark Twain could hear his own minstrel show version of southern black speech, but Bambara's stories would be entirely foreign to him. How much more unrealistic is it then for Tedlock to believe that his readers will hear a Zuni narrator in an English translation with unconventional grammar and stage directions?

Reading does depend to some extent on having heard the language one reads. But one does not hear the performance dimension of a script with any particular performance in mind. It matters little that readers of Shakespeare hear lines spoken as Burbage, Kemp, or Shakespeare himself would have spoken them, but it does matter that readers have some sense of how the lines sound when spoken with understanding and a degree of technique. Deloria presents her stories as prose fiction per se, conforming to the *reading* expectations of an audience she expects to be literate in Lakota. Though Lakota stories begin as oral events and are still performed that way, Deloria has adapted them to written prose, a non-Indian form, in the expectation that many aspects of the oral tradition can be both preserved and creatively expanded through writing.

The idea of adaptation and expansion justifies writing in Lesley Silko's *Ceremony*. An old, very traditional medicine man from Laguna, Ku'oosh, believes that only careful language can preserve a fragile world: "no word exists alone, and the reason for choosing each word had to be explained with a story about why it must be said this certain way" (Silko 35). But another far from fragile Navajo medicine man, Betonie, begins the hero's cure by affirming change:

> They think that if a singer tampers with any part of the ritual,
> great harm can be done, great power unleashed . . . But long ago
> when the people were given these ceremonies, the changing
> began, if only in the aging of the yellow gourd rattle or the
> shrinking of the skin around the eagle's claw, if only in the
> different voices from generation to generation, singing the
> chants. You see, in many ways, the ceremonies have always been
> changing. (Silko 126)

Silko's novel is a form of ceremonial narrative that appropriates English, as the Navajo took Spanish horses, to carry tradition into the future.

From this it might be assumed that Deloria was not adapting to change by devoting her gifts to written Lakota. Singer was once asked if he felt he was writing in "a somewhat artificial or illusionary context," as if a large Yiddish speaking readership had survived the war, when in fact most had perished in the Holocaust:

> There was a famous philosopher, Vaihinger, who wrote a book called *The Philosophy of "As If,"* in which he showed that we all behave "as if." The "as if" is so much a part of our life that it really isn't artificial . . . Every man assumes he will go on living. He behaves *as if* he will never die. So I wouldn't call my attitude artificial. It's very natural and healthy. We have to go on living and writing . . . Every man who creates something does not and should not worry about being understood. I would say I write for the best possible reader no matter how many readers there really are. (Blocker and Elman 7)

At the time Deloria wrote, few fluent Lakota speakers could read and write the language. While readers who only secondarily speak the language now study Yiddish literature, Lakota flourishes as a spoken language among many young people who have learned it from books. This generation may well learn to extend the literary practice and interpretation begun by Deloria. As this development unfolds, the blank verse mode of Hymes and Tedlock will gradually become less obligatory. A Lakota story was and is a performance but not an overacted one. Frank Fools Crow's record, "Fools Crow" (Tatanka Records, 1977), gives some sense of an older, perhaps a nineteenth-century style of oral delivery, as do his unpublished tapes (nos. 453 and 121 at the South Dakota Oral History Center, University of South Dakota). My conversations with Father Paul Manhart (9 June 1990) suggest to me that narrators do not presently observe formal rules of delivery. Nor, according to Deloria, did they do so half a century ago:

> In storytelling, the voice, its pitch, inflection, etc., is very flexible. The same word may be enunciated differently in different sentences, depending on the mood and intention of the speaker to give a certain effect.
>
> The glottal stop is frequently muffled. We know it is intended, and it is there, but it is in *parentheses*, as it were. Not every time; but much of the time. Also *lo*, (i.e. other terminals) even though they take an accent, may be whispered. This feature

is the hardest part of recording this kind of speaking, this natural individualistic kind. I have many instances in these tales which look like inconsistencies, mistakes and oversights, on my part, but they are intentional.

I can best say the whole matter is very irregular and individual and for that reason, it is to be taken as it stands. Another storyteller might stress other points, and play with his voice in tone and pauses, etc. according to the feeling he has, and wishes to put across to his hearers. I have honestly tried to recapture these tales as they sing themselves to me, from my memory of the way they sounded as various storytellers told them. They can't be absolute; but they are as true to the speaker as I remember, as I can humanly make them. ("Dakota Tales in Colloquial Style" 5:59)

Reflecting this narrative flexibility, Deloria's Lakota prose has greater range, more subtlety of inflection, intonation, and affect than most transcriptive poetry. Prose is a larger, freer form, and the modern Native American novel is a testament to its virtues. Imagine Welch's *Fools Crow* in free verse. We would have a creative presence using plot and character to demonstrate technique, as Dell Hymes's imagined narrators use their traditions, but we would not have a story. Deloria unassumingly retells the story as she remembers it and never assumes that writing will corrupt it. Her prose has several distinctive rhetorical and punctuation devices. She divides each story into numbered units, composed of one or more sentences within standard prose paragraphs. The units usually contain some significant action but they do not structure the story. They simply assist in referring the Lakota transcription to the English translation. She also uses dashes in an unusual way to convey some of the oral flavor. For example, speeches in a story are not introduced by "he or she said"; the quotative *eya* usually comes after the speech. The oral narrator's change from his own voice to that of the fictional speaker is usually signified by a dash, rather than a comma or a colon. On the other hand, her English translations adhere scrupulously to standard usage.

For the most part Deloria relies on the usual techniques of English written prose to bring her Lakota prose to life. Commas and periods provide pauses in reading (regardless of what Tedlock says), and most readers expect to hear rhythms of sound and silence in good prose. While Momaday, Silko, and Welch consciously transfer the spirit of ancestral wisdom to a new language, Deloria and Singer have preserved their oral heritage *and* their language. In this case writing rather than oral delivery preserves and creatively adapts the tradition in a significantly different way than either the Zuni storytellers videotaped by Evers or the American "indigenous" novels written in English (see Krupat, *Voice* 214).

For over forty years Deloria worked in an unprecedented form for an imaginary audience with little encouragement or reward. Even this critical study is undertaken, to use Singer's phrase, *as if* the Lakota language literature she produced will be studied by readers of Lakota on a larger scale than at present. As with any comparative literature study, advanced analysis and understanding requires knowledge of the original language, but non-English literature can be productively read, up to a point, in translation.

Literary criticism is usually written under the assumption that its readers have already read the work in question. This book is an introduction to a representative group of stories in *Dakota Texts*, Deloria's published collection, itself representing only a small portion of her overall achievement. The original bilingual edition is now extant in an AMS reprint (1974), and a paperback edition of the translations has been published by the State Publishing Company of South Dakota (1978). Neither edition is widely known, and therefore I have included the full English translation of each story discussed here in appendix 1. Readers who know Lakota can consult the AMS text, but most English-only readers unfamiliar with Deloria's version should interrupt their reading of the critical essays to read each story in full whenever a new story is introduced. Then, having the story in mind, the reader can follow my efforts to place the story in its cultural context and to interpret its meanings.

Much of this discussion can proceed without considering the original language, especially since Deloria's translations are so painstakingly accurate (as explained by her own annotations). But selected untranslatable textural elements will be examined. These descriptions are meant to help all readers, including those without Lakota, learn more about a story's meaning and technique. Perhaps some will be prompted to acquire a reading knowledge of Lakota (see appendix 2 for suggested texts and tapes).

After individual stories are discussed in terms of thematic continuity and stylistic complexity, a brief chapter on Deloria's 1948 English language novel, *Waterlily*, follows, since it has recently been published and is finally accessible to many readers. *Waterlily* contains themes discussed in *Dakota Texts* and specific comparisons will be drawn to show how the works complement each other in creating a greater understanding of Lakota culture and narrative technique.

Having demonstrated a method of thematic interpretation, emphasizing ethnographic background and close reading, I will then compare this practice to that of Dell Hymes, Dennis Tedlock, and Barre Toelken. A description of Elaine Jahner's treatment of Lakota stories concludes chapter 8. In order to further state the case for Deloria's Lakota prose, a final chapter explicates a relatively long story with reference to the critical issues raised in the preceding chapter.

Any interpretation of Ella Deloria, the creative writer, will be enhanced by considering the methodology of Ella Deloria, the ethnographer. Still unpublished, *Camp Circle Society* (1954) might receive mixed reviews today with the current emphasis on allowing individual informants to compose polyphonies untouched by synthesizing voice. Clifford praises the recent University of Nebraska editions of the James R. Walker papers for presenting a wide spectrum of Lakota opinion (Clifford 15). He does not mention, however, that Walker himself freely combined sources to create "ideal" accounts, and that he collected the documents primarily for this purpose.

Walker would commonly merge separate narratives to provide *the* tribal version. The Nebraska introductions do not indicate the strength of Deloria's negative reponse to Walker:

> It would seem much easier for "future generations" to get a notion of "all their ancestors believed and practiced" if the holy men were to tell them privately by word of mouth than to allow it to be written down by an outsider. This sounds crazy to me
> . . .
>
> This word "Vicar" and others; and many expressions throughout the Walker material are very suggestive of Christianity and Church language . . . ecclesiastical language was

very much a part of Walker's thinking, and he explained what he thought the Dakotas said, in terms he knew best. But the Indians who heard all this were mildly amused, and sometimes impatient. (Deloria, "Dakota Commentary on Walker's Texts" 37, 41).

The Walker question demands a separate forum, but suffice it to say that Deloria always tried to remain true to individual versions of stories as Lakota narrators told them, thus preserving the polyphony of individual tellings in the oral tradition. And as an ethnographer Deloria scrupulously mentioned exceptions to her accounts of tribal custom and belief. Perhaps the dialogic principle can be taken too far. However varied, the cultural traditions of a people have common describable charateristics.

Though Deloria does not synthesize her oral narratives, she does divide her ethnographic informants in *Camp Circle Society* into two groups, each composed of numerous unnamed individuals. The first include Teton, Yankton, and Santee elders, "who could say, 'I saw' and 'I did'" (*Camp Circle Society* 2). A second group had not actually lived in the prereservation camp circle but had "nevertheless grown up imbued with the flavor and feel of it, through their parents" (*Camp Circle Society* 2). These "younger" informants could at least say that their grandfathers or grandmothers had done and seen the things of which they spoke. Though DeMallie has described *Camp Circle Society* as "ahistorical, not grounded in time" (afterword to *Waterlily* 237), Deloria's description of her informants indicates that the book specifically concerns Lakota life from approximately 1860 to 1890.

While the chronological limits are explicit, Deloria draws generalized knowledge from the sum of her interviews, and she is careful to mention that certain legends such as that of the creation and of tribal origin were not conveyed "in any absolute form" (*Camp Circle Society* 3), contrary to Walker's impression of a cosmology and genesis known unanimously by the medicine men. In *Camp Circle Society* stories are valued more for their sense of truth than for their verifiable factuality. To the question of when the Lakota first crossed the Missouri River, narrative rather than history supplies "the only vivid and plausible account" (*Camp Circle Society* 4). The story was told to Makula, the "best informed all-round" of all her informants, when he was a boy by his grandfather: "how much further back it began, he could not say. He himself was in his middle 80s when he told it to me" (ca. 1937). The story tells of a group of Oglala, who kill buffalo on the ice of the Missouri River, and take them to the nearer, western bank for slaughter. While they are engaged in making the meat portable, the ice breaks up, forcing them to remain on the west side of the river until later in the spring. As a result, they discover the value of expansion to the west, and the whole camp crosses the river as soon as it becomes fordable.

Though Makula (under the name Left Heron) spoke earlier to Walker (see *Lakota Myth* 109–33), and to Martha Warren Beckwith ("Mythology of the Oglala Dakota" 377–98), only Deloria understood and wrote his stories without utilizing an interpreter:

> The position of an outside investigator looking at an alien scene with cool objectivity did not seem altogether becoming or desirable for one speaking from within the culture. Such a position might not be entirely impossible to maintain, though only with considerable artifice, but since the effort to remain convincingly impersonal for page after page would be too preoccupying, whereas the important thing was to tell what must be told, I chose the less exalted role of plain mouthpiece for the numerous Dakotas who gave this material, and have tried to write it simply and directly, and, I hope, lucidly enough. (*Camp Circle Society* 15)

Since she is part of the culture she describes, she is also able to include herself as an informant. "I have not hesitated to give instances out of my own experience wherever I thought they might throw further light,—with a total lack of reticence, for which I hope to be forgiven" (*Camp Circle Society* 16).

In light of current literary-anthropological theory, such forthright subjectivity is more than forgivable, it is a virtue. However, some might question *Camp Circle Society* and *Dakota Texts*, because individual statements are not attributed to their sources: "In the interest of space and word economy, those findings on each subject were best brought together in single digests" (*Camp Circle Society* 16). At the same time she has the *laissez faire* attitude implicitly praised by the dialogists: "it was not for me to manipulate this source material to

the extent of untwining, isolating, and classifying its various elements
and then naming them by scientific terms" (*Camp Circle Society* 17).
Nor does she impose structures on the material in order to validate
an ethnographic theory. In preference to systematics, she narrates
culture personally and often metaphorically:

> To me it [Dakota culture] is no simple woven fabric at all, really;
> but more like a marble cake. Dough in various colors—pink,
> green, brown— is mixed together and then baked. No matter
> where we lay our knife, we cut through every color, not once but
> many times. And that's the kind of thing I felt I had to talk
> about in this book. (*Speaking of Indians* 12)

Practically, Deloria trusted English to describe the interrelated-
ness of Lakota culture. Her philosophy of translation is standard: "I
saw no reason to limit or otherwise alter my own vocabulary; no
reason to translate correct Dakota into broken English . . . my single
purpose was to transfer their thought content as accurately as possible
with the best English tools at my command" (*Camp Circle Society* 17).
At the threshold of literary translation, Deloria modestly forgoes English "authorship" and refers her readers back to the Dakota, Nakota,
or Lakota original:

> Nor have I tried to translate into English the many terse
> idiomatic phrases and graphic figures that pepper the language
> and give it zest and sparkle. Translated literally, they lose their
> "punch" anyhow, no matter how effective they are in the
> original. But I have translated certain words not in their absolute
> sense, but in their idiomatic usage, wherever they were so used in
> the Dakota. (*Camp Circle Society* 17)

While taking translation seriously, she realized that English,
whether formal or idiomatic, could rarely do more than suggest corresponding Lakota distinctions. Some fundamental experiences do not
translate at all:

> When she'd tell the legends, she would tell them first in
> Lakota, and then in English. I remember that Emma
> Featherman, who was the only girl who knew the language in our
> class, would always be laughing very hard at some of the stories.
> When Ella would translate them she'd say they were not as funny

in English. Emma agreed with her, but they were funny in
English too. She often said, "Now, you see, girls, in order to
appreciate these legends even more, you should try to learn to
speak your own languages. (Sharon Stone, qtd. in Murray 152–
53)

Throughout her professional career Deloria worked to establish the
study of Dakota grammar and literature on an equal footing with
English for all Sioux children. In the late 1960s she trained teachers
in academic methods of using formal grammar and written texts on
the secondary level (Murray 156). Perhaps she would be gratified to
know that Lakota is now a respected "foreign language," but in later
life she focused on teaching her own people.

In the 1930s, however, her energies were largely given to research
and writing. She describes how Makula told her stories that she could
only "imperfectly recall," and she felt that she had not heard them
"often enough or systematically enough," to be "correct" ("Dakota
Tales in Colloquial Style" 30). Since these are the extraordinarily
long stories referred to earlier, Deloria's confession of scientific inadequacy is actually a profession of her artistic talent. If the stories
are not thoroughly Makula's, then not only the gaps, but an unmea-
sured proportion of the rest must come from the other "informant"—
Deloria herself. In *Dakota Texts* the narrators are unnamed, though
Makula may well be among them. Agnes Picotte tells me that the
elderly male and female contributors did not offer their names, because
they did not want to "push themselves forward," to appear as though
they were seeking some special notoriety by appearing in a book.
Many people of that generation were reticent about seeming to rise
above their fellows, especially in the white society's eyes. Even Black
Elk had been criticized for doing so.

Because of her unique relationship to the objects of her study,
Deloria's need for funding was more than personal. As she explained
to Boas:

I can not tell you how essential it is for me to take beef or
some food each time I go to an informant—the moment I don't,
I take myself right out of the Dakota side and class myself with
outsiders. If I go, bearing a gift, and gladden the hearts of my

informants, and eat with them, and call them by the correct
social kinship terms, then later I can go back, and ask them all
sorts of questions, and get my information as one would get
favors from a relative. It is hard to explain, but it is the only way
I can work. To go at it like a white man, for me, as an Indian, is
throw up an immediate barrier between myself and the people. I
can't explain further, but this is so. (letter to Boas 11 July 1932)

Deloria's dual role as ethnographer and informant required her
to receive the stories in some unusual ways. The relationship between
fathers and daughters-in-law and mothers and sons-in-law required
complete avoidance. Under no circumstances were they to speak or
even look directly at each other. In the Lakota extended family this
rule would have to be observed between people who hardly knew
each other. In 1928 Deloria interviewed a man who was the father-
in-law of her half-sister: "That makes me also his daughter-in-law and,
of course, he is obliging enough to talk to us. But his son, my sister's
husband, is our medium, for he is an old time Indian [Deloria's father-
in-law and the interpreter's father] and does not speak to me directly"
(Murray 103).

In Deloria's life and work varying conceptions of truth synthesize
without obscuring (as in the marble cake) the original ingredients.
Most of the "true" reminiscences that Deloria selected to write down,
though commissioned as scientific records, have the feel of modern
fiction. There is the story told by Mrs. White Rabbit whose traumatic
memory of dragging her father's corpse for miles through waist high
snow froze her emotionally for the rest of her life, so that she sought
only comfort and despaired of love ("Dakota Autobiographies" 4: 1–
32). Another woman recalled the suicide of a "handsome" three-
hundred-pound woman who falsely believed that her husband planned
to return to his former wife. One of her relatives reproachfully mourns
her (the story is given in Lakota and in translation): "'It is horribly
that you have done! it wasn't worth it! What's so important? even
were he to leave, you could have come home. Men are not scarce!'
So saying she scolded the dead, yet all the while she stroked the face
and hair with great affection as she wailed" ("Dakota Autobiographies"
5: 18).

But perhaps the most unforgettable of the autobiographies was given by a mixed-blood woman, Emmy Valandry, recalling reservation life around 1890. She tells of being honored at a *Hunka* (making of relatives) ceremony and a Sun Dance, commenting only on her resistance and embarrassment at being asked to participate ("Dakota Autobiographies" 6: 1–26). Later, arriving with her husband to help victims of the "battle" at Wounded Knee, she is again overcome by her hatred of Indians, to some extent certainly self-hatred: "I didn't like them, so I didn't go again. Smelling of blood, looking so dirty, they were spoiling our church; they were yelling so hard now, when really it was their own fault for being untractable" ("Dakota Autobiographies" 8: 41–42).

When she and her white husband, an employee at the agency, return home, she is infuriated to find that the hostiles have ransacked their possessions:

> and my sewing machine, which I prized highly, since I had been the very first to own such a thing, had been dragged out to the water, and it stood in midstream now, utterly worthless, and rusty all over; evidently the raiders had not known just how to make other use of it. Then especially I did not like the hostiles at all. I cried and cried, until at last he told me that I should have another sewing machine . . . The wonder of it all is that they did not set fire to our homes. ("Dakota Autobiographies" 8: 45)

Recalling the earliest phase of the reservation period, Emmy Valandry's reminiscence ironically speaks to the tricksterish "blood" rivalries that have plagued reservation life through much of the twentieth century. Mrs. Valandry unforgettably represents assimilative shame, while her sewing machine is the bait that has numbed Lakota kinship.

While "stories" such as these have the ring of twentieth-century fiction, no aesthetic justification is necessary for reading Deloria's work. The criticism of Arnold Krupat has sensitized me to the risk of seeming to validate Lakota literature through comparison to Western "great works" (see "Identity and Difference" 2–13 and *The Voice in the Margin* 196–201). Nevertheless, I have offered some comparative discussion of Shakespeare in order to more sharply delineate certain Lakota values. In the light of Bakhtin's influence on current theory

I can no longer say that Shakespeare is "representative" of Western writing, but some Western attitudes, significantly different from Lakota attitudes, may be noted in his works.

It may be that Deloria will illuminate Shakespeare more than she reflects him. Krupat predicts that increasing knowledge of "new" writers will renew the old ones:

> To understand better what Native American artists know and think and feel . . . to understand better how a certain traditional commitment to speaking or singing such knowledge and thought and emotion has adapted itself to writing, may well provoke a rereading, even a reevaluating of other American writers, both older, canonical authors and newer authors on the verge of canonical status. (*The Voice in the Margin* 91)

Perhaps the work of Silko, Momaday, Welch, and others could best be compared to "American" writers, but I would emend Krupat for my purposes by striking "American." Most of Deloria's material is no closer to American writing than to any other non-Dakota literature.

2
Lakota Oral Narratives:
The Sexual Theme

FOR INTRODUCTORY PURPOSES I have selected the theme of sexuality in *Dakota Texts*, because it is an especially striking example of traditional Lakota priorities in comparison to those of Western societies. In Lakota culture love for the whole nation of relatives superseded and validated individual relationships. As a result, promiscuity, excessive longing for one person, adultery, and jealousy were not sins. Such behaviors were regarded as repusively regressive in adults, who by nature and training should have been thoroughly devoted to their children's future, like the buffalo, eagle, and other species that the people revered and emulated.

Restraint in sexual relationships reflects the subordination of individual gratification to feeding, clothing, and teaching one's relatives. A preference for personal satisfaction was tantamount to child abuse or abandonment; even incestuous seduction was an appropriate metaphor for adult selfishness in some trickster stories (see *Dakota Texts* 11–19). More than a virtue, moderation was a social and physical necessity. A nomadic people could not transport large numbers of small children. As a result individual families ranged from one to four in each tipi, and the children were spaced approximately four years apart. The group held fathers in contempt if children were born more frequently, "since continency was expected of strong men" (*Camp*

Circle Society 83), and "stability, control, and moderation in all phys-
cial appetites were expected of men of strength" (84).

Although men assumed responsibility for birth control, women
were expected to guard their virginity before marriage. To prepare
girls for harmonious relatedness in the camp circle, the society sanc-
tioned a form of courtship that was virtually a contest. In this game
girls were always the defenders, while the young men "played" at
being enemies disguised transparently as sincere suitors. No matter
how attracted a girl might be to any particular young man as she stood
under his courting blanket, she dared not risk an open display of
affection. Until she knew him better, she assumed that her intimate
confidence would become his vaunted coup.

Most girls were well prepared for this, and courtship was one of
the many rituals that tempered the nerves of a people exposed to
frequent dangers. The "game" also prepared the players for the trib-
ulations of marriage itself. Occasional cruelty can mar any close relation, and Lakota men and women made it familiar by ritualizing
resilience. When a young man caught hold of a girl's blanket as she
returned to camp with water or wood, it was not a surprise attack,
and the girl destined to take her place as a strong Lakota woman
knew her part well:

> when the man did talk, and seemed in earnest, she affected not
> to hear but stood looking off yonder, showing interest in
> everything but him; giving an appearance of being bored or
> hostile or unimpressed. Thus, young courtship started mostly in
> parrying as between two opponents,—the girl ever on the
> defensive and alert to escape because "man's role was to pursue,
> woman's to be pursued." (*Camp Circle Society* 139)

As part of his invader's role, the young man often employed word
games to make the girl say "yes" to something trivial, so that he could
triumphantly say, "There! You have said yes to me for the question I
am asking in my heart" (140). Girls had to be alert to restrain their
feelings and their words. If they neglected any part of themselves,
they left the door open, in the ritual's prefiguration, to other threats
later in life—a carelessly tended fire, an undisguised food cache, an
unwatched for Pawnee or Grizzly bear:

Some men liked to get a lock of a girl's hair by trickery and then parade it off as a secret gift before their male companions . . . It was not safe to drop a handkerchief for a man to pick up; he kept it. If his friends got the ambiguous impression that perhaps it was such-and-such a girl's ribbon or handkerchief that she had given him, he let them imagine what they liked. But wary girls generally saw to it that their personal items did not get into a man's hands. (*Camp Circle Society* 148–49)

If Lakota girls were not likely to receive much sympathy for being frank in their affections, Lakota boys could only embarrass themselves by being "openly wistful" over a girl. Male bonding was (overtly at least) the priority, and divisive competition among young men upon whose cooperation the food and security of the nation depended was unthinkable:

Of an evening, the suitors of a popular girl sometimes clubbed together to await her coming outside and meanwhile they lay in the tall grass side by side, talking of irrevelant matters in entirely friendly fashion. And while one man was detaining her to plead his case, the others waited their turn to detain her next before she could elude them. And, it is said, sometimes one who had finished his courting kept hold of her wrap and consigned her to the next man! (*Camp Circle Society* 149)

On occasion, however, girls could reverse the momentum of the game. Deloria tells of a girl's chance meeting with one of her suitors in the woods or prairie far from camp:

She knew that she had no business out there, and that if seen, she would be criticized severely. So she stopped short and said to the man, coolly and directly, "What is it you want of me? That I marry you?" He said, "Yes." She replied, "Very well, then. I will,—but later."

The man was so astounded at her extraordinary directness that he believed her and let go his hold. But when she was beyond his reach she called back, laughing, "*Iye tuwa heya ške c'un!*" which means, "As they say someone once said!" She had quoted from a legend; the words were not her own. The completely nonplussed wooer could only shout back in frustration, "You *Iktomi!*" [You trickster!] She had been resourceful

enough to gain the advantage, and it shamed him too much to
have been so neatly outwitted by a woman that he did not make
up a song about her. (*Camp Circle Society* 152)

When a Lakota man sang about a woman, he meant to insult
her. Serenades in praise of the beloved did not exist (the flute was
used seductively). A man never sang about a woman he really cared
for or wished to marry, and the words were not meant to be his own
but a mocking version of a girl's bold declaration or invitation. The
love song genre is known as *wioiste lowanpi* (in mockery of women of
women they sing), but the words by themselves will appear to the
modern reader to be the singer's sincere appreciation of the girl's love:

> I came out barefoot
> Only to trick my aunt.
> So I will go with you,
> So arrive. (*Camp Circle Society* 142)

By repeating what the girl said to him in hushed urgency, the singer
shames her before the whole camp. He implicitly warns other girls to
remember that marriage maintains larger kinship relations and that
the feelings of parents, brothers, sisters, and other relatives should
not be ignored.

Happily-ever-after is not possible for people obsessed so strongly
with each other that they neglect those who depend on them. The
purpose of "love songs" offers a condensed, focused area of comparison
between Lakota courtship and Euramerican romance. The following
song might suggest admirable sincerity to the uninitiated ear:

> Dear I'm crying.
> I love you and want to be with you.
> I know all about the other girl.
> In the future
> You will be with a girl of sterling repute.
>
> (Song learned from Kevin Locke)

But in the context Deloria supplies, the female *persona* is being mocked
for her selfishly petty feelings of rivalry, and the punch line is her
boast of perfect virtue, when in fact such virtue would be a contra-
diction in terms if self-proclaimed for a seductive purpose.

Sometimes such songs were sung prior to the Sun Dance, when the annual gathering of bands enabled the singers to broadcast a woman's shame to the largest possible audience. Sun Dances, like other major Lakota ceremonies, include varied rituals of purification. The *wioiste olowan* sweeps away the diversions that might weaken the people's will to renew themselves. It is possible that Frances Densmore misunderstood a Sun Dance song about a woman who committed suicide when her warrior lover was killed (see chapter 5). Her interpreters gave her to understand that the man and woman had been engaged and that the surviving lover leaped to her death from romantic despair. Deloria's story in *Dakota Texts* indicates that the woman was married, that she mourned a lover, and that the camp regarded her with horror rather than sympathy. To this day the following song is sung:

> Wiciśala wan
> tewahila k'un
> wan weglakin kta hunśe

> There was a man
> I loved so dearly
> yes, I will see my man again
>   (Around Him and White Hat, Sr. 24)

Although some modern Lakota interpretations of such songs are idealized, most older "love songs" at Sun Dances and elsewhere were intended to wash away possessive thoughts and redirect an individual's devotion to his or her relatives:

> At the 1928 fair at Rosebud agency, it was part of a reenactment of the Sun Dance. The telling words set to a familiar old melody ran thus:

> > Grey Eagle woman,
> > Your tipi stands empty,
> > Your children are hungry,—
> > Your hearth is cold . . .
> > Where have you gone?

And this was not alone for demonstrating the various features of an ancient festival. Upon inquiring, I learned that there was such

a woman as Grey Eagle Woman and that she had left her
husband for another man the previous season. (*Camp Circle
Society* 145)

Deloria deepens the tone of ritual drama in their song. They were
merciless to the individual but wholehearted in the protection of the
group:

> As they sat drumming away, neither smugness nor apology for
> what they were doing could be read in their placid, sculpturesque
> faces. But after all, it was the Sun Dance that was taunting the
> woman; not they. Individually blameless, and free of all
> responsibility, they were but its instrument. (*Camp Circle Society*
> 146)

Lakota men did not mock women because they hated them, but
because they were strengthening those they hoped to marry, making
them more reliable, more lovable. However, occasional misjudgments
could be made and corrected. As an elderly Lakota man said in the
early 1970s of another man whose song he had repeated: "And, you
know, he married her; you're not supposed to marry the one you sing
about, but I guess he got to liking her after all" (tape obtained from
Kevin Locke). Several of the stories from *Dakota Texts* to be discussed
in chapter 4 indicate that a "fallen woman" could recover, start over,
and live a full, productive life. The stories also show that she might
suffer some humiliation for a time. Though elopements often ended
disastrously because the man did not respect a woman who let herself
be swept away, some such marriages could be successful.

Once a marriage had been made, the same ritual drama had to
be played out on a different stage. Both men and women assumed
new roles, but as before they were expected to demonstrate public
devotion to their children and family, now extended through marriage, rather than to each other:

> when both bride and groom were in a crowd together, one could
> not know without being told which two were recently married to
> each other. And all through life, the married couple did not go
> about where people gathered "as though they were tied together."
> Each moved independently of the other, among those of their
> own sex. Nor did they slip away from the group at any time with

the obvious desire to be exclusively alone. Outside the privacy of their tipi, they aimed not to exclude others from their normal necessary activities. If they must confer privately, they withdrew from the crowd to one side for a moment. (*Camp Circle Society* 180)

A mature man would never affectionately touch his wife in public, and newlyweds were so shy that even in private they barely spoke (177).

Great care was taken for years after marriage to build mutual respect and trust. Marriages were so easily dissolved that they could not survive even minor disregard. Early in the marriage depression might be extreme:

One young husband committed suicide because, as he confided to his male cousin before going off to do away with himself, "She spoke to me as though she despised me . . . I want to get out of her way." Another, who had always prided himself on his riding skill, was so hurt when his girl-wife laughingly doubted his ability to ride a certain outlaw horse, that he went off and was never seen again. (*Camp Circle Society* 188)

The necessity for harmony arose from the obvious dangers of nineteenth-century Lakota life. A long story from *Dakota Texts*, "The Lovers" (224–32; see this volume, chapter 5), emphasizes the care taken in marital relationships. Shouting matches were not acceptable as a "venting" of hostility or a displaced expression of love. The mythical lovers who never say an unkind word to each other represented an approachable, not an impossible ideal.

Should a truly serious grievance arise, men were expected to be as unshakable in their dignity as they were strong in spacing their children. A man could injure his adulterous wife or her lover, but he would be considered weak for doing so. He might forgive the woman for one offense, but he would not forgive habitual unfaithfulness, and if he chose to break off the marriage, he would do so quietly—only "a vain or short-tempered man might go so far as to 'throw away a wife' at a public gathering" (193). Women, of course, could always simply leave a philandering husband, and most had relatives who would take them in.

These events, issues, and problems of life in the hoop reflect Deloria's particular interest in the culture's domestic relations. Neither *Camp Circle Society* nor most of the transcribed stories concern details of hunting and war. Though Black Elk had become a man of peace by the time he spoke to Neihardt, many of his stories concern the predominantly male endeavors of war, hunting, and receiving supernatural power. DeMallie sees *Camp Circle Society* as a "cultural description in a Boasian sense, an idealized and generalized synthesis of the past, a testament to the old and valued customs of the Sioux" (afterword to *Waterlily* 237). But Deloria does not generalize. She does not need to emphasize that the Lakota were warriors, since that fact is so well known. Instead she includes the exceptional as part of her "synthesis":

> there were actually men who chose life-occupations far removed
> from the warpath because they refused to "spill human blood."
> When asking about some detail of warfare, I sometimes got the
> answer, "I can not say, for I do not know from experience . . . I
> have always been a man of peace. Ask my cousin (naming him).
> He was a fighting man." (*Camp Circle Society* 59)

In describing marital relationships as well, Deloria frequently qualifies the Boasian ideal with a significant digression. When a jealous man "gave away" his wife to anyone who would take her in his warrior society, the woman appeared to be unmoved:

> "Where is your pride?" her relatives asked. "Don't you know that
> women have hanged themselves with shame because of such
> unfair treatment?" But she remained unimpressed. Laughing, she
> said, "He'll be back!" And he did come back, knowing she was
> innocent all the time, and they lived harmoniously together to a
> ripe old age. And then, although neither seemed seriously ill,
> they died together on the same day. (*Camp Circle Society* 101–2)

In this instance the man has acted contrary to the dignified Lakota ideal, but the culture at large forgives failures that do not endanger the group.

Stories directed to young men reminded them of their primary responsibilities—hunting to supply food, maintaining horse herds through reciprocal theft with other tribes, and clearing breathing space in frequent skirmishes with the Crow and Pawnee. For fifteen to twenty years of their lives these young men had to be in peak condition, ready to respond to any physical demand. They also had to be mentally disciplined, so that they could concentrate on necessary tasks in varying forms of chaotic motion, in isolation or in groups, among their enemies or in their own camp circles. Such activities seldom conformed to plan. The ability to improvise corrections was socially valued and cultivated. Storytellers created expectations of weakness and recovery, thereby making it possible for listeners to endure defeat or humiliation should they make the same mistakes as a fictional hero or heroine.

Stories of and for young men warned of losing social identity and purpose through excessive erotic fantasy or obsession. A frequently told story concerns an isolated hunter meeting a female spirit, who appears both as a deer and a beautiful woman, often the same woman the man has been courting. Far from the protective ritual the apparent woman openly expresses desire for the man, and if she seduces him, he will be insane for the rest of his abbreviated life. On the other hand, if he perceives a "deer" trait before they have intercourse, he will temporarily capture her until she gives him her power. Usually this Lakota version of sublimation results in his becoming a better horse taker or warrior. The story allows for erotic fantasy but brings the protagonist back to serving the people. Selfish indulgence is an aberration from both maleness and humanity.

The same warning occurs in stories told of and for young women. In the courting process a girl learned to concentrate under pressure and gained confidence to harmoniously negotiate kinship after marriage. When she stood under a suitor's blanket, or when his family formally proposed to hers, both personal observation and reports helped her to decide wisely: "To run away with a man was not so respectable, because it showed that a girl was willing to take too much of a risk with her reputation, which would cling to her forever . . . (*Dakota Texts* 159n).

Lakota society cultivated patience and judgment in women through granting them ultimate responsibility in a process crucial to the culture's survival. Although her parents could invite a young man into their tipi to begin the last stages of courting, only the girl could accept the suit: "if a woman looked in the face of a man and smiled, this signified that she was willing to accept his advances, or if she turned her back toward a man, this signified that she would repulse him." If she was inclined favorably after having had more opportunity to observe him,

> she brought water and gave him to drink and invited him to come wooing again. When he again came wooing, if she still favored his suit, she prepared food and gave him of it to eat. If she desired to become his wife she made and decorated a pair of moccasins and gave them to him. If he immediately in her presence put the moccasins on his feet, they two were considered as betrothed to each other. (Walker, *Lakota Society* 51)

Women were also trained in patience by the women's arts, therein creating both material necessities and an atmosphere of cohesive esteem. But despite the careful upbringing of men and women, youthful impulsiveness was sympathetically portrayed in the stories. Many cultures recognize that surviving adolescence is always a partial miracle for girls as well as boys. Lakota culture recognized danger as sudden physical attraction, more powerful than social and psychological discipline, and able to make a girl suddenly agree to elope with a man she barely knew. Of course, such marriages could work, but the stories implant a sense of self-preservation in girls to help them distrust elopement and to feel they can start over should they make that mistake.

A girl who elopes makes herself vulnerable to every kind of harm because she no longer has the protection of fathers, uncles, brothers, brothers-in-law, and cousins. Since she cannot fight a man who becomes abusive with a man's weapons, the stories reveal that she has her own resources for escape and defense, particularly the concentration developed by her training and discipline in the women's arts. Many stories concern a woman drawing on characteristically female strengths to undo her mistakes and start over in a good marriage.

In both Deer woman and elopement stories, young men and women lose their primary identities as contributors to the life of their extended families, only to return to their best selves at the end. The stories of adultery and jealousy also present characters whirled away by confusing emotions so that they become dangerous to the whole society. If a man catches his wife and her lover together and impulsively kills them, he is not likely to be convicted of first degree murder in our society, at least in certain states or circumstances. In nineteenth-century Lakota society, any murder of another Lakota was an unforgivable crime, regardless of the cause. Some men might beat their unfaithful wives or "throw them away," and women could divorce their husbands for being abusive or unfaithful, but the murder of a tribal member was an unmitigated evil, because the resultant feuds between relatives, all of whom were armed, could leave the people divided and defenseless. Here, as with sexual obsession and impulsiveness in youth, sexuality's danger was primarily though not exclusively a social matter.

Stories of jealousy in Western culture also have this theme, but they emphasize the destruction of the individual soul. Othello's murder of Desdemona is thought to be tragic, not because she is his wife and closest relative, but because he is mistaken about her infidelity. Had Cassio and Desdemona been lovers after all, presumably the murder would not be tragic. In Lakota culture a man's abuse of his unfaithful wife betrays weakness. Having allowed himself to be so shaken as to misdirect his warrior powers against a woman, he will never be trusted again. For a chief in particular revenge is out of the question: "'At your tipi a dog will make water, and if it happens, take your peace pipe and remember these words and your will power.' (Meaning there are a lot of things that are insulting, but if I am a chief and someone elopes with my wife, I have to stand it. Take your pipe and control yourself)" (Black Elk, *The Sixth Grandfather* 390). Leaders were not the only ones expected to show such restraint. A member of a warrior society was expected to "raise no fuss even if a man runs off with his wife," and therefore in at least one society, the Miwatani, "no young men belong because [they are] too easily tempted; middle-aged men alone are firm enough for membership." If a society member's wife is stolen, "he sings, 'Who would fight over a woman?/ It is only the dogs that will fight,' and he is respected" (Antelope of Greenwood in Beckwith 423).

In Shakespeare's works, the characteristic Western tension between sexual freedom and restraint typically precedes the destruction of a passionate individual in this world and perhaps in the next. Or, conversely, depending on the characters and the interpretation, ir-rational acts lead to a rueful acceptance of "sensual faults" with com-passion for human frailty. The larger society in the plays, however, is rarely safe. When Cassio replaces Othello, or Caesar supplants Antony, the world is as subject to the effects of original sin as it has been since the outset of both world and play. In Lakota stories enough individuals learn the lesson to maintain the community. Individuals may have troubles, but the community at large is more stable at the end than in any of Shakespeare's tragedies. If Othello or Macbeth can become monsters, then nothing can protect any descendant of Adam and Eve from a like fate. Antony's weakness for Cleopatra can be condemned or pitied, but it cannot be cured. And even if it could, his full strength would exist for the sake of its own glorification rather than for the benefit of plebians, or even soldiers, except perhaps in their vicarious elevation through his triumphs.

In this study comparisons between Lakota stories and Shakes-peare's plays reflect these focal points of identity and difference: 1) the disorientation caused by erotic obsession, 2) the importance of courtship, 3) the danger of elopement, 4) the destructiveness of jeal-ousy, 5) the ideal of harmonious relationship.

3

Sexual Dangers for Young Men: The Deer Woman

A YOUNG MAN'S ENCOUNTER with danger in the midst of solitary travel occurs frequently enough in the oral narratives to suggest a conventional metaphor of adolescent fantasy. In Deloria's version of "The Deer Woman" (*Dakota Texts* 163–64), the young man's initial direction has specific Lakota overtones. He is heading home, the completion of all circular excursions for hunting, war, or horse taking. But blocking his road to his relatives and his identity as provider and protector is a figure whose ability to plunge him into confusion is foreshadowed by the time of day, just before nightfall. His vulnerability to losing both self and home is suggested by his trying rejection by a woman he had attempted to "buy," but who did not regard him seriously.

In such a state of mind it is easy to lose the rest of oneself and to become only one's fantasies of possessing the beloved. In the "low comedy" version of such an obsession, a Plains trickster is typically reduced to his enormous penis which he must ingeniously transport to its object (see Dorsey and Kroeber 62–67 and Bushotter 15: 94). Iktomi is driven by pure physical desire and frustration, while the young man meeting the Deer woman is more confused by romantic longing and social humiliation. These feelings can overwhelm his abilities to remain male in the full Lakota sense of effecting specific

33

tasks for the people. The deer that the young man should hunt for food becomes the image of the girl (rather than the girl herself) and that image absorbs his energies. Instead of hunting for the people's food, he dreams of possessing a woman for himself alone. The rope that he might use to take wild or enemy horses now links him only to this dream.

The fantasy is briefly interrupted by the appearance of another woman with a dog, a domestic rather than a romantic figure. The second woman is probably gathering wood, food, or medicine, and her dog's bark exposes the young man's fantasy of his beloved as a destructive dream sent by the Deer woman. Once the deer is "caught" long enough to be recognized, it will generate rather than absorb potency. The man cannot kill the impulses in his own maleness that have caused his pain. Acceptance of natural expression is always present in the narratives, in that all harmful spirits are immortal. The speed with which the Deer woman runs, when the young man releases her, conveys the power he himself will have once his erotic daydreams have disappeared. His doubting of her promise simply reflects his inexperience. Having felt betrayed by the girl he courted, the Deer spirit, and by life itself, he has a feeling of hopelessness, and in fact he will not recover from his ordeal for quite a while.

He barely reaches "home," and when he does arrive he finds it difficult to act as someone who belongs there. His vomiting reflects the natural process of healing, the return to equilibrium. But for a time he cannot relate to others as a human being. The deer sounds he makes express love sickness rather than the communal bond of human speech. Some basic healing rituals of Lakota society help him to complete the transition from the shadow of the woods to the light of the camp circle. The sweat lodge is like the vomiting, but also different in that the vomiting is the natural instinct of the person to right himself, and the sweat lodge is a cultural means of assisting that process. The same can be said for the exploding gun powder, a Lakota means of spiritual shock treatment.

Restored by his own instincts and by ritual wisdom, the young man's prowess in horse taking concludes the pattern for young listeners. The obsession that took the man into the shadows left him in the form of the catapulted deer. The sweat lodge further externalizes weaknesses within the person and returns him to harmony at the center of the four directions, and their associated virtues—courage, fortitude, generosity, and wisdom (see Hassrick 32ff.). The gun powder suggests the urgency of his resuming the proper use of his body for provision and defense; the people live in a dangerous world, and they cannot allow their young men to be "sick" indefinitely.

A Deer woman story related by Bushotter suggests that the warning matters. Bushotter's young man heedlessly has sexual relations with a beautiful woman in the woods after which she springs up and runs off into the "wild country." The young man never returns from a wild country within himself: "then the man grew suddenly 'groggy,' went reeling about and finally he fell to earth. Thereafter that man was never well, but was always somewhat insane, and in all his behavior was no longer the man he once was" (Bushotter 248: 1). Bushotter's conclusion is quite explicit on how male powers of hunting and war can disappear under the sway of eroticism:

> It is not established that any man ever shot one of these
> mysterious deer; for if one saw one in the form of a beautiful
> woman, he would be rendered dizzy by the sight, and so he would
> be too paralyzed to shoot, and so instead, he would be made to
> suffer. Nobody knows why, but it is that spirit's nature to confuse
> men, so they fail to shoot when they would. Such matters my
> father told me long long ago, my grandfather warned him, and
> he passed it on to his sons. (Bushotter 248: 2)

While Bushotter's young man dies of love, and the one in *Dakota Texts* is sickened by it, the Deer woman story in Buechel's *Lakota Tales and Texts* (273–74) is told in the first person by a narrator whose encounter with the Deer woman was less difficult. This man has not undergone rejection by the girl he loves, but when her band of Cheyenne separates from his own band of Lakota, he is "icante śica," 'sick at heart.' He follows the girl's people until their tracks show that they are only one day ahead of him, but suddenly near their abandoned campsite, he sees the Cheyenne girl weeping on top of a hill. She tells him she stayed behind because she had been scolded for loving him. She is, of course, the Deer woman, enacting a young man's fantasy of discovering his beloved unprotected and alone before they are married.

But as he approaches he is warned by his horse's sensitivity to danger. Earlier the horse had been given the single adjective, "luza-han" 'fast,' so that its valuable skittishness at approaching the Deer woman is part of the young man's own instinct to preserve his future as a warrior and hunter, one whose energies are usefully expressed on fast horses rather than one who seeks only to gratify his body. The young man immediately lassos the deer and extracts her promise to give him power. In this story the young man's reciprocated love makes his encounter with sexual fantasy less difficult. He arrives at the Cheyenne camp having overcome the Deer woman and adolescent confusion. Immediately thereafter he marries the girl and becomes an adult: "Le waniyetu amake napciunka el hecel ecamon na hetan mi-tawicu ake zaptan" 'I was 19 years old when I did that and my wife was 15' (Buechel, *Lakota Tales and Texts* 274, my translation).

In another story in *Dakota Texts*, "White-Plume Boy" (106–13), a young man's extraordinary strength is contained in a white plume worn in his hair. He loses this power in his first excursion from the camp circle, not to a Deer woman but to Iktomi (the trickster) dis-guised as a woman. After lulling him to sleep while removing lice from his hair, "she" steals his plume and he awakens as the image of adolescent obsession, an itching, whimpering puppy. The association of seduction and sexual weakening with the removal of lice may have come into this and other Lakota stories by diffusion from tribes where the metaphor is more elaborate. Carr and Gingerich report on a Pueblo story in which an old woman delouses twin hunters "before she bites their necks and roasts them" ("The Vagina Dentata Motif: A Com-parative Study" 195). After dining, the huntress again takes on the image of the hunted and becomes a deer.

In several Nahuatl stories the "old woman" demon appears as a beautiful young woman, who seduces the boys before tearing them apart and devouring them. These girls then turn into pieces of flint. In a Blackfeet story collected by Grinnell, Blood Clot Boy must wrestle with a girl who kills her opponents by throwing them on razor sharp flints (*Blackfeet Lodge Tales* 37). The Blackfeet version in Lowie's *Crow Texts* is more explicit about the sexual warning. The girl insists that she and her opponents be naked as they wrestle, so that she can distract them by pressing her sexual parts directly against theirs. Then after leading her victim to lie down, she suddenly pushes him over on the flints. In Lowie's version, Blood Clot Boy, being superhuman, sweeps her up, hugs her deceptively, and deftly drops her on an edge so sharp it slices her in two (Lowie, *Crow Texts* 347–449).

This victory over the seductress resembles many Lakota Deer woman stories, though the heroes in these stories are not immune to erotic power. The threatening female goddess in the southwestern stories assumes varying shapes, but, like the Plains analogues cited, is occasionally associated with flint and almost invariably with deer. The Deer demon, however, is more physically aggressive and violent than in the Plains stories, though sometimes the Plains Deer woman does kill a man by making him sick. In both areas, however, the warning against sexual excess is one of the dominant oral tradition motifs. Carr and Gingerich quote a Nahuatl father's advice to his son:

> And if you ruin yourself impetuously, if too soon you seduce, you
> discover, women on earth, truly the old men went saying, you
> will interrupt your development, you will be stunted, your tongue
> will be white, your mouth will become swollen, puffed . . . you
> will be enfeebled, weakened, emaciated . . . And you are like the
> bored maguey, you are like the maguey: soon you will no longer
> give sap. ("Vagina Dentata" 198)

Practical advice is offered in the *vagina dentata* stories told throughout North America. The women so equipped can mutilate and kill the unsuspecting youth, but the man who listens to his elders knows enough to grind down the woman's "teeth" with a stick or a stone before committing his own body to the same passage. Psycho-mythography may conceive a "terrible mother" in these stories, but Carr and Gingerich include a more obvious anxiety: a young man's fear of being unable to satisfy a woman ("Vagina Dentata" 199). Given the biological difference between male and female sexual function, *vagina dentata* episodes may have delivered humorously practical advice to adolescent listeners. The young man who is subject to the natural male "impotence" of adolescence, i.e. not being able to forestall his orgasm long enough to satisfy the girl, will "die" in the sense of being humiliated. The woman will seem like an insatiable monster wishing to ingest him.

On the other hand, the stories in which the young man "kills" the girl who would kill him may mean that he knew how to bring her to repose, as in the Shakespearean metaphor of death as orgasm. The following passage from a Lakota story promises peace for the man who knows how to satisfy his wives:

> There were two beautiful girls there. Each had a bed on opposite sides of the lodge. When night came each invited the brother to bed. As he did not move, the girls fell to disputing as to which he would choose. At last the brother settled the argument by going to one of the beds. Now these girls had teeth in the vagina, and when they were in erethism the teeth could be heard grating upon each other. The brother heard the noise. He took his crane's bill, thrust it into the vagina and upward, killing the girl. Then he went over to the other bed and did the same. Soon he went on his way. If he had not done this to these girls, all woman would be dangerous to their lovers. (Wissler, "Some Dakota Myths" 198)

The Lakota stories of the Deer woman and the *vagina dentata* do not emphasize the terrors of the female demon but assume an attitude of assurance, simultaneously warning of real danger, and portraying growth beyond the anxiety. Fearing one's mother as a murderer coincides with the melodrama of the Freudian nursery and to some extent the classical mythology on which Freudian critics regularly draw. Fear of the female in Lakota stories would not focus so exclusively on a single Medea figure, since a male child had many mothers. Sexual fear in Lakota stories depends less on guilt than on physical weakening, mental distraction, and social humiliation. In the few stories we have already looked at, a young man is distracted from hunting, obsessed with a single woman and the fear of losing her. Since he is physically sick from being in love, he loses his identity in relation to his other relatives as well as his function on behalf of the tribe. By neglecting kinship and provision the man has incapacitated himself, but in the end he is stronger than he would have been without the lapse.

Psychological diversion is also portrayed in stories about chivalric expeditions for a sacred object. In some tellings the familiar European reward of marriage is conferred, while in others the girl requiring the quest is revealed to be a Deer woman in disguise. Although the young

men go on fools' errands at the behest of a falsely idealized human
being, they thereby learn not to risk their lives for an unworthy
purpose. The Beckwith and Wissler versions are long and so similar
in detail as to suggest the same narrator, Eagle Hawk, identified by
Beckwith but not by Wissler. Eagle Hawk begins with a young man's
effort to determine what the *pte-he-iya(ya)pi* (they-go-after-the-buf-
falo-horn) is and how to find it, since a beautiful girl has promised
herself to any man who brings it home.

His father indirectly warns him by suggesting that he ask Iktomi,
as if to say that a child learns to avoid fire by burning his fingers. Ikto
says even he does not know what it is, but of course, Ikto is always
off on mad quests for unworthy objects himself. At a feast called by
the young man's father, an old woman supplies the perspective supplied by the rest of the story and many other stories on the possibility
of the permanent loss of identity and function that infatuation can
cause: "It comes from where the sun goes down and is very far away.
Many a young man has gone after that and never returned" (Beckwith
401).

Accompanied by a friend and by his younger brother, the young
man discovers that impulsive chivalry is foolish but endurable. The
tripled (tribal rather than individual) hero makes allies of a bear,
buffalo, crane, and bird, and they carry such additional spiritual shields
as paint, eagle feathers, beaver's skin, and buffalo sinew to elude panic
and fatigue. In taking the buffalo horn the three young men maintain
the steady nerves of horse-takers, and their return is a harrowing flight
from Thunder beings, much as horse-takers were pursued by angry
enemies. Several old women equip them for their final skirmish with
the Thunder beings, and the grandmothers themselves amazingly rush
out of their tipis killing many of the enemy. The young men are
preserved by dependable values personified by relatives who are decidedly not sex objects.

Upon their return, the girls of the camp play a ritual game of
shinny in which the one who ordered the quest suddenly runs the
ball out of the game, becoming a wood deer before she disappears in
the east (Beckwith 405). This act reveals her to be a spirit of division,
one who does not initiate play toward the west according to the rules

of the game, and according to the ritual order of social affirmation permeating Lakota culture.

The young men have thought only of gratifying a desire for the girl (vicariously, for the two helpers). The last word is ostensibly recalled by Eagle Hawk as having been spoken earlier, as if such wisdom, though always present, can only be revealed at the point of maturity for each listener: "And by the way, the old women, the Moon and the Sun, had said, 'They have sent you on a dangerous journey. You will get what you are going after but you will not marry the girl.' The Indians believe this story; they will not eat the wood-deer" (Beckwith 405).

As with the stories associating foolishness with sexual enthusiasm, Bushotter's representation of a young man's courting rhetoric satirizes its strategic excess. Since it has not yet been published, the speech and the woman's skeptical response are worth quoting at length:

Just a moment, (he says), won't you please stand still, I
would like to talk about my affairs, and declare myself pitiful;
throw my case on your pity. Now then, ever since I was born I
have never had anything good, and I was not brought up rich,
and I lived, going about and spending the night in any home
where I happened to be, as a rover; but one thing at least I can
say of myself, and that is: I have joined all warpaths which young
men undertake, and I have roamed about, suffering, seeking for
black face paint. (He wants to achieve renown by killing an
enemy, which would entitle him to wear black face paint as a
warrior). And I seek for the right to marry, and it has cost me
sleepless nights, wandering in war; and now, that which I am
thinking about, I think of with my entire being; and when I do
that, no matter how hardship is involved, I try to achieve what I
want, because I have my mind set on it. Next, I beg you, if you
feel kindly disposed towards me, that you will think seriously of
what I say, and when I see you, you will tell me what you think
about it all.

Now, O sister-in-law, you are well aquainted with the family
from which I come, so it is not fitting I should speak about it,
but I should like to hear what you feel towards me, in the light
of all these matters.

Human nature (purpose, etc.) is one; the branches are

many; but if one does not take care of the one, which is the root of all the branches, they, the branches, are of no use.

But come now, I am not saying I am handsome, and brave, and of a real family, or that I am rich. But look at me for myself, as a person, that is what I want you to do . . . I feel myself competent to cope with matters in the pursuit of the necessaries of life, and to the end that we should not suffer for want of anything, I can work with all my might. I try to be a man among men, and so, I continually think to myself, "would that some woman would take pity on me, and help me to live as I would like to live, as a real man; and would that she would accept my proposal of marriage!" But so far nobody has yet held that feeling of kindly goodwill toward me, but now on this day I would know what yours are like; if you are agreeing with me, and accept my proposal, you will look up at me."

But the woman would stand not looking at him. Then he would say, "I'll change that; if you are accepting me in your heart you will *not* look up at me!"

The woman would then answer, "That is too many things to say. By saying all that, will he get anybody to accept him, anyone who would trust a man giving all that about himself?" she would say as to herself.

Then he may say, "Well, because (for my part, I want) you must say now what you want and I shall do it. And whatever you want me to think, concerning all this, I shall do. Now is the time for you to say outright what your wishes are.

But now, because you said the words you did about me just now, I am coming again . . . Then I want an answer to my words. (Bushotter 258: 3–5)

The young man declares himself "pitiful," not because he longs for an impossibly perfect woman in the European sense, but because he has sacrificed himself on behalf of the people, showing the courage necessary in a provider. In addition, he alludes to the uprightness of his family, since the girl, should she consent, would marry into many relationships besides the one with her husband. He also mentions his devotion to her family to show that he knows that the "branches," a husband and wife, are useless without the "trunk." In this way he assures her that he puts human relationships ("real family") ahead of prestige and material possessions. The length of the speech is itself a way of representing loyalty, as is the concluding ploy to keep her from saying no—"if you consent, you will look up," adapted to "you will *not* look up," when she does not look up the first time. Her response seems to say she is unimpressed, but it may also be a test. The man shows that in refusing to accept a first rejection, he forecasts perseverance later when hunger or danger threaten.

The young man in Bushotter's courtship speech recommends himself as a useful person: he has proved his courage in war; he is a member of a strong though not necessarily prestigious family; he values family and tribal survival before individual satisfaction, the trunk rather than the branches; he has courted other women because it is marriage and its opportunity to contribute to the tribe that he seeks, not an idealized individual woman. As a married man he will also be privileged to sit in council with other men, and with the help of a wife and her family he will be able to perform the give-aways that accompany the honors he hopes to gain for himself and his children.

The most obvious contrast to Western courtship for most readers will probably be the absence of flattery. The Lakota girl is likely to be persuaded by her lover's qualities and accomplishments rather than his praise of her own. Shakespeare's foremost courtship play presents Romeo as initially infatuated with Rosaline, but obviously more in love with love than any real person. He appears to be "love-sick" because of social convention, though he himself will not admit it (*Romeo and Juliet* I.ii.87–98). His love for Juliet, of course, is another story, a love-at-first-sight one, that turns out unhappily in at least one group of interpretations, because the lovers worship each other instead of God. They are not to blame in this but are victims of the original sin that accounts for the feud between their families, and ultimately their deaths, along with those of Mercutio, Tybalt, and Paris.

Juliet's love for Romeo is "naturally" passionate, against her better judgment. For that very reason she is portrayed sympathetically, as a person of deep feeling who cannot dissemble. Though she feels this passion to be "too rash, too unadvised, too sudden,/ Too like the lightning which doth cease to be/ Ere one can say it lightens" (II.ii.63–64), she knows she can do nothing other than "follow thee my lord

throughout the world" (II.ii.148). While interpretations differ on
whether or not Romeo and Juliet can be forgiven for loving so un-
wisely, Lakota stories do forgive youthful mistakes, and such mistakes
rarely lead to tragedy. Young men made sick by Deer women recover
to become stronger and wiser. Girls who elope with seductive and
ultimately abusive men find the strength to escape and make a better
marriage. In both cases the happy ending shows them contributing
to the life of their extended families. In *Romeo and Juliet* the human
family cannot control their destructive tendencies, and the individual
protagonists, having the potential for love, are unable to heal the
divisions among human beings and between their fallen nature and
a perfect God, at least as long as they are in this world.

As suicides Romeo and Juliet are tragic, because for reasons only
God can know they destroy their individual souls, and only secondarily, unlike the Lakota stories, because they are lost to their families.
But there is an important likeness as well. Friar Laurence distinguishes,
as do the Deer woman stories, between loving a person and being
swept away by a fantasy:

> These violent delights have violent ends
> And in their triumph die, like fire and powder,
> Which as they kiss consume: the sweetest honey
> Is loathsome in his own deliciousness
> And in the taste confounds the appetite:
> Therefore, love moderately; long love doth so;
> Too swift arrives tardy as too slow. (II.vi.9–15)

One of the most constant motifs in Lakota cultural expression
is the praise of an endurance that sustains clear judgment under pressure. The Deer woman stories set the temptation for instant gratification over against the courtship process that develops patience and
the confidence to persevere through rejection and setbacks. Elopement stories jolt a woman, accustomed to predictable kinship exchange, into galloping emotions—from the rush of preparation and
flight to the realization that she has married a "monster." If the
protagonist is to recover from this disaster, she must draw upon lessons
learned from the stories she has heard. Presumably they would resemble the one she finds herself in. Storytelling might dispel actual trag-

edy. Bushotter's verbose courtship speech contains a message derived
from narrative: people marry in paired branches, but they must remember the whole tree.

Othello's courting of Desdemona also recalls a tree in the Garden
of Eden, and is meant to ironically reflect the idealization of romantic
individuals who ignore that tree. But while the Lakota tree is that of
a healthy culture, some descendants of Adam and Eve externalize in
a branch the poison incepted in the seed. In loving Othello "for the
dangers" he passed, Desdemona does not remember humanity's sub-
jection to sin and cannot halt its unleashed momentum before she is
suffocated by the man she loves. She and Othello worship each other
because they believe they are invulnerable to danger:

> My story being done,
> She gave me for my pains a world of sighs:
> She swore, in faith, 'twas strange, 'twas passing strange,
> 'Twas pitiful, 'twas wondrous pitiful:
> She wish'd she had not heard it, yet she wish'd
> That heaven had made her such a man. (I.iii.158–63)

That same man is brutalized because he begins with a notion of his
own perfection. His wars against the Turks and his final murder of
Desdemona have been undertaken to maintain the collective illusion
of being "as Gods."

Just as Desdemona and Othello, like Romeo and Juliet, are too
sudden in declaring love and deifying each other, so they jump to
conclusions after decontextualizing their roles. Romeo's suicide and
Othello's murder of Desdemona occur because the heroes are unable
to slow down long enough to consider alternative possibilities to their
despairing thoughts. Once Romeo and Juliet are moved to discard
the protection of social conventions, and once Othello's mind is set
in motion by Iago, the pace of each play quickens until the characters
are unable to see a real source of danger while blindly striking an
imaginary one. Tybalt kills Mercutio; Romeo kills Tybalt, Paris, and
himself, and Juliet kills herself because Romeo did. Similarly, Othello
kills himself because he has killed Desdemona. Once the mind begins
to run, it can leap from romantic eroticism to wrathful revenge or to
the helplessness of virtual insanity.

Such intensity appears in *Antony and Cleopatra,* when Antony follows Cleopatra's ship in retreat in the midst of a naval battle. The warrior is unable to fight while captivated by the erotic object, like the swine of Circe, or the dizzy, tottering young man returning from an encounter with the Deer woman. Antony makes Cleopatra a "goddess," because she makes him a "god." Love is mutual illusion, as it is in sonnet 138: "O, love's best habit is in seeming trust,/ And age in love loves not to have years told:/ Therefore I lie with her and she with me,/ And in our faults by lies we flattr'd be." Antony tragically loses his manhood, becomes "effeminate" and incapable of political greatness. Being weakened by love harms his military prowess, but whether he is militarily or erotically satisfied, for him the mass of people exist to populate kingdoms, acquired and pillaged for the jewelry he gives to Cleopatra. Nothing is said of Antony's responsibility to any group of people other than the soldiers of his mercenary army.

Even military reputation is an illusion, as his officer, Ventidius, says: "Caesar and Antony have ever won/ More in their officer than person" (III.i.16–17). Though he counts his coups from earlier battles, Antony is a Roman (and Elizabethan) warrior whose energies have only bolstered his ego. Cleopatra too lives only for the erotic illusion Antony helps her to create. When he doubts her at one point, she says she would rather sacrifice her children than see her love for Antony diminished (III.xiii.158–67). Though interpretations of such sentiments vary, Antony and Cleopatra lament their losses for reasons entirely foreign to Lakota culture. They are "stars," like the nobles of Shakespeare's days and the celebrities of our own, and for Cleopatra death means the loss of her *persona,* should she be paraded in Rome. The thought of this disgrace impels her suicide as much as the loss of Antony. In preparing for it in the last scene she never mentions her children, dwelling only on her fantasies of having achieved a final triumph by depriving Octavius Caesar of glory.

Perhaps Shakespeare is depicting a world so far gone in folly that human beings are merely pathetic. Certainly the characters themselves show little pity for anyone but themselves. In Lakota society, the *oyate* (nation) is exalted when young men count their coups, since they have risked their lives for the people, but nowhere does an individual beloved or leader evoke or invoke the grand extravagance of Cleopatra's final tribute: "His face was as the heavens; and therein stuck/ A sun and moon, . . ./ His legs bestrid the ocean: his rear'd arm/ Crested the world: his voice was propertied/ as all the tuned spheres . . ./ For his bounty,/ There was no winter in't" (V. ii. 79–87). Antony's "bounty" was after all only a display of wealth and self-congratulatory praise for those who praised him. Perhaps Shakespeare means to condemn this. Or perhaps he means us to be moved to terror and pity at the deterioration of greatness, an emotion still prevalent in commoners of the tabloid press. Regardless of interpretive sympathy, the lovers in the plays mentioned are presented as victims of passion (original sin, tragic flaw) rather than as human beings learning to become useful by trial and error.

4

Sexual Dangers for Young Women: Monsters and Rivals

WOMEN WHO CHOOSE the wrong man, even in a courting ritual giving her the best possible opportunity to judge, are not themselves judged negatively in Lakota stories. Instead they are usually given a second chance. In real life, however, Lakota women had to be very careful both physically and emotionally. The husband of an unfaithful wife might cut her nose to disfigure her for life, or at least remove one of her braids as a public disgrace. He might even publicly "throw her away," making her available to any man who would take her.

Laws did not protect the woman who did anything to divide the people. Girls were trained in self-control because the inner strength of the community depended on their loyalty to their husbands. Hassrick mentions rawhide "chastity belts" that bound a girl's legs together as she slept (*The Sioux* 124) to protect her from young men able to reach her tipi as quietly as they entered an enemy's horse corral (see also Deloria, *Dakota Autobiographies* 3: 11, 16). The adolescent boys and girls were involved in a game of stealth, alertness, and self-control, qualities they would direct to other purposes in later life.

The testing of a young man occurred in various physical ordeals from the hunt to the Sun Dance. The testing of a young woman required her to protect herself from emotional turmoil and to preserve her strength of mind and body for the next generation of children.

Young men were expected to bolster the girl's ability to protect her identity and purpose by ingeniously devising appeals to her emotions and arousals of her sexuality. Like Lakota men, Lakota women learned of their vulnerability early on and knew that survival meant remaining within certain limits. The society taught her how to make self-preserving choices. Through stories she learned that the man who tries to bypass courting and marriage rituals is not to be trusted, because he has no respect for the collective purpose of sexuality. In the stories he is portrayed metaphorically as a monster, intoxicatingly attractive in his initial disguise, horrifyingly ugly as himself. The man who waits for the woman in courtship and offers horses to her family proves that he possesses the qualities of a hunter and a father. Patience, fortitude, respect for the family of the girl, not just the girl herself, indicate a mature sense of male adult identity, one who is indeed ready to assume the responsibility of caring more for others than for himself.

The young man who receives favorable signs from the girl he courts may ask her brothers if he can buy her with a gift of horses. Even so, the final decision is up to her, but the brothers are the girl's protectors and the man shows that he wishes to be allied to them, to bring them food and defense, rather than to take someone for his own service and pleasure. In young women chastity was a primary virtue. It showed that she was strong enough to remember that her body, and everything else she was, existed to serve the people, not to satisfy herself or another individual. In later life fidelity could be a matter of life and death. Upon her loyalty rested the strength of the tribe to defend itself against enemies. Virgins had the honor of cutting down the Sun Dance tree and carrying the most sacred symbols at warrior and society dances. Rituals of proving virginity defended girls against slander. If a man accused a girl of improperly participating in a ceremony for virgins, he had to bite a sacred knife to validate his accusation. If he lied, he would mysteriously die. Many older women, especially widows, were honored for having lived their whole lives with only one man. Societies for such women exemplified continence (see Deloria, *Waterlily* 139–40).

Stories like "Double-Face Tricks the Girl" (*Dakota Texts* 46–50) should be read in light of the strong social pressures women had to bear. The story's forgiveness of its heroine for forgetting paramount ideals of behavior typifies the difference between a Lakota persona's youthful mistakes, arising from adolescent inexperience and predisposition, and a Christian persona's sin, arising from deliberate choice or supernatural predestination. This story of youthful passion is decidedly not tragic like *Romeo and Juliet,* nor is the happy ending like a fairy tale. Women who were promiscuous before and after marriage were badly treated because they were a threat to society. A girl who naively follows her heart or her hormones on one occasion is not ruined in the Victorian sense. As the story tells its listeners, mistakes are allowed if they are not repeated and may ultimately serve to make a young woman stronger and more alert in protecting and advising her children.

Although the circumstance is not stated at the beginning of "Double-Face Tricks the Girl," courting often took place at the summer Sun Dance where a large gathering of different bands brought eligible men and women together. Since the men of her own *tiyospaye* (community) would be too closely related to her, a girl could expect to be courted by many men she had never seen. In such conditions she might well decide on the basis of physical attraction, since she would have no information about the man to mitigate that appeal. The story presents the girl as a person unlikely to be impulsive in her choice. She is a good woman, well-liked, even "ksapa" 'prudent,' and these qualities make her especially attractive as a wife and relative to a prospective husband's family. Though they all want her, she will consent to none of them.

But suddenly her prudence and goodness are blown aside by a stranger who inexplicably convinces her to run away with him. The lack of narrative preparation for her unaccustomed impulsiveness implies its potential emergence in any girl of that age. That it doesn't follow from anything she has ever said or done is just the point. The girl who has obviously done everything right all her life doesn't even speak to her parents about her choice of a husband, thus ignoring the idea of marriage as a family alliance. With ironic foresight she prepares dried meat and moccasins and mentally rehearses their secret departure. The narrator's attention to detail accentuates the part of the journey she is not prepared for—the reality of a man turned into a monster when his courting blanket is dropped. In the shadows of her ignorance the imminence of unlooked for hardship is suggested by the man's throat clearing. As a preparation for speech, it holds the potentiality of a story the girl could not imagine.

Since every young person encounters unexpected trials of some sort, the narrator shows how the girl is psychologically equipped for survival. Before starting the journey she takes her pet beaver with her: "The spirit of the beaver was the patron of work, provision, and domestic faithfulness" (Thomas Tyon in Walker, *Lakota Belief and Ritual* 121). A pet is "waniyanpi," literally 'a living possession,' and the qualities represented by the beaver—the disciplined habits of work, endurance, and loyalty—live in the girl. Carrying these qualities in herself she goes out to meet her enemy, still hidden by his blanket.

The speed with which they travel corresponds to the impulsiveness of her act, the beating of her heart, the excitement of danger and sexuality. The deep lake that he forces her to cross, though she cannot swim, represents the depths of betrayal she has not been prepared to face. Probably the girl has never been forced to do anything against her will; Lakota children were not bullied or intimidated by anyone. The man provokes a fear unfamiliar to a girl surrounded by many brothers, brothers-in-law, and cousins. The entry into the lake while riding the man may also be a sexual euphemism.

In the midst of the crossing the horrified girl sees her husband's second face in the back of his head. This discovery is not a simple reversal of expectation, as the narrator presents it, but a comment on the psychological value of the courting process. The monster is not the man with whom she agreed to elope. That man too might have become a monster if they had not married in the proper way. Breaking the rules can cause even a sincere husband to mistreat a woman whom he feels he can no longer trust.

And as a man transformed by the loss of discipline that creates Lakota identity, the Double-face immediately evokes repulsion. Once inside his tipi he asks her to pick the lice out of his hair, perhaps the same sexual metaphor used in "White-Plume" (see chapter 3). As she puts him to sleep, she herself becomes alert. The toads that serve for Double-face's monstrous lice magnify her recognition and lighten the tone, foreshadowing escape. They also present a workable task for her feminine skills. While men are at their strongest in swift motion outside the camp circle, women are trained to be calm, intent, and dexterous in the tipi.

The girl systematically ties the monster's hair in a spider web pattern to the tipi poles, symbolizing the women's virtue of industry, traditionally associated with the spider (M. Powers, *Oglala Women* 68), a psychological habit that allows her to concentrate confidently in all circumstances. In addition the spider is associated with deception—Iktomi means spider—and here with poetic justice she has temporarily tricked a trickster.

Her Lakota upbringing also helps her to accomplish her tasks resourcefully and quietly; she does not bang the stones together to kill the toads but carefully puts one down and crushes the toads with the other one. (Deloria's translation does not include the technique described in the original): "Canke inyan blaska nunp gnakin na wanzi oyuspa canśna hel kaslisli-kat'a ke', inyan kin oko ogna ewicagnakin nanśna inyan kin iciyapa un" 'And two stones were lying there and she took one and whenever [a toad came out] she killed it by crushing it to death, they say; she set one stone between [herself and Double-face] and used the other stone for crushing' (my translation). When she sets out for home again, she again carries the pet beaver, as she has carried the resources for survival throughout, from the meat and moccasins to the quietness and manual skill imparted to her by others. Now she heads back to the people to make their survival the consistent purpose of her life.

But first she must learn that any one person's resourcefulness has its limits. Every person must remember that being at home in existence requires the protection of relatives. The beaver, "waniyanpi" 'the kept alive one,' is also the consciousness of interdependence that returns to the girl. A girl should not forsake the protection of her brothers to gamble on the promises of a strange man. Only the beaver, as a representation of her protectors, can bring her back from the deep lake of unfamiliar emotions to the solid kinship relations that define Lakota life. The beaver, like the bridge he builds, is an extension of the male power the girl must remember to respect. His loyalty and industry are also her own female virtues; *she* is the one that weaves the monster's hair into the spider pattern. But the ability to think on the run, in a state of rushing turmoil is typically a male power, and in the end the beaver represents a separate male being rather than a "side" of the girl.

The Double-face falls from the bridge because it is so narrow he is unable to cross it before the beaver destroys it from the other side. Calm, deliberate action is not the Double-face's strength, and he is overcome in the midst of trying to effect it. The narrow passage from immature egoism to the community is impossible for him to negotiate. Although he swims across the lake on the way out, he drowns in its depths at the end because the girl's attraction to danger has now dissolved. Double-face sinks in the recognition of the woman who knows what he is and is glad to return to those she can rely on. Her parents arrange her marriage to the young man with whom she had originally wished to elope, and they are formally united with much honoring of all concerned.

The people's praise of the beaver has the narrator's final attention, since he is an alter ego for the male children listening. He is rewarded for loyalty by being made to feel like the best person in the camp. Of course all children are supported by adults, "waniyanpi" 'kept alive' like pets, but they are also raised to keep others alive. When they have proved their ability to do so, they will grow from being helpless children to honored heroes. On her homeward flight the girl carries the beaver in her arms until she stops in despair beside the lake. A "boy" then completes the journey by building a bridge to the future. In another manifestation of real life the bridge might be made of food, horses, or coups to keep starvation or an enemy at bay. In the end home is cooperatively established by the defensive alertness of both men and women. Having learned the hard way, the girl can transmit the strength to help children surmount their own captivations.

As in most of the stories in *Dakota Texts* narrative conventions are used to augment meaning in "Double-Face Tricks the Girl." The quotatives, *śke'*, *keyapi'*, and *ke'* (it is said, they say) are phrases used to conclude sentences and to indicate continuity from teller to teller through the generations. The quotative has been recognized as serving these purposes in many Native American languages (see Wiget 329). But it has not often been seen as a structuring principle in the sense that Dell Hymes has given to initial particles in Clackamas Chinook stories. Of the sixty-four stories in *Dakota Texts*, an intentionally aesthetic use of the quotative may be observed in twenty-eight. In these the strong sound *śke'* concludes approximately the first and last two to six sentences. Most of the intervening sentences end in the less emphatic *ke'*, the shortened form of *keyapi'*, though at the end of an episode or after a decisive action, *śke'* may be selected.

The meaningful use of *śke'* is a storytelling style, rather than the practice of a single narrator, since the technique is found in stories Deloria collected from both Rosebud and Standing Rock (for the differentiation, see *Dakota Texts* x). The other major method of using *śke'*, at the end of every sentence throughout a narrative, occurs in twenty-four of Deloria's texts. At the end of a sentence, *śke'* and *ke'* both take the terminal glottal stop, accenting the narrative pause with a physical cessation of breath. When *keyapi* refers to characters speaking within a story, it has no glottal stop (see Deloria, *Dakota Grammar* 106–7). While the glottal stop strengthens sentence endings, the fricative *ś* makes *śke'* a stronger sound than *ke'* and a more emphatic sentence ending. A story told with *śke'* at the end of each sentence may be both more intense and more ritualized. Although Deloria notes that *śke'* is used particularly in myths, and *keyapi'* or *ke'* is used in "tribal tales, war, and other stories" (*Dakota Texts* 1), this distinction does not match the texts. In many *ohunkakan* (myths) *śke'* is used variably with *ke'*, though in others *śke'* is used consistently.

Intensely dramatic stories like "The Deer Woman," "The Feather Man," "A Woman Kills Her Daughter," "A Woman Joins Her Lover in Death," "The Elk Man," and "Double-Face Steals a Virgin" are well served by the use of *śke'* at the end of every sentence, but other short, suspenseful stories like "Meadowlark and the Rattlesnake" use *śke'* only after the first and last sentences. Narrators expected irregular choral responses from the audience such as *hau* and *ohan* (see Jahner, "Stone Boy: Persistent Hero" 178), particularly after statements affirming fundamental values: "After each *śke'* or *keyapi'* the pause is to allow all who are awake and listening to show their interest by saying *han*. Sometimes the boys will say *Ha o* but *han* is acceptable from either sex, in this situation—replying to the storyteller" (Deloria's notes in Bushotter 16). The glottal stop after each quotative contributes to this rhythm by clearing the space for response. When *śke* or *keyapi* are not used as quotatives, they do not evoke response and they do not create an automatic pause because they lack the glottal stop.

While *śke'*, *keyapi'*, and the latter's shortened form of *ke'* may be used to evoke audience response rhythmically throughout a story, some narrators distinguish *śke'* and *keyapi'* and *ke'*. *Śke'* signals the beginning and end, while an alternation between *śke'* and *ke'* creates dramatic emphasis. "Double-Face Tricks the Girl" has a symmetrical arrangement of *śke'* and *ke'* endings. The first and last four sentences of Deloria's transcription end with *śke'*, while all the intervening sentences end in *ke'* except the two that express the shock of recognizing that her "husband" is a Double-face:

> Wana nunwan ya canke cankahu akanl yankin na nazute kin el etunwan yanka yunkan heciyatanhan nakun ite *śke'*. Le anunk ite ewicakiyapi kin heca *śke'*.

> As she sat on his back while he swam along, she looked at the back of his head, and on that side, also, there was a face! This man was what is known as Double-face. (*Dakota Texts* 47, 50)

In her translation Deloria does not translate the quotative but much of the narrator's tone and effect may thereby be lost.

Elaine Jahner has theorized that in the Lakota "Stone Boy" story she translates ("Stone Boy" 178), *śke'* marks major pauses and *keyapi'* minor ones. She distinguishes between the two quotatives in her translation by putting *śke'* (so they tell) in separate lines each time it occurs, while *keyapi'* (they say) is set off by a comma at the end of a line. Although this is an improvement on Deloria's complete omission, the one syllable *śke'* with its fricative *ś* signals a more distinct pause, enhanced by the glottal stop, while "so they tell," even when set off in a line by itself, is comparatively neutral. The subtle relaxation from *śke'* to *ke'* is also lost in the unrelated sounds of "so they tell" and "they say." Because it includes the glottal stop but lacks the fricative *ś*, the pause after *ke'* is a half beat shorter.

"Double-Face Tricks the Girl" appears to be structurally formal in using *śke'* four times at the beginning and again at the end, since four is the pattern number in Lakota culture. However, most of the stories using both *śke'* and *ke'* adhere to a general pattern of *śke'* at the beginning, end, and dramatic points to emphasize reversals without being exact in the number of *śke'* endings used. Approximately four pauses precede each *śke'*, as in the first sentence of "The Deer Woman": (pauses are marked by a slash); "Wicaśa wan maninl omani-i na/ wana ḣtayetu aya canke/ tiyatakiya ku yunkan/ canmahel ugnahanla winyan wan ataya *śke'*" 'A man was walking away from camp and/ now evening came and so/ toward home he went and then/ suddenly in the woods he met a woman' (the Lakota is from *Dakota Texts* 163; my literal translation indicates that in Lakota the pause comes after "na" 'and,' "canke" 'and so,' "yunkan" 'and then,' rather than before, as in English).

In "Double-Face Tricks the Girl" the use of *śke'* and *ke'*, though symmetrical in structural placement, has an irregular number of pauses between each occurrence. As in English the emphatic phrases are short, but in Lakota the pauses are modulated from *śke'* to *ke'* to no ending. The staccato effect of two successive *śke'* endings is reserved for the story's most dramatic reversal quoted above. But the girl's increasing fear is expressed by longer phrases with several unsounded minor pauses before *ke'* demarcates the flow of emotion, halting the current she must ride: "Kośkalaka wan waśtelake c'un ehank'un he eśni kin nakeś hehanl sloyin na lila waḣtelaśni nakun hinyans gla *ke'*. Iyuweḣ kinazinpi na canmahel wakeya wan lila tanka ca etanhan sota izitanhan yunkan el kipi *ke'*" 'Now she knew that this was not that handsome young man she loved; and she despised and loathed him. They stood on the farther shore now, and walked from there to a large tipi in the wood from which smoke was rising' (*Dakota Texts* 47, 50).

Thereafter the story proceeds as a steady description of action punctuated by unspoken pauses and by *ke'* until the increasing fear is finally quenched by the monster's death. Then *śke'* ritually wraps the last four parts: 1) Double-face drowns; 2) the girl enters her camp; 3) the girl is married; 4) the beaver is honored. With corresponding symmetry, *śke'* had unwrapped the story's beginning: 1) the girl is virtuous and well liked; 2) she is unwilling to accept the young man who courted her; 3) she is suddenly courted by a handsome young man; and 4) she happily agrees to marry him. Thereafter the narrator uses *ke'* to establish pauses that are stronger than the unspoken ones, though the infrequent use of spoken stops contributes to the quickening pace of the story. The longer the phrases, the more literally breathless the action. The longest interval between spoken stops begins with the story's climactic event—Double-face begins to cross the bridge and the beaver rushes to collapse it from the other side.

Ke' marks the girl's frightened awareness that the monster is in pursuit, but the next spoken pause is the first of the four concluding *ske'*(s), coming ten pauses after the story's most violent event. The three concluding *ske'*(s) that follow are conventional, anti-climactic, and confidently ritualized in tone, the first two separated by only two pauses, the last by three, while the conventional "hehanyela owihanke" 'that is all' equals the *finis* of written prose. The diminishing length of phrases in the final *ske'* groups also corresponds to the disappearance of the story itself, in the same way that fading drumbeats end a Lakota song.

Additional uses of *ske'*, *keyapi'*, and *ke'* will be cited in other stories. Questions of style and translation will continue to be discussed in the context of each story. Deloria identifies the girl at the beginning of the preceding story as "virtuous," but the Lakota "narrator" (also Deloria, see introduction) was probably being more precise when he/she uses the word "ksapa," meaning prudent or self-protective rather than generally virtuous. After all, her attention to being "ksapa" did not protect her from forgetting the maidenly reserve that had made her so attractive as a prospective wife. In this case a single word suggests the narrator's use of irony and dramatic reversal.

In other instances the narrator's psychological insights are not precisely expressed in Deloria's translation. When the girl sees the monster as himself, Deloria simply says she "loathed" him, but "hinyans gla" in the Buechel dictionary means "to be afraid on seeing something terrible," i.e she feared something strange or unexpected, an emotion appropriate to the larger meaning of recognizing one's own vulnerability and others' deceit, realities one might have preferred to remain unknown. Similarly when the girl feels physical revulsion from Double-face in his tipi, Deloria says she "cringed at his nearness," differing again from Buechel's definition of "aloshingle" 'to become suddenly frightened' and 'to feel a scorched sensation suddenly.' The last meaning makes the phrase as intensely dramatic as the situation.

Dramatic intensity was supplied vocally as well as verbally. Words spoken by fictional characters are not preceded by "he or she said," which usually comes after the quote. The shift from third person narrative to drama is accomplished entirely by the voice: "K'eyaś wikośkalaka kin ecun cinśni yunkan hecena wicaśa kin lila canze na,— El iyotaka yo, epe lo" 'But the woman did not want to ride across the lake on Double-face's back, so then right away the man was very angry and,—"sit there," he said' (Lakota passage, *Dakota Texts* 47, my translation.

As in Shakespeare, punning provides an especially appropriate technique for oral expression. At the end of the story the beaver is described as "waunkaicilala," glossed by Deloria as "to feel important, as a spoiled child." Buechel supplements this definition with "to be proud, to think one is all 'it.'" A similar sounding word "waunka" means to 'fell a tree by sawing.' The beaver is proud because he has performed this activity. The grammatical breakdown of the words is not identical but close enough to create the pun:

waunkaicilala	*wa* (one) *unka* (the best) *icila* (makes himself) *la* (diminutive)
wawakiciunkalala	*wa* (one) *wakiciunka* (saws down trees for another) *lala* (diminutive reduplicated)

(Deloria has commented elsewhere on Lakota punning; see *Dakota Play on Words* 1–19).

From the finer details of language to the general art of recombining plot and character motifs, Lakota oral narratives reveal many distinctive refinements of technique. The following story, "Heart-Killer," has thematic and symbolic similarities to the Double-face stories. It opens with a familiar scene of four brothers making a sister of a strange young woman at their campsite. The mutual dependence of brother and sister is established at the outset, and the girl sustains their respect and her security with the practical virtues attributed to the heroine of "Double-Face Tricks the Girl." Together they live well, dividing their labor on the basis of gender; the brothers bring home meat and skins, and the sister turns them into food and clothing. But as must always happen at a certain stage of a young girl's life, the brothers "went away," or were not foremost in her consciousness, and she was distracted from the discipline of work to chase an elusive feather. She finds herself in "can oteȟika" 'dense woods,' as Deloria puts it, though "oteȟika" connotes 'tryingly difficult' rather than 'thick' in Lakota. In this confusion she is pulled (by her own impulses, as it were) into an alien family of beavers who drain hot fish on her face, a probable metaphor of sexual abuse. The revenge raid by her brothers and the sparing of the smallest beaver resemble similar poetic justice in other stories (see "Blood-Clot Boy," *Dakota Texts* 116), but the thematic implications change with the context. Here the beaver is adopted as a brother because he has acted as one, and the girl survives in captivity only because he comes to her aid.

Her second departure from fraternal protection suggests the difficulty of applying knowledge and the inevitability of danger. The girl is now named Heart-killer, a name connoting both desirability and imperviousness to courtship (see Deloria, *Camp Circle Society* 147). Like the girl in "Double-Face" she carries a pet beaver that grows into a resourceful defender. The extent to which identity depends on relationship is shown by the beaver's depression over losing his beaver brother. Like the girl, he has yet to fully appreciate the new relatives he has. Both the girl and the beaver are adopted, but perhaps the narrator suggests that every child is born as an individual and then "adopted" into a social group.

Like the feather coveted in the first episode, the promise of a husband temporarily distracts the girl from helping her family. She knows that she is risking something valuable, but the other girls take her pet beaver away, forcing her to join them. In this "seduction," the narrator demonstrates the power of peer pressure against even a wise girl's better judgment. Because the other girls seek only prestige in a husband, they wind up as wives of Teal Duck, the name of the trickster (usually Iktomi) in this story. Of course, they think the trickster is the hero. Heart-killer gets the real hero, Blece, but even with a good man as her husband, she is endangered because she has no brothers to protect her. Jealous of Blece's reputation, Teal-duck has him killed by Iya, a monster representing primitive appetite and brutality. With such forces existing even in a Lakota *tiyośpaye,* Heart-killer needs more than one protector.

She escapes over a bridge the beaver builds and unbuilds, as in the Double-face story. Iya does not drown but is simply portrayed as incapable of crossing a stream. Perhaps the storyteller means to say that the danger Iya represents cannot exist in a community that is truly a home. A young woman is advised to think twice about following any man from that home, but should she do so and regret it, she will always be welcomed back by the relatives she has known the longest.

In Lakota society being unmarried was not a fate worse than death for a young woman, but living without the protection of brothers might very well have been miserable: "Hetanhan nakeś tokiyani yeśni śunkaku op ti *ke'.* Kośkalaka kin nakeś lila tankeku awanglakapi canke inunpa hecel taku otehika akipaśni *śke'* " 'and after a long time they arrived at her brothers' home, where they were very happy to see her. From that time, she never went anywhere again but lived with her brothers. The young men kept closer watch of their sister now; so that never again so terrible a thing could come to her' (*Dakota Texts* 132–33). Note the use of *śke'* in the concluding sentence. *Ke'* is used throughout this relatively long story to mark all the pauses until the amazing vision of Iya holding the head of Blece high up in the full moon. This is followed by *śke',* as is the joy of her brothers upon her return. Their resolve to prevent her from being lost again is followed by the story's third and final *śke'.*

Heart-killer's vulnerability derives from wanting something (the feather) so much she forgets about danger and being pressured into feeling she will lose something valuable (the beaver, her security, and family identity) by not joining in the competitive husband seeking of the other girls. Marrying a stranger initiates another lesson in adolescent survival in "The Feather Man" (*Dakota Texts* 142–45). Elopement leads the heroine to discover that she is only a trophy to a man for whom spiritual purification in the sweat lodge means nothing. His taking of her scalp, an ironic reference to a sign of victory over a male enemy, means that he counts seductions like coups.

But even if a girl loses her virginity to such a man, the narrator mitigates future despair for listeners who make the same mistake.

Seeing a pretty "feather," she chases it as she had followed the first man, but this time the "feather" (also a symbol of male honor) is a complete human being. He cures her by teaching discipline and restraint. She will become whole but not unless she can learn to hold her breath under water. The return of her hair suggests the return of her identity as a Lakota woman, i.e. one respected and respecting of others.

Having found a real husband who will provide her with her own identity rather than just a handsome or even a brave "feather," the woman advances to another lesson in kinship and respect. Lakota women ritually thanked the mice whose gathered earth-beans they took, always taking care to leave some in the cache (see Deloria *Waterlily* 9). As in all good relationships respect was reciprocal. The mice respond by offering more food. But the Feather Man already had a first wife who is selfishly unwilling to share the duties of provision with a partner. Plural marriage tested the possessiveness of an individual woman and her willingness to put the extended family before herself. The first wife is a bad woman because she wants material objects for herself ("the brown swing is mine"), and because she competes for everything from the pursuit of pleasure to the gathering of food.

The heroine prevails because she has learned to value all relationships, not just those that result in pleasure or praise. She addresses her mouse friend as "Tunkaśila" 'Grandfather,' and he gives her all the food she needs, while the first wife exerts herself only to win and so comes home empty-handed. When the selfish woman emerges from the tunnel as an evil bear spirit, the narrator shows that her way of life has not been human, that she does not belong among the people. Killing her is almost an afterthought since she has never lived for others, and has therefore never been alive in the Lakota sense. A human being is a relative to other beings—people, mice, and badgers. Their powers supply the force that moves a person's story forward. But the meaning of particular animals was flexible. In this story the bear is an enemy animal, outside the network of relationships constituting the woman's mature home.

In "A Woman Kills Her Daughter" (*Dakota Texts* 166–71), the bad woman's unnatural competitiveness is more pronounced, since she envies her own daughter as if she were jealous of a rival wife. Although her daughter and son-in-law prevail, the focus of attention for the first half of the story is on the woman. She serves to negatively define a woman's kinship role, beginning with her scheme to seduce her son-in-law—a relationship ruled by strict avoidance (see Bushotter 253: 2 and Hassrick 116). She plans to effect this design by killing her daughter, an especially heinous crime in a society that made protecting children the paramount purpose of adult life. Childishness in an adult threatened survival. The plot she devises symbolizes the connection between evil and blocked maturity. Swinging represents her replacement of parental protectiveness with a regressive fixation on pleasure. The depth of the water next to the swing foreshadows the woman's disappearance in the crevice at the end of the story. Selfish passion removes the ground of mutual support and trust, on which the people depend and live. The narrator's comment on the "hacked rope" makes it into another symbol of the woman's breaking of kinship bonds: "ecin taku un suta kta wanica canke he un" 'for what was there about it to make it strong?' (*Dakota Texts* 167).

After thinking that she has killed her daughter, the woman assumes her daughter's identity, wearing her clothing and face paints, and tries to live unnaturally as one younger than herself. The narrator may be guiding the listeners into appreciation of all of life's stages. Only a semi-monster would wish to stop time and remain permanently youthful. This idea is immediately developed when the woman who can assume a youthful appearance cannot nurse a child. The unsuspecting husband initially expresses irritation that his "wife" is allowing his infant son to cry. In so doing he is expressing the natural instinct of an adult, but the unnaturally childish mother passes her grandchild to her son, another child, discarding both of them. Crying out his helplessness, the man's young brother-in-law carries his nephew to the river bank. In response his sister swims to the surface, retaining even in her metamorphosed state the maternal care her invisibly monstrous mother lacks.

The daughter's form as half-fish, half-human represents the mother's division of her own body into separate functions of feeding and pleasure. In the depths resembling the chasm where her mother ultimately disappears, the girl is non-existent except when she surfaces to heed the child. She can become a whole person, in whom sexuality and nurturing harmoniously blend, only if she is made confident of her husband's love.

Symbolic male powers are brought to bear on behalf of the woman in the same way that the beaver builds a bridge in "Double-Face Tricks the Girl" and "Heart-Killer," and as the husband empowers his wife with a tunnel-digging badger in "The Feather Man." In "A Woman Kills Her Daughter" the man's powers are expressed in metaphors of horse stealing and rescuing captives. The captive in this case is his wife, drowned by the chaotic selfishness of the mother. The man's rescue represents other unselfish acts of physical courage performed by warriors. Many stories use the tree stump transformation as a symbol of the invisibility assumed by a Lakota man in proximity to an enemy (see Beckwith 403; Buechel 389–90; Dakota Texts 83, 85; Wissler 130). The convention usually has somebody notice that the stump was not there before, only to be assured by someone else that it was always there. In this case, the man adjusts his identity to the situation, manifesting a resourcefulness evoked by danger. His ultimate purpose is to change an oppressive reality by employing his imagination. But in addition to having the personal will and intelligence to recover his wife, he draws upon the ritual means of restoration most widely employed: "Śkośkope eyaś agliyakupi na tiyata inikicaġapi na gluecetupi śke'" 'The body curved and jumped like a fish, but they managed to get it home where they made a sweat bath and restored the young wife to her former self' (Dakota Texts 170).

Again "home" is the place where a woman feels protected by her male relatives, while the depths of the water or the open places represent a state of emotional limbo. Men, of course, are accustomed to keeping their identities intact on hunting or war expeditions, but even they need spirit helpers to travel with them. The man obviously has supernatural powers, as evidenced by the doctoring of his wife and the manner of punishing his mother-in-law. Just as the Sun Dance and Vision Quest require unquestioning dedication, so a threat to social cohesion elicits a decisive, unsentimental response. But before destroying the enemy he secures his wife's safety in the action to come, "Mikiyela ece ku wo" 'stay near me all the time.' She immediately agrees, since he has already proved himself to be a husband in more than name.

In her initial state of abandonment, she had wished her mother had simply taken her husband. She would gladly have forfeited him: "Wicaśa kin he tuweka ca! Cantiheya hecinhan owotanla keś oglake śni wakukta tka; wana le nitehepi kin hehanyan hoġa imacaġe" 'Who is that man anyway? If she wants him so, how much better, had she told me; gladly I would have turned him over to her! But alas, I am now a fish from my waist down' (*Dakota Texts* 168). While the mother has never been deepened by marriage, the girl discovers the value of a husband in depending on him for life. A newly married girl will not know what love means until she recognizes that a husband sooner or later will spell the difference between life and death.

Both men and women have their own responsibilities and each must trust the other absolutely in the performance of specialized skills. The literal line drawn by the man divides those who perpetuate the future of Lakota culture from those who selfishly endanger that future. The telling of this story extends Lakota kinship, while the mother disappears into her customary oblivion, now physically realized. Because she has never lived for others, she has never become real as a human being, and as she has lived a fiction, so fiction vanquishes her. The husband becomes the stump. The storyteller becomes the story. In the process the mother's sick obsessions are artfully erased: "canke ekta mahel oyusnapi s'e iyaya śke'" 'So she disappeared into the abyss, as if someone had dropped her down' (*Dakota Texts* 171).

The storyteller uses *śke'* throughout rather than concentrating it at the beginning, end, or key dramatic points, nevertheless his frequent use of *śke'* and an occasional *ke'* is not random. The first *śke'* occurs after the first two pauses but thereafter occurs at relatively long intervals. In general the less frequent stops speed the story's action (see Tedlock 50). Eight unvoiced pauses occur between the girl's asking if the tree stump was always there and her husband's dramatic severing of her body from the fish. That action is immediately concluded by a decisive *śke'*. Thereafter the efficient enactment of the husband's plan is expressed with frequent *śke'* endings; the statement of the wife's restoration is followed by *śke'* and comes only three pauses after her separation from the fish.

The revenge sequence is intensified by the sound of *śke'* accompanying the man's clear direction, the wife's prompt and undeviating response, and the cleansing disappearance of the mother. The mother's meat pouch, the propensity she might spread to others, disappears with her. The perpetrator's ability to multiply greed is temporarily quelled by storytelling, with the final *śke'* as the narrator's last coup:

Hecena ake maka kin ecel naokiyuta canke hetanhan winunhcala wantakośku akiscu k'un he e ca talo k'in ka ca tunwan tuweni inunpa wanyankeśni *śke'*.

At once the ground came together once more. So from that time on, that old woman who was in love with her own son-in-law, was never seen again by anyone; neither she nor the pack of meat she carried. (*Dakota Texts* 171)

The woman's disappearance like that of any trickster, is tacitly understood to be temporary despite the narrator's assurance that she never returned. The dangers she represents are always present or the story would have no purpose. Divisions among the human family form the tragic substance of Shakespeare's major plays, especially *King Lear* where the family metaphor predominates. In the light of the narrator's conclusive solution to the problem of evil in "A Woman Kills Her Daughter," as well as in Shakespeare's overall perspective, Lear's gigantic lament at the presence of evil everywhere and even in his own family seems childishly overblown. What did he expect? Certainly his general curse on life, arising from an immediate experience of betrayal, would be less probable in a fiction uninfluenced by the concept of original sin. He curses all women, not just Goneril and Regan:

Down from the waist they are Centaurs,
Though women all above:
But to the girdle do the gods inherit,
Beneath is all the fiends';
There's hell, there's darkness, there's the sulphurous pit,
Burning, scalding, stench, consumption; fie, fie, fie! pah, pah!
(*King Lear* IV. vi. 126–32)

In Lakota culture betrayal by a relative would be shocking but not contagious. If a person's words or actions revealed them to be a trickster, then that person broke the bond of relationship and was treated accordingly.

In "A Woman Kills Her Daughter" an evil woman is discovered and dealt with, even though she is a mother and mother-in-law. Lear's violent incredulity proceeds from being unprepared for the presence of tricksters close to home. So does Hamlet's fury against his mother. So does Othello's deluded rage against Desdemona. Conversely, the disillusion of Lear and Hamlet goes to the opposite extreme: life is doomed from the beginning as proved by the present actions of individuals. Regardless of Shakespeare's intended meaning, Lear and Hamlet express the Western extremities of starry-eyed idealism and Puritanical realism, a consolatory pessimism extending in Western culture through Freud.

"A Woman Kills Her Daughter" combines Goneril, Regan, and Edmund in one figure. Repeatedly referred to as "wicaśaśni" 'tricky' or 'crafty,' the woman is the trickster in female form. Since a trickster is routinely encountered in the oral tradition, listeners will not be shocked by his/her challenges in real life, and scourging them will be the delight of storytelling. But Edmund and Iago are not as funny as Iktomi, nor so comically preposterous as the woman who violates the strictest rules—avoidance of her son-in-law and nurturing of her children and grandchildren.

Her plotting is both grim and absurd, but Edmund's is mostly grim:

> To both these sisters have I sworn my love;
> Each jealous of the other, as the stung
> Are of the adder. Which of them shall I take?
> Both? one? or neither? Neither can be enjoy'd,
> If both remain alive. (*King Lear* V.i.55–59)

In Lakota stories tricksters are dangerous but so lacking in self-respect as to evoke more contempt than revulsion. Lear and Hamlet, on the other hand, are especially incensed when they perceive women as tricksters. Rather than have Ophelia grow into a woman, Hamlet rhetorically removes her to a nunnery:

> I have heard of your paintings too, well enough; God

has given you one face, and you make yourselves another:
you jig, you amble, and you lisp, and nick-name God's
creatures, and make your wantonness your ignorance. Go to,
I'll have no more on't; it hath made me mad. I say, we will
have no more marriages: those that are married already,
all but one, shall live; the rest shall keep as they are.
To a nunnery, go, (*Hamlet* III.i.148–57)

For a long time before and after *Hamlet*, Western culture had considered asexuality to be a feminine ideal. In "A Woman Kills Her Daughter," both women wear face paint, but the mother is condemned because she tries to escape being maternal, not because she decorates her face. The paints are her disguise, rather than a sign of sluttishness, since good women too can wear them. But Hamlet uses medieval antifeminism as a metaphor of the hypocrisy he has not been prepared to encounter. He is angry at his mother because she, like the world at large, embraces unworthiness: "Ha! have you eyes? . . ./ . . . and what judgment/ Would step from this to this?/ Sense, sure you have,/ Else could you not have motion; but sure, that sense/ Is apoplex'd . . ." (*Hamlet* III.iv.67–73). In "A Woman Kills Her Daughter," the narrator does not condemn the woman for bad taste or not conforming to an ideal role but for breaking up a family and endangering her children and grandchildren. Hamlet pities himself because his world view has collapsed. He refrains from reversing his losses, not because he is weak but because he has no one he cares enough to fight for. Lakota heroes risk their lives for people rather than ideals.

When Hero is slandered in *Much Ado About Nothing*, Shakespeare emphasizes the ease with which the male characters, even Claudio to whom she is betrothed, accept the trickster's (Don John's) lie. Tragedy threatens because seemingly rational human beings can be fooled into sin, just as their first parents were in the Garden of Eden. And like Adam and Eve, Claudio, Don Pedro, and the rest are so hysterically proud (honorable) that they lack the fortitude to make patient judgments. Moreover, they have no responsibility greater than making their reputations the pretext for the wars they professionally fight. Souls are lost to anger or doubt in the tragedies and nearly lost in the comedies, but societies remain intact. Kings may come and go but the life of the larger group is a minor concern compared to the bliss, wedded or immortal, of the principal aristocratic characters.

Othello contains societal values and attitudes toward sexuality most fully and clearly different from those of Lakota society. The first wife in "The Feather Man" and the mother-in-law in "A Woman Kills Her Daughter" fixate on the objects of desire rather than on their rivals. Some stories do include sibling rivalry, as we shall see, but this is simple coveting, not the monumental self-hatred that supports Othello's jealousy. Self-hatred is largely absent from the Lakota oral tradition in any character type. In Shakespeare's plays individual self-hatred is a corollary of the collective self-hatred of original sin. Human beings must struggle against their nature to achieve faith in God's love. From Satan onward, the inability to keep faith has been painfully transmitted through the generations. Lakota culture assumed that life was good from the beginning. People could be fooled, but they were innately resilient enough to adapt and prevail.

5

Sexual Dangers for Everyone:
Adultery, Jealousy, and Revenge

Othello depicts a human race doomed for lack of faith, or, depending on the theology, lacking faith because they are congenitally doomed. Lakota stories of sexual jealousy do not forgive the killing of relatives, i.e. any other Lakota person, even when the crime is adultery. Men are expected to exhibit strength by letting their wives go and ignoring the wife-stealer. A leader especially "belongs to the people" and cannot act upon a private provocation. When Crazy Horse's wife returned to him after an affair with No Water, the latter was so incensed he shot Crazy Horse in the face. Although he was one of the most remarkable fighters of that time, Crazy Horse did not retaliate because he was a "shirt wearer," an honored executor of tribal action determined by a council of elders (Ambrose 341).

Othello is such a leader, the military governor of Venice, but Shakespeare uses his position to imply ironically that people cannot govern their passions, and that Othello's murder of his wife is only a variant of his occupation as a soldier. Venice has engaged in long wars against the Turks, because like Othello they are trying to prove who they are. Iago exploits Brabantio's fear of "an old Black Ram" covering his "white ewe," giving him "coursers for cousins and gennets for germans" (I.i.88–89, 113–14). Western culture fears the resemblance between human beings and animals. Animals are seen as subject to impulse and circumstance, more vulnerable to suffering than human beings who have free will and reason to control their fate. More importantly, animals in the Western view can die, while human beings have an immortal soul.

When Othello courts Desdemona, she is moved by his rehearsal of the "dangers he has pass'd," including an encounter with "cannibals," foreshadowing the universal fears that will consume them both. Shakespeare reveals the psychological basis of war. Following the Satanic paradigm, jealousy expresses an inability to love the self, compensated only by an act of revenge against the Creator or the established condition of one's life. In rituals of competition or "justice," the winners are actively autonomous, while the losers are passively impelled. Iago reminds Othello that he is "black," or animal-like, and that he is "old" or mortal. Othello fights for Venice to conceal this collective fear.

When the fears become personal, they are still the same, only less hypocritically concealed, closer to consciousness. Observing Othello's verbal brutality toward Desdemona, inappropriate in a social situation for a man of his standing, the Venetian envoy, Lodovico, is shocked and saddened. Ironically, Lodovico and others applaud Othello's brutality in war:

> Is this the noble Moor whom our full senate
> Call all in all sufficient? Is this the nature
> Whom passion could not shake? whose solid virtue
> The shot of accident, nor dart of chance
> Could neither graze nor pierce?

> (*Othello* IV.i.275–79)

The ideal Othello Lodovico mourns resembles the shirt wearer Crazy Horse remembered himself to be. But the assumptions accounting for Othello's fall were not held in Lakota society.

Othello kills Desdemona because humanity is unable to see straight since Satan "opened" their eyes in Eden. Iago repeats the cycle and Shakespeare implies that invisible forces, supernatural or psychological, manipulate human beings in every generation. The other characters in the play parallel Othello closely enough to make his guilt universal. The marriage of man to God and the Renaissance hier-

archical bond between human beings is broken by eternally active
satanic forces, variously construed to be natural or supernatural. Evil
thrives on an individual's need to maintain an illusion of control,
and being cuckolded or insulted without effective reprisal is a fate
worse than death. On the most ephemeral of provocations nations
will attack nations, the human family will destroy its own. Emilia's
temptation of Desdemona parallels Iago's seduction of Othello, though
Emilia is a good loyal servant and Iago is the devil. Desdemona is
urged to take revenge by realizing Othello's suspicions in order to gain
the "whole world," just as Satan told Adam and Eve to eat the apple
and be as gods.

Adultery here symbolizes the disloyalty to God and to his in-
junctions that all human beings will sooner or later manifest. Even
Desdemona is proud:

> *Desdemona.* Wouldst thou do such a deed for all the world?
> *Emilia.* The world's a huge thing: it is a great price
> For a small vice . . . why, who would not make her
> husband a cuckold to make him a monarch? I
> should venture purgatory for't.
> . . .
> . . . have not we affections,
> Desires for sport, and frailty, as men have?
> Then let them use us well: else let them know,
> The ills we do, their ills instruct us so.
> *Desdemona.* Good night, good night: heaven me such uses
> send,
> Not to pick bad from bad, but by bad mend!
> (*Othello* IV.iii.67–69, 75–77, 101–6)

Although Desdemona rejects adultery or revenge, she is caught in
the "web" of pride along with other characters as diverse as Brabantio,
Roderigo, and Cassio. Her childish insistence that Cassio witness her
ability to manipulate Othello into rescinding his punishment "plays
into" Iago's expectations. The best human beings share attributes of
the worst inherited from their first parents. In this sense Desdemona
eventually kills herself.

Iago's song for the drunken Cassio and other "gentle" officers
reflects the general intoxication of civilized society:

King Stephen was a worthy peer,
    His breeches cost him but a crown;
He held them sixpence all too dear,
    With that he call'd the tailor lown.

He was a wight of high renown,
    And thou art but of low degree:
'Tis pride that pulls the country down;
    Then take thine auld cloak about thee.
                             (*Othello* II.iii.92–99)

In the same scene in the dark, an inebriated Cassio staggers after an elusive enemy, shouting, "I am not drunk," becoming even more incensed when another soldier tries to protectively restrain him. In Shakespeare's plays God may or may not control the action but man not only doesn't—he can't. And if he learns the truth of the situation, even if the voice is the garbled one of his own bad dreams, he will kill other members of the human family to silence it, making every murder a self-murder.

Othello redefines "triumph" as self-destruction. As he had turned his weapons against others in the name of justice, so justice in the end is only his last desperate retreat from self-knowledge, this time through suicide. The "hero" fights victoriously for his own ignorance and (unintentionally) for someone else's enlightenment. Strutting and fretting his hour upon the stage, he is tragically "great," while the anonymous awareness of the audience confirms the wisdom God simultaneously allows. Salvation is the overview from the galleries (the heavens) and is not granted to actors predestined for the mouse trap:

I have done the state some service, and they know't.
No more of that. I pray you, in your letters,
When you shall these unlucky deeds relate,
Speak of me as I am; nothing extenuate,
Nor set down aught in malice: then must you speak
Of one that loved not wisely but too well;
  . . .
And say besides, that in Aleppo once,
Where a malignant and turban'd Turk
Beat a Venetian and traduced the state,

I took by the throat the circumcised dog,
And smote him, thus.   (*Stabs himself.*)
                                   (*Othello* V. ii. 339–56)

In Lakota stories the revenger is weak, but his weaknesses do
not represent those of man in general, as in *Hamlet* or *Othello*. In the
tragedies the audience accepts with fear but ultimately with resig-
nation a world that has been created to teach man's absolute dependence on God for personal salvation. The actions of the world's
great men bespeak folly and the spectators are left feeling grateful that
God's Providence has enlightened them. Lakota stories show listeners
that certain kinds of misfortune are to be expected, especially treach-
ery, betrayal, and personal humiliation. Any suffering that may result
is part of life's natural difficulty and is to be borne, if not always
stoically, at least without hysteria and above all without acts of violence toward a tribal member. Adultery was a fact of life, but it was
never a cue to go crazy. The deceived man might in some cases take
terrible revenge upon his wife. In an incident reported by Bushotter
as factual, a man left his unfaithful wife in a marsh where swarms of
huge mosquitoes ate her alive before he finally killed her (Bushotter
214: 1–2). The attitude in the oral narratives is usually against justice
of that sort.

Certain Lakota men had the power of the elk from a vision or
dream. The Elk power was useful in war, since the remarkably agile
male elk could run through thickly wooded areas even when his antlers
were at their widest span. But Elk power was most notable for its
erotic influence on women. While buffalo bulls and stallions were
believed to have hypnotic power over their cows and mares, and the
spider was invoked for its skill in weaving courtship schemes, the
male elk was in a class by himself:

He travelled alone. At times he would stand on a hill and call or
whistle in tones similar to those of the Indian flageolet. This call
would bring the females to his side . . . The flageolet thus
becomes a courting charm, but it is the power of the mythical elk
that is appealed to and symbolized by the music. It is well to note
that while the elk is taken as the incarnation of the power over
females, the real elk is regarded only as the recipient of such
power. (Wissler, "The Whirlwind and the Elk" 262)

Wissler goes on to tell the story of the first flute. A poor boy, ridiculed in courting by the daughter of a wealthy man, pierces his chest and stands tied like a Sun Dancer to four poles on a high hill. There he fasts and prays for coups, horses, and women until a mysterious man appears and gives him the flute with instructions for its ritual use. The music so disorients and excites women that soon the young man, Shoots at the Mark, and the friends with whom he shares the power, seduce most of the women in camp. But the triumphs end abruptly when Shoots at the Mark forgets the purifying sweat that should always follow intercourse, according to his vision. The next time he plays his flute he rises into the air until he disappears. The young man's fate reflects not erotic power as such but the destruction of anyone who forgets to acknowledge his supernatural benefactors and confuses a received ability with an innate or self-made virtue (see the discussion of Deloria's "Incest" later in this chapter).

Some Lakota men trusted material containers of erotic power, just as most wore a *wotawe* (war charm) into battle or carried a sacred stone for health and wisdom. The white of an elk's eye was part of an aphrodisiacal medicine bundle intended to sway a girl's affections (M. Powers 76):

> Another powerful charm was made from a mirror. In a small mirror was drawn the figure of an elk and around the edge a zigzag line to represent the lightning. Through the middle of the mirror a broken line was drawn to represent the trail of the elk, and sometimes his tracks were drawn along the trail line. In use the mirror was flashed so that the beam would fall upon the girl. The trail in the drawing implies that the girl must follow the footsteps of the owner of the mirror like the females of his kind follow the male elk. The lightning symbol is added to represent the thunder, or according to some accounts, to imply that this is a charm object. The flashing of the beam of light upon the girl is supposed to have something like a hypnotic effect and to put her into a state of submission. (Wissler, "The Whirlwind and the Elk" 266–67)

While Wissler's account implies that the Elk power was almost irresistible, several descriptions of the Elk dreamer ceremony mention four virgins leading six "elks" in a procession and conspicuously *not* looking back at them, while the elks flash mirrors at the onlookers to represent erotic distraction. This drama of sexuality portrays a girl's recommended response to a man's seductive tricks (see Black Elk, *The Sixth Grandfather* 242–44 and Fletcher 286). In a version of the flute story, quite different from the one reported by Wissler, the man's first performance causes all but one of the women in the village to follow him in rapture. He marries that one rather than the one he had avidly sought before (M. Powers 77 and Deloria, *Camp Circle Society* 146, 172). But while a girl who resists seduction is honored, preceding stories permit deceived girls to start over.

Some narratives pragmatically portray ingenious seductiveness as here to stay and never worth an Othello-like overreaction. In "The Elk Man" disciplined women who have "oteȟiicila" 'held themselves dear' and rejected many suitors, unaccountably run off with the same handsome man. His success narratively acknowledges that sexuality can sometimes overwhelm societal restraint. However, the chiefs initially mishandle the situation. They plot to kill the Elk man, less because they are humiliated than because of the social chaos he threatens. But their solution to the sexuality problem poses a greater problem. When they seek to promote social unity by dividing brother against brother, they themselves succumb to spiritual unchastity. To enable their design they violate kinship loyalty, the center pole of Lakota society. The older brother also proves a negative example. For a promise of horses, a home, and a beautiful wife, he agrees to sell out the man with whom he was nursed, a metaphor of any intratribal betrayal. The chiefs and the brother break rules more profound than those of sexual propriety. The *ȟaka* (hoop and stick game) they order should ideally channel competition into partisan support and permitted gambling. Its interruption by a political murder is a far more serious threat than a sexual adventure outside of marriage.

The Elk man's crimes are not judged by his youngest sister-in-law, who agrees to act in his drama of death and return. He tells her to say "le miś'eya śicaya makuwa s'a k'un" 'this one used to abuse me too' (*Dakota Texts* 160–61), probably a literal untruth, to show that the sexual impulse is part of everyone's nature even when not acted upon. If the people are to live, the Elk man must live among them.

Though his body is dismembered and burned, the social threat he poses will always recur.

The narrator specifies this acceptance when the resurrected Elk man returns to his brother "canzekeśni" 'not at all angry' (*Dakota Texts* 162). If sexuality cannot be absolutely controlled, so the wisdom of Lakota society counterpoises folly. The Elk man teaches his brother, as the narrator teaches the listeners, that loyalty to one's relatives must always take precedence over anything that can be possessed— women, horses, tipis. When he fails to receive the prizes promised by the chiefs, the older brother learns what the eloping girls learned in preceding stories: lose your brother and you have no one to protect you. The Elk man stands up for his brother as the brother had not done for him. The chiefs are forced to share the wealth, not by rule of law but by force of the kinship bonds that guarantee fair distribution.

They learn to "fear" the Elk man in the sense of respect for conditions they cannot change or exploit. Chiefs must prevent dissension and promote harmony even when ordinary people personally insult them (Black Elk, *The Sixth Grandfather* 390). As the governor of Venice, Othello is responsible for more than his own household. Yet responsibility to the society that has lionized him does not slow the momentum of personal rage. The narrator of "The Elk Man" accepts the Elk man's crime and the chief's urge to remediate, but he unconditionally rejects internecine killing. The story protects future generations by shaping character through fiction. Instead of saying crime does not pay, or that crime is universal, the storyteller says some acts are inevitable, and though they may be considered crimes, they are best let alone. But, he concludes, some acts really are crimes and the majority of people can fully refrain from them.

Tales of murder committed within the tribe conventionally carry a tone of awe. "A Bad Deed" (*Dakota Texts* 246–53) condemns a man's murder of his wife's lover though he virtually catches them in the act. The narrative's first line emphasizes that the deed is "wotehika" 'tryingly difficult' (Deloria translates it as "tragic"), because it is committed in the tribal circle. The man should have cared more for social harmony than the loss of a wife, especially a younger second wife that he has probably taken only to keep sisters together (see Hassrick 132). The first wife and the mother have no one else to hunt for them, and he has done the proper thing by marrying both girls and caring for his mother-in-law. Still it is not surprising that the younger wife might be sexually susceptible, living in such proximity to a younger man. Since the husband goes every night to the council tipi, he is theoretically mature and at least peripherally of leadership status. Following the discovery that his younger wife has taken a lover, the magnanimous gesture would have been to give her away if the young man could take care of her.

His revenge is emotionally sparked, but its cold execution is graphically described down to intestines unwinding from a gashed abdomen and the hurled body sliding down the side of his tipi. That such horrific bloodshed could occur in immediate proximity to a Lakota tipi constitutes the nightmare of a people generally safe from enemies though they lived without walls or fortifications. If a Lakota could be killed this way in the circle, no one was safe. The man realizes the implications of his deed immediately, but when he rantingly threatens his weeping wives with an arrow, the sense of horror is compounded. The story is a *wicowoyake*, a true account, rather than an *ohunkakan*, a fiction of mythical nature. But if the story is not tragic in the *Othello* sense, it is threatening enough in a Lakota *tiyośpaye*.

A sense of irrevocable harm falls over the man and his wife when they discover the proximity of the lover's relationship. The young man was his brother-in-law (or cousin, the narrator does not specify) as the adopted son of one of the girls' uncles, a member of their own immediate community. It is the body of that community's safety that has been ripped open by a mature man, not by a boy's adolescent lust. Moreover, boys were expected, even encouraged, to gain sexual relations as furtively and cleverly as they stole horses (Hassrick 124, Deloria, *Dakota Autobiographies* III:2, 1–19). When they succeeded, the woman usually bore the blame. The double-standard trained the boys in stealth and concentration and the girls in self-control and self-respect. A man with two wives might expect a younger wife to be vulnerable. But the mature man's own emotions should be made of sterner stuff. The boy's death in the midst of headlong flight symbolizes an attribute of adolescence, while the man's coldly surgical dexterity is a warrior's virtue misapplied. Jealousy is contemptible in a warrior; possessiveness was censured among people who continually circulated food, horses, material goods, and supernatural power. Considering the murder's consequences, not spelled out by the narrator, the man has no choice but to leave for good. He will either be killed or continue to live among the people under an unbearable burden of isolation and shame.

In addition the murderer has made himself, his wives, and mother-in-law orphans with little likelihood of survival on their own. But the fact that his wives and mother-in-law agree to escape with him suggests that he must have been a kind and conscientious provider most of the time. No mention of hot-tempered abuse is otherwise made. The man has not only launched himself into an apparently infinite darkness, but his dependents must also depart into the night. The narrator suggests the desperate feeling of exile, the ultimate punishment. Perhaps the consequences of the crime metaphorically objectify his state of mind upon committing it. The narrator includes the information that the imprudent boy was an orphan. His adoption by the uncle throws the protagonist's act of murder into brighter relief. The murderer has no children, but his first concern should be for the children of the community. Instead it is as if he had killed his own child. And in his banishment he is himself an orphan.

A series of metaphors indicate the loss he has sustained. Although his wives are with him, and although they have food, a blizzard makes pursuit impossible. On the one hand he has food and life; on the other hand, his own rage, objectified by the snow, has obliterated his life as a Lakota. The narrator's tone is not vindictive, however. He emphasizes the cherishing of kinship more than retaliation for sin. The husband is nearly destroyed by his own act of retribution. Providence, or the hypothetical Lakota equivalent, does not pursue the murderer; his own feelings of emptiness and disorientation are horrible enough. The storyteller allows him to learn from his mistakes and from a man who has as much *cause* (Othello's ironic word) to kill him, as he had to kill the boy.

Since the Crow and the Lakota existed in a state of perpetual hostility, the murderer might himself have been a victim of any Crow war party bearing the memory of their own relatives killed by the Lakota. The narrator establishes symmetry when the Crow war leader sits "hosanpatanhan" 'on the opposite side of the tipi,' just as the boy had lain with the younger wife "hosanpatanhan," across from the elder wife. But this time the man's enemy has the same power to determine his life or death that he had held over the boy. Outnumbered five to one, the man has no more chance by himself than the boy had against his professional attack.

By contrast, the Crow leader is a model of cool, deliberate manhood. He and his men stamp the snow off their moccasins as if they were entering a tipi in their own camp. The Lakota man impulsively reaches for his gun, but it is of no use without supportive male relations. Unable to defend his family from an enemy, he offers them food, an automatic gesture of hospitality within the tribe. But the Crow leader's response only deepens his sense of loss: "Heca wicaśa ca wicaśa wanzi el hi can okipaġi na kici canunpe unśto" 'When man meets man, when they visit one another, they fill the pipe for a smoke together!' (*Dakota Texts* 249). The Lakota man then recounts his story to explain his apparent lack of courtesy: "He un le ocicipaġikta owakihiśni yelo. Lakota kin tuwa ti wicakte can he nape śiceunyawa pelo" 'That is why I cannot fill a pipe for you. Among us Dakota, a murderer's hand is bad' (*Dakota Texts* 250).

The consequences of the murder are emphasized when the man declines to smoke with the Crow, since the pipe is the best way for men to establish life-ensuring alliances. On the other hand, his refusal to smoke shows that he still respects the pipe and its power to connect. The man that has broken his bond to another Lakota who should be a son, brother, brother-in-law, or cousin is not fit to touch an instrument creating those ties. Without the right to handle a pipe the man must roam about—living, but not like a human being, and finally not caring if he lives or dies. Yet he does care about his family and asks the Crow to spare their lives. Although he is a murderer, he has been raised to protect the helpless ones.

The narrator has the Crow leader respond properly, by conferring first with his warriors, respecting and depending on their opinions before making a careful decision. His surprising proposition advances the symmetry of the story, since he now formally asks for the woman the boy had simply taken. His desire to restore a dead relative is greater than his desire to kill a Lakota, a direct reversal of the Lakota man's Othello-like revenge. The killing of an enemy was legitimate among the Crow and the Lakota, but his supposed enemy makes kinship and generation his priorities rather than glory and vengeance. Having received acceptance from the women, who again express the severity of exile by immediately agreeing—"Nakun heciyani unt'api k'eyaś hecetu we" 'Even if we die there, it will be well'—the Crow leader ritually purifies the Lakota during a four-day ceremonial period that includes renewal in the sweat lodge and a symbolic change of clothes (also a common symbol of tribal adoption).

As a Lakota, the murderer had become a "buried man," the term used for someone of no standing and little worth (see Walker, *Lakota Society* 55). The narrator does not begrudge him the opportunity to start over as a Crow. His "sin" is washed away in the sweat lodge, and although no Lakota would perform this rite for a *tiwicakte* (one who kills at home), the rite in and of itself can cleanse the man. The Crow leader has essentially refused to kill a man who is already dead. In bringing him to life, the Crow leader trusts that the man will never forget how it felt to be dead and that he will always remain appreciative. Accordingly, the Lakota helps the Crow war party to steal some Lakota horses.

As they approach the herds, they pass the scaffold where the dead boy lies and next to it the dead body of his horse. The detail helps the narrator to express the impact of the Lakota man's good fortune. As the horse accompanies the boy to the spirit world, so his killer has died as a Lakota but lives on as a Crow. While the men are taking horses, the women, protected by one Crow, pack all the necessary provisions at a location just far enough from the Lakota camp to facilitate their escape. Even here the emphasis is on safe return to the larger group. The group of former enemies now functions as a family. The Lakota man had put his pride first, as Othello did, and instead of proving his strength against one he feels to have mocked it, he feels the abject helplessness of any man forced to stand alone. The act of stealing horses is also carefully described in further contrast to the murder. Horse stealing was an accepted way of life rather than a crime. It required control and courage, qualities the Lakota has misemployed against one of his own. Here cool premeditation results in more life—horses for defense, food, and transport.

While Othello as Everyman suggests a universal inability to avoid self-destruction, the Lakota narrator shows that creation can supplant destruction through his Crow hero. When they arrive together at the Crow camp, the Crow leader again respectfully speaks to his people before telling them to treat the Lakota family as relatives rather than captives. Like a storyteller he tells the welcoming assembly how the new relationships came about. He instructs them in his own version of Desdemona's will "Not to pick bad from bad, but by bad mend!" (*Othello* IV.iii.106). The bad had been his first wife's death and the Lakota man's crime. The good expresses one of the foremost messages of the Lakota oral tradition—whatever happens, remember that an enemy can only destroy you if you hate him more than you love your own family or your own people. The Lakota man had almost taken his wives and mother-in-law down with him. The Crow man's replacement of his wife fulfills a man's obligation to think first of the people's future and to restrain personal obsessions. The storyteller consistently reminds the listeners not to be overwhelmed by failure, as in the stories of girls who elope with monsters only to eventually return to the circle as respected wives. By having the girl who caused the bad deed save the family, the narrator affirms the people's ability to live well.

Shakespearean tragedy affirms the opposite. Even the comedies are populated by people who turn out all right only because in the overtly contrived endings God's grace cancels out original sin. *Much Ado About Nothing, As You Like It,* even *The Tempest* might not have ended well if the characters were not thrown into mysterious circumstances or suddenly blessed by inspired thoughts. In "A Bad Deed" survival does not require an invisible *deus ex machina.* Instead the Crow leader values the future of his people and wants a wife. He knows that individuals die and that his first duty is to think of the future of the whole people. He knows that rituals work, that they have a lasting effect in a culture that respects them. He knows that individuals grow and change and that in his society banishment is a greater deterrent than execution because it is a living death of isolation, an Indian version of hell.

The resurrection of the buried man affirms the only life that really counts. Having created a society of relatives rather than citizens, people are loyal to each other for better reasons than ethnicity or patriotism. A bad deed becomes the good deed of tribal origination, and the story is the narrator's version of the social contract:

> canke iyuha ptaya takukiciya unpi na ecel sanp cincapi kin
> Lakotapi k'eyas Kangi wicasa iyecel icagapi sanpa igluotapi k'eyas
> ektana unpi na heciyanna t'api.

> So the families of the two men lived together in a happy group and were as closely related as if they were natural relatives. And that was how, after a time, the children, and the children's children, though they were Dakota, grew up as Crow Indians; and there they multiplied, and there they died. (*Dakota Texts* 252–53)

As the Lakota characters become members of another tribe, so the Lakota tribe itself is an alliance of independent bands. The word *Lakota* means "the friends." "A Bad Deed" is a microcosm of tribal formation. Relatives are not determined by blood but by behavior (see Walker, *Lakota Society* 6).

At the beginning it is mentioned that the Lakota man "toki-yatanhan hi" 'arrived from somewhere else.' Similarly the boy who sleeps with his wife forgets that he has once been an orphan, and that the husband and others in the community have accepted him as a trusted relative. The general meaning of adoption here implies that every human being is adopted into a community they must learn to regard as their own, though conscious gratitude may temporarily lapse. While sexual desire can cause forgetfulness, adultery is not a cause for Puritanical hysteria or libertine defiance. It is a natural likelihood and a source of danger when it impels violent jealousy or habits of laziness and indulgence. None of these are collectively fatal, but if the jealousy provokes murder, the murderer has effectively committed suicide.

"A Bad Deed" dwells less on the proper punishment for murder than on the culture's ability to heal its effects. The narrator also promotes intertribal peace. Just as the man who killed the boy has grown into one who "igluotapi" 'multiplies' instead of destroys, so the Crow and Dakota have outgrown their feud to recognize shared values and customs. The narrator practices friendship by portraying the Crow as an ideal embodiment of Lakota ritual, respect, and wisdom.

The balancing and transformation of characters in this story is its outstanding technique. An immature boy dies but his killer becomes mature. A Lakota girl commits adultery and dies in the sense that she is banished from the group identity that defines Lakota life, but she becomes the chaste wife of a Crow leader whose own dead wife she resembles. A man destroys an immature relative but then is spared by a man more mature than himself. People prevented from contributing to the future of the tribe by their own acts enter a new life where they and their children multiply.

The idea that retribution for lust is a lust that cannot be allowed also appears in "Incest" (*Dakota Texts* 175–80), another long story containing additional perspectives on the subject. While "A Bad Deed" has some parallels to *Othello,* this story also offers a Lakota view of a problem raised in *Measure for Measure.* Anyone who remembers the harshness of Isabella's answer to her brother's plea for life will notice the analogy in the following text where sexual dishonor is measured against kinship loyalty (*Measure for Measure* III.i.136–51).

The story identifies its protagonist as a "boy-beloved," a child specially groomed for leadership. But the narrator suggests that a boy who has known only approval and never suffered failure may turn out to be dangerously self-righteous. His temptation by a sister may represent his entry into puberty. All girls are in some sense like sisters, and if one of them acts like a Deer woman, she is not worthy of punishment by a chief. Most will be loyal and virtuous, sisters to the whole people, like his younger sister. In the darkness of adolescent naiveté he overreacts to the crime. Although he is clever about discovering the culprit, his emotions are intemperate and his strategies misfire.

His inability to identify the girl on the first try corresponds to his inappropriate responses to her threat. Burning her with a hot brand, like cutting off the tip of an adulterous woman's nose, may have a certain justice but the narrator implies that the one who enacts such revenge has raw emotions like a child and may or may not grow up to be the rock a leader must resemble. The young man's moralistic arrogance develops from the deference his father shows him, even though he has not merited it. Though he wonders, the father does not wish to show disrespect for the boy's odd requests. The narrator does not question such permissiveness, since it was customary to bolster youthful independence. Instead he suggests that boys become chiefs when they learn humility the hard way, not because proud parents have dreams.

The boy feels anger and shame after branding the girl, because she is his sister. The narrator means to instill shame for inflicting violence on any "sister" for this sort of crime. The image of being glued to a rising tree portrays the boy's excessive and misplaced sense of justice. He has correctly been repelled by a close relative's gross selfishness, but he has gone too far in implementing his verdict. When the tree grows through the tipi, the young man's perfectionism has placed him above the people, a danger in any future leader. In fact the people's fear of the rising tree suggests the implied threat to the tribe from leaders able to inflict overly severe punishment for crimes they themselves define and measure. Lakota society did not allow individual leaders to punish law breakers. Disputes were usually mediated by families. Groups of families would simply pack up and leave a potential tyrant (Walker, *Lakota Society* 24).

In this story the young man returns to reality and effectiveness through the influence of the younger of his two sisters. The balance of one sister being a Deer woman and one being true reflects types of women expected to be present in each generation. Just as Deer women are immortal in the oral tradition, so the virtuous sister or future wife typically brings the male hero a vitalizing lesson in loyalty and sacrifice. The Deer woman's identifying brand is safely visible once her immortality is recognized. A young man who learns that such women always exist can return from the heights of judgmental elevation to feeding his people on the ground. But first he himself must be fed by certain stories. The Thunder man instructs the young man in adversity. First he recapitulates the young man's rise by having the girl feed him deer meat. After all, obsession with the Deer woman has put him in this predicament. But then the Thunder man directs the young man, now a captive audience, to concentrate on the other kind of woman when he proposes to marry the younger sister. Since he is a

Thunder man he is likely to present a frightening image, but the girl understands that her brother cannot come down to earth unless she consents. She agrees to this sacrifice because her love for her brother is greater than her fear.

The Thunder man's destruction of the tree, while the girl is covered by a blanket, represents the acts of a warrior performed away from women. He teaches the young man by example where and when to exercise warrior power, not on a Deer woman (or a wife-stealer, as in "A Bad Deed"). The power to destroy is finally channeled into killing buffalo and even to the usual woman's work of grinding meat and bones into *wasna*. Teaching by example, he imparts to the young man the will and ability to supply food, the first duty of a chief.

At the distribution, a woman dissatisfied with her share of the *wasna* resembles the young man in his perfectionist phase. But when she almost chokes to death on her greed, it is cut out of her mouth just as the narrator and other Lakota teachers, helped by inevitable setbacks to youthful ambition, could transform an appetite for prominence into an unstinting will to provide. The young man then leads the people back to the place they had left, an inhabitable home once again because its leader has become a man.

The Thunder man gives his last lesson when he frees the girl and returns to his home. As a chief, the story's hero will protect his own as a Thunder man among Thunder men. He will use the power of the lightning to burn away greed and selfishness, not to pursue minor enemies already branded as Deer women by their actions and punitively shunned. A "crazy sister" might become an adulterous wife. In any form she fuels the hollow pride of the seducer or the swollen rage of the deceived. And the man who feeds her with desire or jealousy does not feed the people. Instead of remembering them as relatives, he starves them by pursuing a private obsession.

The loyal sister and the Thunder man enact the ideal models for men and women. The young man is hardly the warrior ideal when he is reduced to begging his sister to marry the Thunder man because he wishes to come down from the tree. But experiencing weakness was intentionally formative in such rites as the Vision Quest and the Sun Dance. Participants did not cry for relief but they may have felt like it. The ordeal taught them limits and helped them to accept those of others. In *Measure for Measure* Claudio's imprisonment teaches him to fear death and value life enough to ask his sister to surrender her virginity to Angelo, so that the latter will revoke his death sentence. Her response to Claudio would have been unthinkable in Lakota society:

> *Isabella.* O you beast!
> O faithless coward! O dishonest wretch!
> . . .
> Die, perish! Might but my bending down
> Reprieve thee from thy fate, it should proceed:
> I'll pray a thousand prayers for thy death,
> No word to save thee. (III.i.136–46)

The Duke knows that Isabella would gladly sell her brother for her sanctity, yet he is deeply in love with her and manipulates the action so that he can marry her in the end. In the last scene the aptly named Marianna forgives Angelo for jilting her and lusting after Isabella, because "best men are molded out of faults;/ And, for the most, become much more the better/ For being a little bad" (V.i.42–45). But Shakespeare is probably being ironic. Marianna represents the irrationality of love, since Angelo is the most unlovable of characters, and she also reflects the infinite mercy of a God who forgives people no matter how proud or corrupt, as all the major characters in *Measure for Measure* prove themselves to be.

In the end the Duke knows how to make it look like he cares for his people when he establishes a society free from anarchy and therefore easy for him to rule. Ostensibly he cleans up a dirty town, beset by sexual corruption of every sort. But his political purpose is disguised, and the people are instructed only in managed news, as the last line of the play's curtain speech reveals: "So bring us to our palace, where we'll show/ What's yet behind that's meet you all should know" (V.i.544–45).

While the Duke will conceal whatever is not "meet" to disclose about his own leadership, the Lakota stories define a leader as one who feeds and protects the people, disclosing his identity in his acts. In a variant of "Incest" in the Beckwith collection the replacement of lust and pride with generosity is more elaborately developed (Beckwith, "The Nation of the Horses," in "Mythology of the Oglala Lakota" 413–14). The Thunder man not only teaches by example, he gives the youngest sister nonsacred dances that elevate social celebrations over private relationships:

> He took a drum, all black, and gave it to the girl and bade her establish such dances as the Omaha, the woman's circle dance, the white horseman dance, the buffalo dance, including the chief's dance called the short hair dance—"We shall be up in the sky watching you to see if these dances are observed." (Beckwith 413–14)

The narrator, Mrs. Susie Hollowhorn, adds in a footnote that the girl never married and "knew things in dreams." While lifelong virginity was not a common goal of nineteenth-century Lakota women, virginity was accorded great respect and was idealized in the tribe's single most important story, the White Buffalo Calf Woman's gift of the sacred pipe (Black Elk 283–85, Densmore 63–68, Walker, *Lakota Belief* 109). Lechery destroys the bad scout. The good scout helps communicate the meaning of the pipe. Here as throughout the oral tradition, sexuality becomes negative when it represents selfish exploitation. Though the sacred woman is a virgin, neither she nor the narrators of the oral tradition recommend celibacy as a morally superior way to live. The virginity of the girl who receives the Thunder man's instruction in Beckwith's "Incest" is so unusual that like other *wakan* phenomena it sets her apart and enables her to have visions. In the story's metaphor, the incestuous sister produces anger and confusion, while the generative sister is spiritually virginal, even though she is willing to sacrifice her physical virginity. The virgins in the Elk ceremony, in Black Elk's horse dance, and in the Sun Dance represent single-minded dedication to healthy life and the shutting out of debilitating distractions, not the spiritual superiority of abstinence for its own sake.

The psychological and social sophistication of Deloria's "Incest" complements its effective use of language and narrative conventions. *Ske'* and *ke'* are used conventionally as well as variably to modulate the story's mood. The first four uses of *ske'* demonstrate the ritual beginning of a story. *Śke'*, as the stronger sounding form of "it is said," gathers the attention of the audience and invites the initial enthusiasm of a vocal response to express appreciation for the fun of any telling. *Śke'* follows the ritual "oyate wan tipi" 'a people were encamped,' and then in succession: the description of a boy so beloved that his parents give him his own tipi, the mention of his two sisters living with their parents in an adjoining tipi, and the high hopes held by the whole community for his future. From the beginning of the action, however, the narrator uses the softer *ke'* to mark the insidious entrance of the oldest sister to tempt the boy. He (or Ella Deloria) then drops the use of all endings for an unusually long interval to describe the boy's response to being tempted, his instructions to his father to slide in the paint, the painting of the girl, the ordering of the shinny game, and the perplexity of the father.

The narrator finally uses *śke'* again to mark the end of this series of preparations for the boy's first test of the woman's identity: "canke wana winyan taṗkapsil wicaśipi *śke'* " 'Immediately a shinny game was arranged for the women' (*Dakota Texts* 176). The *śke'* closes the preparatory action and precedes the moment of truth. But the woman simply changes her clothes before the game, and the man cannot find her. Accordingly the description of this failure is verbally indefinite—it has no ending. The next line describing her second attempt at seduction also has no ending, but the announcement of the second shinny game, as the boy's next attempt at decisive identification, has the lesser ending of *ke'*.

By dropping all endings again for a long sequence, the narrator lends speed and excitement to the boy's recognition in the next game that the girl with red paint on her face is his sister, and this recognition leads breathlessly into his plan to brand her. Even after he connects these acts, the narrator does not use *śke'* or *ke'* to divide the deed from its consequence, the imprisonment on the rising tree. *Śke'* is finally employed to emphasize the helplessness of the boy's plight: "na can kin he lila oḣankoya wankataḳiya icaḣ aya canke ikoyak iś'eya sanp wankataḳiya ya *śke'* " 'Of course, since he was part of the tree, he was rising higher all the time, too' (*Dakota Texts* 178). Now that a supernatural event has occurred, the narrator uses the strongest ending more frequently, repeating *śke'* again after a repetition of nearly the same statement: "canke iyowaśinya kośkalaka k'un lila wankatakiya ya śke'" 'Then the tree grew even faster, elevating the young man higher and higher' (*Dakota Texts* 178). Then again at briefer intervals *śke'* follows the people's fearful retreat. In these uses *śke'* divides separate actions, whereas before, the absence of *śke'* marked the flow of the young man's emotions into his attempts to control it, attempts not requiring a *śke'* because they are unsuccessful.

When the subject changes from the boy to the people, the narrator marks the change with *śke'*. Then when it changes again from the people to the youngest sister, he/she uses it again to mark that change: "Canke tankśitku unma hakakaia wan ksapela k'un hecela can huie kin el nazin na ceyahan śke'" 'Only the good little sister of the young man stayed at the base of the tree and wept' (*Dakota Texts* 178). The next episode involving the taunts between the oldest sister and the brother is then set in motion. It is not suspenseful like the initial sequence describing her attempts at seduction and his attempts at revenge, and so it is not fast-paced without endings, but on the other hand it does not include decisive turnings, and so the narrator uses *ke'* rather than no ending (for speed) or *śke'* (for intensity). *Ke'* is used three times in a row to punctuate the oldest sister's insinuation that the youngest sister too is attracted to the brother, and twice for the brother's reply that he has permanently disfigured the oldest sister. The punch line, however receives *śke'* when the oldest sister reveals herself to be a Deer woman:

> Canke wicincala wan waeyeśipi k'un he ecel eya yunkan
> hecena,—He wotehi wakila k'un,—eyin na tahica wan canmahel
> wahpe yusnapi s'e kigla śke'.

> So the girl called back as her brother had taught her, and
> straightway the one in the wood called back, "O, that's the thing
> I resent!" and a deer ran back into the wood amid rustling leaves.
> (*Dakota Texts* 178)

The story then turns after *śke'* concludes this episode. It is used again after a brief interval to mark the brother's release and the beginning of his instruction by the Thunder man:

> Wicincala, le nitiblo cekipa yo,—eyin na tahica talo wan

hiḣpekiya canke inazin na ceunpi na wankatuya nazin k'eyaś ekta
iḣpekiya canke yuta *śke'.*

"Young girl, roast this for your brother," and he threw her a piece
of deer meat. So she rose and cooked it and tossed it up to her
brother, though by now he stood very high. Her brother ate it.
(*Dakota Texts* 178–79)

Ke' immediately precedes the Thunder man's proposal of marriage
and follows the young man's begging his sister to consent. *Ke'* again
precedes the quoted and fearful instructions for her to lie under a
blanket and then follows the description of her imprisonment underneath. For the mysteriousness and force of the Thunder man's
actions, however, the narrator reserves *śke':* "Hecel un hingnaku tokel
ecun kin wanyankeśni canke oyaka okihiśni *śke'* " 'Thus it was that
she did not see how her husband worked his magic, and was unable
to tell it' (*Dakota Texts* 179). While the narrator had used neither
śke' nor *ke'* to describe the immature actions of the young man in
seeking to punish his sister, the mature power of the man's Thunder
strikes is sounded in a more compressed use of the ending, *ke'* building
power through repetition, until *śke'* expresses the culmination of the
effort:

Yunkan leyalaka, he wakinyan wicaśa hunśe ca wakinyan tunwan
hingnin na iyakiglegle wakinyan hotun yunkan can k'un
naśleślecin na kaweḣ gliḣpaya canke kośkalaka k'un he glicu *śke'.*

He was actually a Thunder man, though they did not know at
first. For the Thunder man opened his eyes (lightning), and
repeatedly he roared (thunder), and the tree was split in two,
and fell broken to the ground so that the young man stepped off.
(*Dakota Texts* 179)

Each description of the Thunder man is treated as an extraordinary occurrence by using *ke'* to intensify a series of statements and
śke' to conclude the larger actions. *Ke'* follows in succession 1) the
release of the girl from the blanket, 2) her greeting of her brother,
3) the Thunder man's provision of meat, 4) his telling the young man
to bring the people back to their abandoned camp site, 5) the dis-

tribution of the *wasna,* and 6) the complaint of the greedy woman. Used six times consecutively, *ke'* accompanies the story's turning away from the teaching of what not to do, to the imprinting of its major positive lessons. Again he saves *ske'* to make one of the story's strongest teaching symbols more memorable:

> Hecun na yate c'eyaś sanp ota ayin na hankeya i kin okipiśni na wana katkinkta canke mila icupi na wasna kin waksaksa ikicicupi *ske'.*

> Then she chewed; but gradually it increased in amount until finally her mouth could not hold it all; and she was choking on it. (*Dakota Texts* 180)

From this point to the end of the story *ke'* is not used at all, while *ske'* is used five times at relatively small intervals to conventionally signal the story's approaching end, and to lend force to the girl's sacrifice and its transformation of her brother to a Thunder man. *Ske'* follows the miraculous filling of many containers from the single morsel, as if to say that a nation takes life from a few wise men. Then *ske'* is used again to express the results of such leadership, "ecekce kiyotakapi na lila waśecapi *ske'* " 'they set up their homes again; and they were very well provisioned' (*Dakota Texts* 180). And again only six words later *ske'* is used to say that these results are lasting: "Hetanhan oyate kin he wicakiześni unpi *ske'* " 'From then on, that people no longer knew want, they say' (*Dakota Texts* 180).

The last two *ske'* endings of the story help to ensure that the Thunder man be remembered as the personified male ideal. First, he does not exploit the girl, magnanimously releasing her from the marriage. His unselfishness should apply to all human relationships. Mature men help other human beings with no strings attached. Their satisfaction is in giving rather than reward or exchange. By initially promising to help the brother only if he can have the girl, he teaches by negation, but he also tests the girl. Implicit in his actions is the release of a girl from a marriage she did not want but has agreed to for the benefit of her family. If a family was poor, they might badly need the horses offered by a suitor, and the girl might sacrifice her personal happiness in such a case (see Deloria, *Waterlily* 149). However, the narrator of "Incest" seems to say that a strong man will release a girl from such a marriage, finding his fulfillment not in having anyone or anything but in helping for its own sake. His speech is so central to the story's meaning that *śke'* both precedes and follows it:

> Yunkan hehanl wakinyan wicaśa k'un he tawicu kin na heya
> *śke'*,—Howo, wicincala, nitiblo awicakeya teyahila un hingna
> mayayinkta yeś ko iyowinyaye c'un, wana wagninkte lo. Eyaś
> wana ociciya ca,—eyin na toki wakinyan tipelaka hecetkiya kigla
> *śke'*.

> Then the Thunder man told his wife this, "Now, young girl, you whose love for your brother was so big that you consented to be my wife for his sake, I am going home. It is enough, for I have now given you aid." And so he went away, somewhere, wherever it is that the thunders abide. (*Dakota Texts* 180)

"Incest" makes it clear that illicit sexual desire can be classified with other forms of extreme selfishness such as the woman's greed for food. Although adultery is as eternal as the telling of trickster stories, the Lakota narratives do not trivialize it. Some oral narratives present a stronger sense of sexual misconduct than those previously discussed. Deloria's "A Woman Joins Her Lover in Death" (*Dakota Texts* 260–62) shows less sympathy for its youthful Cleopatra than a version recorded by Densmore:

> A young woman had promised to marry a man, but he wished "to make a name for himself" before the marriage took place. He had been on the warpath, but he wished to go again that he might distinguish himself by valor. When the war party returned, they said that he had been killed by the Crows. Sometime afterward in the course of tribal wanderings a camp was made at the place where, according to the report of the war party, the young man had been killed. Dressing herself in her best attire, the maiden went to the edge of a cliff, and after singing the following song and giving the shrill "woman's tremolo," jumped into the river below. (Densmore 494)

The Densmore story concerns a woman's dashed hopes for marriage and her romantically distracted response. Like the young man she grieves for, she demonstrates courage in her death. Both are sympathetically regarded. The Deloria story, on the other hand, treats the woman with little sympathy and tells her story as a complex lesson in value. To begin with she is not betrothed to the man she dies for, but engaged in an adulterous affair with him. She and the man are therefore as dangerous to the peace of the camp as the enemies who kill the man.

Deloria says the man's war party was "aoglutewicayapi" 'held at bay,' but "aoglutewicayapi" means 'surrounded' and the woman herself is surrounded by a society unwilling to approve her affair or her death. The narrator verbally emphasizes the sense of hopelessness for one in her situation by referring to the war party with an intentional redundancy avoided by Deloria's translation: "canke wanzini niśni iyuhaḣcin hena t'api śke'" 'and so none lived, they all died' (*Dakota Texts* 261, my literal translation). To avoid this fate, the narrator implies, the people must not do as the lovers have done but remove themselves completely from idealizing such behavior, as they do at the end of the story. Near the beginning the narrator associates the event with *ḣmu*, the buzzing sound accompanying the presence of evil spirits, another word and idea not translated by Deloria: "canke ḣmu s'e lececa" 'and so there was a buzzing all about' (*Dakota Texts* 261, my literal translation). *Ḣmu* here may be a metaphor for the bustling of setting up tipis, but the connotations of the word make it an appropriate one to immediately precede the woman's song. As a psychological metaphor *ḣmu* expresses the cultural association of uncontrollable emotion with the inability to survive, the suicide of the individual that must not become that of the nation.

The woman herself initially appears apart from the people. They are camped at the bottom of the hill on which she stands, further removed from them by the concealment of her head in a blanket. The spatial arrangement objectifies the way she has lived—putting herself above the people, thinking only of herself and her lover, becoming invisible to them as a contributing member of the camp circle. Deloria's note on the woman's song as resembling in tone a song to give a man an honor name is especially helpful, but her translation lacks this idea. "Wocazeyalya," the 'sentiment' of an honoring song is ironic in relation to the dishonorable attachment of the lovers. While a person honored gives the people life, these two have destroyed themselves and weakened the community.

By dancing backward off the cliff, the woman recapitulates the blindness of her life to this point. The word "kaĥleĥlel" 'bruised and broken' further reflects the effect on the community, should enough of its members emulate her romantic intoxication. The nation cannot live if bitterness becomes so intense and widespread that families hate their own. The husband's refusal to accept the body of his wife is a horror because the unclaimed one is eternally in exile, a fate unreversed by circumstances or compassion, as it had been for the man who killed his wife's lover in "A Bad Deed." Deloria's translation of the husband's wish that her bones should "rot" with those of her lover misses an additional meaning of "aîakunikteśni," to become "enfeebled" or "ruined," according to the Buechel dictionary. The word connotes the spiritual deterioration that pervasive cultural warnings have taught the people to avoid.

The woman in the end has her wish; her bones are mingled with her lover's; so in life they combined as semihuman beings to produce weakness and death rather than new life. In gaining a lover, both have lost a family that retains the wisdom not to lose itself. The leader declares that the camp must not stay near the influence of the lovers and must be immediately moved. Although Deloria translates this directive simply as "we must move from this spot," the word "unkiglakapikte" precisely means "we must go home," a term especially striking since it immediately precedes the reminder that the camp had just been made. The selfish acts of a few can turn a circle of tautly stretched tipis into a besieged place where none can survive. The symbol of security can surround its inhabitants with death, like members of a doomed war party. The camp leaders have the same protective will and influence demonstrated by the storyteller. He or she takes a well known song (see chapter 2), capable of inspiring sentimental pity, and performs it through and beyond that kind of darkness: "iyuha iglakapi na ĥtayetu hankeyela aîaya îokel iyayapi śke'" 'they all packed in haste and moved away that same evening' (*Dakota Texts* 262). Traveling all night, the people eventually reach clarity and consensus. Like many others the story emphasizes that any individual's loss may be the nation's gain. The stories are told and retold so that the *takoza* (grandchildren) will recoil from values and emotions that rot the circle from within.

In stories that are mythical, *ohunkakan,* rather than based on a historical event, *wicowoyake,* such as "A Bad Deed," the metaphors of adultery are not necessarily more emphatic than in the preceding story, but they do have a more horrific tone. In "The Woman with a Bear Lover," collected by Wissler ("Some Dakota Myths" 195–99), a husband witnesses the sort of bargain that might have been struck in real love affairs. In return for her sexual submission, the bear presents food—in this case his own body. Once satisfied, the bear lets the woman kill him with an axe. With grotesque justice the husband waits until the woman cooks the meat and then stuffs it down her throat until she chokes to death.

As in the preceding stories lust for revenge is more perversely destructive than adultery. Still, the consequences of the woman's appetite, as in "A Bad Deed," are as grave for her family as for herself. She has forgotten about the safety of her children in satisfying her bear-like appetites. Dehumanized by rage, the father sends them off to die:

> Then the man said, "Now children, you are to go back to your father [the bear]." He gave them the skin of an oriole and a whetstone. Then he sent them out to look for their father. "Go home," he said; "you do not belong here." (Wissler 132)

Soon after they depart, they discover that they are being chased by the rolling skull of their dead mother. As they are about to be overtaken, one of the children throws down the whetstone, which becomes a mountain. The skull bribes a snake to make a hole through the mountain but instead of giving him anything he wants, as she had promised, she breaks him in half. The symbolism suggests that children are protected by custom but that some women can circumvent both custom and maternal instincts. The snake is an obvious male symbol, and her promise to reward him recapitulates the fate of the bear. Men as well as women can be destroyed by adultery.

The children are saved, however, by societal adoption. First, a supernatural voice places them in a flying bird's nest to represent tribal nurturance transcending individual neglect. Then after the nest lands, the children, still pursued by the skull, have to swim into a river where an anonymous man takes them into his boat before beating the head under with his oar. Although the children are abandoned by their unnatural parents, Lakota society makes sure that the sins of the fathers and mothers are not visited upon their sons and daughters.

If the preceding stories delineate the worst kind of sexual relationships from cold blooded seduction to incest to adultery, one story in *Dakota Texts*, "The Lovers" (224–32), describes an ideal marriage as one that not only benefits two people and their children but serves as a model for the tribe. At the outset, however, the young man must disobey a tribal directive meant to ensure that the tribe will explore the full range of hunting grounds to have sufficient meat for the winter. Though the young man should contribute to this hunt with his own band, the narrator obviously forgives him for deserting his immediate relatives to be with the girl. Her death results from his apparent abandonment of her and the subsequent breakdown of her health. The young man's remorse is profound but his dilemma had been serious. If he had hunted for his immediate relatives he would have helped them to live; but by not going to the girl sooner he has apparently caused her death. Obviously their relationship has not followed the prescribed course of fulfillment, through courtship to a union of their families, but its very atypicality foreshadows the *wakan* event that creates its central meaning.

The young man in effect brings the girl back to life. Full vitality and expressiveness exist only in people needed and respected by their families. The girl who dies for lack of love not only revives after the young man demonstrates the depth of his grief, she returns as a mature person with mysterious power to guide others. The scene inside the death tipi directs detailed attention to the young man's unwrapping the girl, warming her with fire, preparing a bed, and then carefully lifting and placing her on it. Apart from physical necessity this demonstration of care is an important way for one person to give another life. The girl in turn offers the young man food. She then prepares to nourish all her relatives in a structured ritual. By having her brothers break the news she softens the effect of marrying without their approval. Her general message intensifies the value of kinship. Reverence for life explains her request not to be touched for four days. For this ritual period she delivers advice that must not be taken for granted:

Tka wowasukiye wanzila ahounpapikte. Le e ye: Tuweni iyopeunkiciyapikteśni, na ohinni unśiunkicilapikte. Tohan unnipi k'eyaś hehan wowaunśila ece unkiciyuhapi hantanhanś oihanke kin ekta sakip unkipikta keyape. Hecel ecunk'unpi hantanhanś wounśpe wan oyate kin wicaunkicagapikta ca heyape. Kinhan wicaśa na winyan tohanl kiciyuzapi canśna iyecel iś'eya unśikicilapikte.

But there is one rule that we must observe. It is this: Neither of us must ever scold or be unkind to the other. If we show only kindness to each other all our lives, then at the end we shall arrive full of years, together. And if we do so, then we shall have built a great lesson for the tribe, so that hereafter, when men and women take each other in marriage, they will be kind to each other. (*Dakota Texts* 231).

In small hunting communities emotional restraint was a necessity. Venting one's emotions was never recommended since the risk of such indulgence was obviously too great in a society where all the men were armed and everyone depended for survival on the ability to cooperate. Respect and loyalty rather than law and order brought each Lakota generation, as Deloria writes, "to a ripe old age," or to translate more literally and inclusively "sakip kaniyagleya" 'to the end together' (*Dakota Texts* 232). The generality of the phrase extends the word "sakip" 'together' to the whole people and "kaniyagleya" 'reach the end' to the collective life of each generation.

The precision of the girl's ritual, like the storyteller's art, gradually discloses its lesson. The story begins with the narrator introducing the voice of a camp crier declaring the considered wisdom of the magistrates. This progression of messengers at the outset generalizes the priority of cooperation and makes the story of the lovers applicable to the disciplines observed in all relationships. The first line, introducing the crier, is followed conventionally by śke'. His actual speech is not interrupted by a śke' or ke' ending, the absence being usual with dialogue, but śke' immediately follows its conclusion, like a spoken exclamation point. The next two lines introduce the major characters and are both followed by *śke'* at short intervals to intensify their identity as protagonists.

But the next five uses of *śke'* occur at irregular intervals throughout the tense scene of the young man's disobedient departure from his own camp and his arrival at that of the girl. When the reported dialogue begins, first between the boy and the girl's relatives, then between himself and the girl, the narrator creates a dramatic effect by softening the quoted phrase with *ke'* instead of *śke'*. *Ke'* is especially appropriate to conveying her weakened state, but when her words cease, not to resume again until after her death, the narrator allows *śke'* to express finality. This *śke'* also carries an added impact, since the gift of moccasins was usually a formal acceptance of courtship, a promise of future union rather than bereavement.

As the story turns out, the moccasins' meaning is fulfilled after all, but the young man and first-time listeners cannot know this. The sincerity of the young man's feeling is expressed in the next line where he weeps for her even though her relatives are watching. Since tears are inappropriate for a man, the narrator again after only a brief interval maintains the sense of grief and shock with another *śke'*. *Śke'* occurs again at irregular intervals to set the stage for the young man's entering the death tipi preceding the story's turning point.

To move from action to the young man's emotion *ke'* returns briefly to modulate the tone downward: "yunkan ceya wakeya kin el hi *ke'* " 'he came weeping to the tipi in which the young woman lay' (*Dakota Texts* 227). The softer *ke'* then creates a hush to precede the next strong affective sentence ending in *śke'*: "Tawicu t'a iyecel tehi akipa *śke'* " 'He carried a sorrow as bitter as if he had lost his wife' (*Dakota Texts* 227). For the physical rigor of opening the death tipi and the young man's need to spend the night there the narrator again uses *śke'*:

Tiyopa kin sutaya iyakaśkapi na pazuntapi k'eyaś yuśkahin na
tima iyayin na—Ito lel hanhepi wanzi ecuhcis amayanpa na
hehanl canku kin otap mninkte,—ecin *śke'*.

He found that the door had been securely fastened and laced, but he worked at it, untying it wherever it was tied, until at last he entered the tipi, thinking thus to himself, "I shall spend at least one night here with her and when morning comes, then I will leave and go on to the camp." (*Dakota Texts* 228)

Just as the young man could not bear to leave the girl when his band left for the Missouri, so he cannot fight the current of feeling that still draws him to her.

For the story's central revelations, however, the narrator dramatically lowers the volume but increases the excitement by switching from *śke'* to *ke'*. Sudden changes of volume or intensity create dramatic tension whether they go from soft to loud or in this case from loud to soft. The use of *ke'* rather than *śke'* continues throughout the scene of the girl's awakening, her reassurance of the young man, his warming and covering her, and her feeding him with *wasna*. *Ke'* continues to punctuate her lesson in the meaning of her return—to live always in mutual kindness—and her instructions for the ritual of that lesson's disclosure. Not until the young man and the brothers have built the ceremonial tipi for the marriage is *śke'* reintroduced: "Cokaṗ ticaǵapi na tokel eye c'un ecel taku oyas'in yuwinyeyapi ca wana hingnatunkte c'un iyehantu *śke'* " 'They set about at once to build the tipi and make the arrangements exactly as the young woman had specified, and soon everything was in readiness for the marriage' (*Dakota Texts* 230). It is important that the tipi be not just in the camp circle, as Deloria has it, but "cokaṗ" 'in the center' since the girl's message creates tribal unity through the metonymic marriage of husbands and wives.

To best describe the fear and awe of the expectant people, the narrator follows the completion of preparation with a series of sentences with no ending. This is the longest such sequence so far in the story, and it causes the four-day waiting period to elapse quickly, considering their common state of mind. The narrator of "The Lovers" consistently employs quotative endings to verbalize abstract feeling. After the description of the waiting period, the opening of the tipi, and girl's invitation to her family, the narrator finally uses *ke'*, ascending gradually from no endings rather than jumping suddenly to *śke'*: "Tanhan, niyepi na niyate nihun ko wana yaupikte lo. Nitankśila hecel eye lo,—eya *ke'* " ' "Brothers-in-law, you and your father and your mother are all to come in now. It is your sister's wish." In due time they all entered the bride's tipi and with great happiness they met the girl' (*Dakota Texts* 231). The softness of *ke'* is the perfect modulation between the joy of the event and the typically quiet voice of familial respect.

The narrator's affirmation of the marriage ascends to *śke'*, immediately preceding the girl's second explanation of her return. Having received supernatural wisdom she transmits her vision-talk in a ritual context. As is customary, her explanation and instruction is not interrupted by a quotative, but when she stops speaking, the narrator uses *ke'* rather than *śke'*, as more appropriate to the speaker, her audience, and her effect on them. When she finishes, the narrator concludes with a forceful reiteration of the story's central event and meaning. The last two statements employ *śke'* as a conventional sign of closure, and characteristically for this narrator, as a major note of emotional reinforcement. The meaning is concisely recapitulated. The quotatives help to make it memorable:

> Ho he wounśpe ca wikośkalaka kin yuha wanaġiyatanhan gli canke hetanhan oyate kin ahopapi *śke'*. He un tuwa nunp unśikicilapi na okiciyuze waśte wanzi kaġapi canśna nunpi sakip kan iyagleya tanyan unpi *śke'*.

> Now, that was the lesson which the young woman brought back with her from spiritland and gave to the people. And so, from then on, whenever two people lived together in kindness towards each other and made their marriage a peaceful one, then it was said they were sure to live to a ripe old age together. (*Dakota Texts* 232).

In the concluding sentences Deloria's translation can again be supplemented by a more literal reading. The first sentence does not merely say that the girl returned from the spirit land and gave the message to the people. It says that thereafter the people "ahopapi" 'kept or heeded' her advice. And, as mentioned before, the lovers did not "live to a ripe old age" together but "kaniyagleya" 'reached the end together' and so "tanyan unpi" 'lived well.' Deloria's translation misses the idea of wisdom in marriage, emotional depth as well as duration. The narrator emphasizes that the people followed her advice, but in the Lakota kinship system they could have done so in many relationships, not just that of husband and wife.

In another version of the returned wife story in Buechel's *Lakota Tales and Texts* the same message is given: "'na letanhan ohinni iyopemaye śni ye,' eya, 'tohanyan unni hehanyan'" '"and never reprove me," she said, "as long as we live"' (Buechel, my translation 112). But the young man fails to remember. Several years later when his four-year-old son is crying, he says to his wife, "He kigna yo! Tokeśke naka he?" 'Tend to him. Why is he shivering?' (Buechel, my translation 113). His reaction to the child's discomfort seems reasonable and compassionate by contemporary Western standards, but the wife immediately reminds him, "heye śni ciśi k'on" 'I told you not to speak that way' (Buechel, my translation 113). The subsequent resolution of the story gives some idea of the extreme importance of treating relatives with gingerly care (see Deloria, *Waterlily* 162 and *Speaking of Indians* 17, 21). That evening his wife has a severe headache that she depressively neglects to bind, and shortly thereafter she dies. The husband dies four days later. The storyteller implies that children cannot be protected if the adults responsible for them are not continually reinforced by other adults. While a child may react mindlessly to fatigue or hunger, an adult must shelter the immediate and extended family. Addressing relatives by kinship terms in a respectful tone is more than etiquette or flattery. The child's literal loss of parents at the end implies that living parents can become shadows if they do not maintain each other in words.

Words split a marriage in Bushotter's "The Woman Who Turned into a Fish from the Waist Down," a variant of "A Woman Kills Her Daughter" (see chapter 4). Here the victim suffers from a husband's harshness rather than a mother's jealousy. While the husband is hunting, the wife tells her younger brother that she is going away to live in the water. The brother is to bring the baby whenever he comes to the water's edge so that she can nurse him there. The brother weeps but complies and when he takes the baby to the shore for the first time, he is horrified to see that his sister has become a fish from the waist down.

The husband's attempt to correct the situation is absurdly inappropriate to the condition he seeks to cure. The brother reports that the woman fears that her bottom half will wither if she returns to land. The man never considers approaching this psychological crisis with soft words. To get his wife back he devises a plan more appropriate to capturing an enemy than bringing a wife back to herself:

> Ho, ake cin nitunśkala ceye cinhan mniyohutata ayin na ake tokel kipan niśi k'un ecel eya omani yo. Heyata hiyu kinhan oluspi na mayakipan kte lo. Tokśa tuktel kiyela cunwoheśma el wakta munkin na kakel yapan kin hecenahcin mila pe wanzi yuha wahiyu na tohanyan hogan icage cin hehanyan waksa iyewayinkte lo.

> Well then, the next time your nephew cries, take him to the shore, and call out as she has taught you, as you walk about. If she comes out to the shore, you must catch hold of her and call me. I shall be lying waiting nearby somewhere in the brush, and the instant you shout, I shall run out with a very sharp knife, and will cut off the part that is fish. (Bushotter 348: 13).

The knife's sharpness, mentioned again later in describing the actual operation, connotes the man's characteristic tone in correcting his wife. When she does not conform to his idea of proper behavior, he tries to excise the problem, not to calm her and strengthen her in the Lakota way. By trying to make her perfect, he accomplishes her death. And even if a wife did not literally die of sadness, she could depressively withdraw from her whole family. Although she can feed children, she cannot nurture them.

The narrator adds that without the woman, the man and the brother were forced to do without many things that they had taken for granted, and that they had learned a bitter lesson. For younger listeners the potential loss of services may elicit some heedful appreciation, but for other listeners the narrator has made the central event the fish transformation, the loss of the person as a whole human being, rather than one who fills the function of physical nourishment. "From the waist down," also has sexual connotations. The woman's sexual function has been divided from her maternal purpose. She thrashes like a fish out of water until the man subdues her with a knife. But though the symbols of the sexual act should bring forth more life like her first child, instead the life drains out of her.

The story says that a woman must be treated like a whole human being if she is to be a source of life for her child, her brother, her husband, all her relatives. She must be more than a feeding aide, keeping a baby quiet so her husband can rest, as in the ghost wife story in the Buechel collection. And she must be more than a sexual object flipping her lower half as if it were not properly a part of her being, or she will not endure as a person. Even if she survives to perform her physical duties, the narrator says she will virtually disappear without the respect and appreciation of her husband. The nature of Lakota society, small intimate communities requiring continual cooperation for survival, made lapses into infantile temper unforgivable in an adult. While the relative security and constancy of a woman's life helped her to maintain tranquillity, men had to be especially careful to modify the intensity and suddenness of their temperaments at home. The fish wife and ghost wife stories warn male listeners to treat their wives with a scrupulously observed softness. The future of the people depended as much on male restraint in marriage as on any other virtue.

6

The Lakota Language Texture: Its Effect on Meaning

IN HER INTRODUCTION to *Dakota Grammar* Deloria describes the Lakota language as having a "peculiar . . . tendency to express approval, disapproval, or indifference" (3). Certain aspects of this tendency do not translate into English any more than vocal conventions of oral narrative can be heard in written form. But Deloria's written Lakota preserves several untranslatable subtleties. Appreciating these forms requires only a reading knowledge of Lakota, especially one developed with the aid of *Dakota Grammar*. The following textual examples do not structure a story in the manner of the *śke'* or *ke'* quotatives, but they do create nuances that affect meaning.

Conjunctions equivalent to English "but" are easy to perceive as expressing the Lakota language tendency to judgment (*Dakota Grammar* 3). Most narrative sentences including a "but" clause employ the word *k'eyaś*, indicating that the narrator reserves judgment of the action or dialogue in the clause to follow. The most common Lakota practice is roughly equivalent to English "but," "however," "yet," "nevertheless." It is only in special instances that a narrator uses less common words for particular emphases. *Yeśa* means "but" and is used only when the narrator means to express disapproval of what he is about to relate.

Since it is a convention for a narrator to explicitly oppose a trickster, the narrator of "Heart-Killer" uses *yeśa* to describe the initial duping of the heroine's companions: "*yeśa* slolyapiśni canke Śiyaka eha kici kipi ke'" 'But they in ignorance went with him' (*Dakota Texts* 131). Even though the girls are not particularly sympathetic characters, the narrator's use of *yeśa* rather than *k'eyaś* makes the statement something like "but unfortunately," though Deloria's translation includes no such qualification.

Another closely related word for "but," *yeś*, precedes an unexpected action but does not imply negative judgment—"it rather exonerates" the actors (*Dakota Grammar* 145). At the beginning of "The Deer Woman," the young man is said to have wished to "buy" a young woman, the most respectful way of proposing marriage: "*yeś k'upiśni*" 'but they did not give her to him' (*Dakota Texts* 163). *Yeś* implies both sympathy for the young man, since he did not receive an expected reponse to a proper procedure, but also respect for the parents' refusal. They and their daughter have the right to refuse any young man, regardless of his conscientious gifts. The narrator's use of *yeś* therefore exonerates them from blame. In the context of a story elevating social discipline over romantic infatuation or self-pity, the use of *yeś*, approval of the parents' decision rather than *yeśa* (disapproval) or *k'eyaś* (indifference), is especially appropriate.

The same approval of an action that might be emotionally disappointing to the character or to the audience occurs near the end of "The Lovers." After the heroine has returned to the camp circle and directed her brothers to establish absolute privacy for her and her husband for four days, the narrator emphasizes that the rule applies no less to her immediate relatives and parents: "Titakuye na hunkake kin epika *yeś* ko itehanyan wanyank nazinpi" (*Dakota Texts* 230). A somewhat more literal translation than Deloria's preserves the emphasis: "They were close relatives and parents, but they too stood at a distance looking on." Though the narrator acknowledges the emotional unexpectedness of her request, the use of *yeś* approves her prior action and foreshadows more from her in the way of conveying wisdom. The word *yeś* helps to communicate the reversal of roles characteristic of the story, as the child becomes the parent, and a woman presents a *hanbloglaka* (a vision talk) of her experience in the other world. Usually travel to other worlds on various planes was completed and related only by men.

In another story previously discussed, "The Elk Man," *yeś* expresses a subtle judgment against the older brother who sold the Elk man for a promise of horses and a wife: "Wana ĥtayetu canke etipi k'eyaś k'un wanzini *yeś* ecunpiśni canke tiihanke wan el uśiyeĥci eti śke'" 'It was now evening, and the tribe was making camp. But the brother who sold his own, not having received any of the favors promised him, went and pitched his tipi pitifully, at the end of the camp' (*Dakota Texts* 161). In this instance neither the brother nor the chiefs are admirable characters, but by using *yeś* the narrator "exonerates" the chiefs for double-crossing the brother, not because they have acted rightly but because the brother deserves no reward. Thus the word *yeś* implies a subtle irony; the chiefs have rightly deprived a traitor of his reward though they have done so unintentionally, acting only out of self-interest. The use of *yeś* at this strategic point is appropriate to the rhetorically even tone of the whole story. From the Elk man's seductions, to the chiefs' efforts at social control, to the Elk man's restoration as an unstoppable force, the narrator's tone is one of mature and pragmatic acceptance of minor disorder, while at the same time firmly maintaining a bottom line of group survival.

Yeś is also used to express or imply attitudes of fictional characters toward a subsequent action. A humorously outrageous example occurs when the mother in "A Woman Kills Her Daughter" excuses herself for being unable to quiet the baby, apparently her child but actually her grandchild: "Ecin le azinwakiya *yeś* hecena ceyahe cin sehan tokel owakuwaktelaka!—eyin" '"I have nursed him, and still he cries; What next can I do?" she said' (*Dakota Texts* 168). Satisfied that she has murderously removed her daughter, she justifies an apparently innocent maternal failure. The narrator's use of *yeś* creates just the right tone of horrifying absurdity that serious evil often bears.

Another word for "but," used less frequently than *k'eyaś* and more often than *yeśa* or *yeś* is *tkaś*, implying that the following verb "has the approval of the speaker or that the results are according to his expectation or hope" (*Dakota Grammar* 145). In "Heart-Killer" the narrator's overt opposition to the trickster accounts for the anticipation of his exposure just before his wives violate his order to remain at home:

> Kigla yunkan tawicu kin wicankin na,—Upiśni po. Tuwa wawanyanka can iśta kin ħca ca tuweni wawanyankeśni yelo,— eya ke'. He iyekiyapikta-kokipin na heye. *Tkaś* iyaya canke iyatap ekta ipi yunkan kul unpapi na nite kin akanl Blece wacihan ke'. Hecena lila canzeka-glicupi na unma tazuska-kinyanpi k'un heca ozuwicatun na unma iś wicayazipa ozuwicatun na henaos Śiyaka ħpayinkte cin itananunk iyepi s'e egnakapi.

> When the man left, Teal-duck told his wives, "Don't come. Whoever looks on, gets a sty in the eye; therefore nobody ever looks on." He feared they might recognize him. But after he had gone they followed him there and saw him lying on the ground, and Blece dancing on his back. They returned, very angry, and one made a bag of flying ants, and one a bag of wasps, and those two bags they laid on either side of Teal-duck's sleeping place as if they themselves were sleeping there. (*Dakota Texts* 131)

The use of *tkaś* rather than *k'eyaś* expresses the narrator's anticipation of Śiyaka's exposure. He "approves" of the following event because in some sense it is both just and fun.

Similarly, when Ikto (Teal Duck) is about to be stung by the wasps the angry girls have bagged for him, the narrator expresses anticipation of Teal Duck's torment with a *tkaś* that expresses both the expected result of a plan (putting the wasps in the bag) and his own approval of it:

> Ecanl unma pazipa canke,—Nawizila owanzi ħpayapi ye,—eye c'eyaś ecanl unma iyotan lila pazipa canke,—Hunhunhe, le lila mapazipe lo,—eyin na unma ecetkiya ikpaptan *tkaś* ecanl ħmu s'e ahiyu canke,—Ya, Ya,—eyaya nakipin na maninl ceya omani śke'.

> Just then, one pricked him. So, "Little jealous ones, lie still, will you?" But, just then, the other stung him. So, "Well, well! This one is certainly stinging me!" so saying, he turned over, but that moment, like a great roaring, they all came at him; so, "yah! yah!" he cried, and ran to the deserted places weeping. (*Dakota Texts* 131–32)

The smaller stings before the onslaught draw out the fun, and *tkaś* releases an energy charged by the artful manipulation of conventional techniques. The audience knows something will happen to Teal Duck. The fun is in the variations of his comeuppance in different tellings.

Variations on the use of *tkaś* occur in varying contexts. *Tkaś* in the preceding example expresses both the expected fulfillment of the characters' plan and the narrator's approval of it. Similarly in "The Feather Man," when the evil senior wife wishes to dispose of the heroine through the hacked swing trick, also used in "A Woman Kills Her Daughter," the Feather man diverts her from the scheme: "na inapa yunkan kici iyaya *tkaś* wiyaka-wicaśa k'un he el hiyu canke wiyaka wan waśtelahcaka ca wicitokap kahwohwok iyaya śke'" 'So she went out but as they were starting, the Feather man interfered, and a beautiful feather fluttered in the wind before them' (*Dakota Texts* 144). The use of *tkaś* here suggests again both the Feather man's fulfillment of a plan in the next clause, as well as the narrator's sense of satisfaction in the hero's consistent control. In each contest between the women, the heroine prevails according to the Feather man's plan, and as the people cheer her, so does the narrator through the use of *tkaś*:

> He un oksantanhan omnica waśteśte tanktanka ece ahitoksupi canke kin glicu na tiyata glihunni na etan itehanhca yunkan winyan unma un he temni t'eyela iś'eya glihunni *tkaś* oyate kin aśapi śke'.

> From all quarters, the mice brought fine large earth-beans, and piled them before her. So she took them home; and a long while afterwards, the other woman came home, all covered with sweat from her efforts, and the people laughed at her. (*Dakota Texts* 144)

Tkaś also assures the woman's reward for following the Feather man's directions. After the evil woman again tries to deflect her to the fatal swing, the girl does as she has been told, and as the narrator wishes: "Hohotela-giyapi kin he mitawa ye—eya pan un *tkaś* iyeśtuka wiyaka kin el etunweśni iyankin na ihunni śke'" '"The swing colored brown is mine!" But the young woman, not heeding the feather, ran on and reached the swings' (*Dakota Texts* 144). Finally when the story

reaches its predetermined but satisfying conclusion, the heroine kills
not only the villain but future evil in a sentence decisively turning
on *tkaś*:

> Canke cankśa wan icu na wiyeya nazin yunkan tohanl wana mato
> cincala wan hinapa *tkaś* kat'a ihpeyin na ehakela hunkuke cin
> hinapa canke ake he kte na hetanhan nakeś canl-waśteya unpi
> śke'.

> So the young woman took a club and stood ready. So first a bear
> cub came out, but she killed it with a blow; and then, after that,
> the woman, its mother, as it were, came out, so she killed her
> also. And from then on everything went well for them. (*Dakota
> Texts* 145)

Certainly it would seem to be a shock to see the bear cub emerge
from the tunnel instead of the woman, but the heroine and the
narrator are unfazed. Their expectations include the possibility that
the future may contain more evil. Dangerous people were once cubs,
and every new "story" will have to contain adversaries. By the end
the woman's actions will always proceed from *tkaś*, that is, according
to outlines prescribed by the narrative tradition.

The wife in "A Woman Kills Her Daughter" also survives because
she follows a plan set down by her husband, guiding her through a
series of actions preceded by the concept of *tkaś*, and at the end,
concluded by a relatively unusual repetition of the word itself. As in
the "The Feather Man" the woman follows her husband's plan perfectly (fulfilled expectation) in her role as the heroine (with the
narrator's approval). Then the evil mother also plunges to her fate
according to plan:

> Yunkan can wan yuha canke ungnahanla un maka kin el icago
> iyeyin na lila glicu *tkaś* tawicu kin ihakap ohankoya iś'eya apsil
> iyaya śke'. Yunkan winyan wan wicaśaśni k'un he wana iś ehakela
> el glicukta *tkaś* icunhan oicago kin ognalahcin maka kin kinaksa
> canke ekta mahel oyusnapi s'e iyaya śke'.

> He was carrying a staff in his hand. With it he suddenly made a
> mark on the ground and started forward quickly, so his wife
> followed directly behind, and jumped over the line. Then the

crafty older woman came along, and as she was about to step over the line, the ground separated right over the line, so she disappeared into the abyss, as if someone had dropped her down. (*Dakota Texts* 171)

Tkaś expresses an intelligent, structured response to evil by strong characters, and in the preceding example, with the narrator's approval of the planned actions he or she describes.

Sometimes, however, as in "The Elk Man" examples cited previously, the actions are too morally complex to say that *tkaś* expresses simple approval. When the boy-beloved in "Incest" receives a red hot brand slipped into his tipi by his father after a throat clearing signal, the narrator uses *tkaś* to express the efficient execution of the plan. But here *tkaś* is also ironic in that the "plan" results in the boy's becoming glued to the rising tree:

Yunkan wana ake winyan wan til hiyu na toyunke kin icaǧla hiyunka *tkaś* hecena hoṗiciya canke aṫkuku k'un wihuṫa kin eṫan maza kaṫa wan hiyukiya . . .

And now, once again the woman entered and came and lay down beside his bed. But that instant, he cleared his throat, and his father, who sat immediately outside the tipi, slid the heated iron in to him, under the base of the tipi. (*Dakota Texts* 177)

Later in the story *tkaś* is used in a dialogue when the word expresses the attitude of the characters toward what they are saying rather than the encompassing view of the narrator. In the exchange of insults between the Deer woman sister and the boy on the tree, the immediate repetition of *tkaś* has the force of repartee. Both the sister and the brother boast of events having gone according to *their* plan. Though the brother has the last word, his situation is ironically far from his expectation since he is still unable to do anything other than argue. *Tkaś* therefore sounds childish in the following exchange, especially since it is so obviously inappropriate to moral approval by either speaker:

yunkan ungnahanla canmahetanhan cuweku wan witkotkoke c'un he ahiyokasin na—Ṫuwa tibloku teḣila *tkaś* can auyewaye!—eya-houya ke'. Yunkan kośkalaka wan wankal nazin k'un he heya

ke',—Tankśi niś'eya leya yo, Ṫuwa tibloku naġi yekiya *tkaś* ite kin
maza kata iṗamamaye: eya yo,—eya ke'.

suddenly, from the wood near by, the wicked sister looked out,
and called tauntingly, "There's someone loves her brother very
much; but I have caused him to grow onto the tree!" And the
young man called down to his good sister, "Reply this to her,
little sister, 'There is someone who tempted her own brother, but
he caused her face to be branded with a hot iron!'" (*Dakota Texts*
178)

In this case *tkaś* corresponds to both uses of "but" by Deloria in the
translation.

A similarly ironic use of *tkaś* appears in "A Bad Deed." The
Lakota man premeditatedly kills his wife's lover as the young man
rushes past in the dark: "Opta iyaye wacin *tkaś* yuziyankin na mila
k'un un tezi capin na glakinyan yublas ahiyu" 'As he came past, the
husband caught hold of him and at once dug his knife into his rival's
abdomen' (*Dakota Texts* 247). A literal translation clarifies the emphasis on *tkaś* here, missing in Deloria's free translation: "He tried to
run past *but* the husband caught him . . ." Although the act fulfills
expectation in the short run, *tkaś* can only be ironic in light of the
story's dramatic reversals. The narrator cannot approve of the murder
of another Lakota, but in the larger view *tkaś* anticipates a surprising
and satisfying outcome.

In this relatively long story the narrator does not use *tkaś* again,
preferring *k'eyaś* throughout. The latter "but" (indifferent) is appropriate to a story that withholds moral judgments in the Western sense
of poetic justice. Killing a Lakota is *the* most serious crime, but the
man is punished neither by other Lakota nor by supernatural powers.
After becoming a Crow and even assisting them in stealing Lakota
horses, he lives a long and happy life with his adoptive tribe. Since
this is reported to be a true story, the narrator remains neutral. *K'eyaś*
occurs fourteen times in the narrative to signal the equivalent of "but,"
while *tkaś* occurs only once, at the crucial moment of truth when the
man kills his brother or cousin (depending on whether the uncle
mentioned was the brother of the wives' father or mother).

To further distinguish the force of *yeśa, yeś,* or *tkaś,* the words, *leyaś* or *leyalaka,* should be comparatively noted. Like *k'eyaś, leyalaka* has the sense of "but" in meaning "contrary to expectation," and has no connotation of attitude on the part of a character or the narrator. The narrative sophistication of "A Woman Kills Her Daughter" may be indicated by the use of *leyalaka* rather than *yeśa* ("but" with disapproval) to precede the information that the woman has hacked the swing's rope to ensure her daughter's death:

Leyalaka winyan wicaśaśni k'un he e ca ehanni hena hecel okaska egle na cunwintku yankinkte un heciyatanhan wikan kin wahunhun canke he un wancagna kapsakaske, ecin taku un sutakta wanica canke he un.

It came out later that the crafty woman had previously set those swings and had hacked the rope in one of them so that it would break at once; for what was there about it to make it strong? (*Dakota Texts* 167)

The narrator's understated *leyalaka* lets the action speak for itself. Deloria translates the word as "it came out later," but the narrator apparently understands restraint as the best way to convey the ultimate crime, a mother's murder of her own child.

Leyalaka appears to have the same effect of intensification by understatement in "Incest," when the good sister's husband is revealed to be nothing less fearful than a Thunder being, who immediately demonstrates his powers in the most dramatic fashion:

Yunkan *leyalaka,* he wakinyan wicaśa hunśe ca wakinyan tunwan hingnin na iyakiglegle wakinyan hotun yunkan can k'un naśleślecin na kaweh glihpaya canke kośkalaka k'un he glicu ske'.

He was actually a Thunder man, though they did not know at first. For the Thunder man opened his eyes (lightning), and repeatedly he roared (thunder), and the tree was split in two, and fell broken to the ground so that the young man stepped off. (*Dakota Texts* 179)

As in Western literature, restraint and understatement accentuate moments of extreme dramatic intensity whereas editorializing, such as *tkaś* or *yeśa*, might push them into melodrama. The young man in "The Lovers," demonstrating true love in his grief for the "dead" girl, is neither praised for loyalty to her, nor lightly condemned for social disobedience. The narrator uses the neutral *leyalaka* to precede his arrival at the burial tipi, a scene prevented from being a sentimental tableau by the spareness of its language, more apparent in Lakota than in translation:

> Kośkalaka k'un iś *leyalaka* hehanhuniyan otiwota kin el un hunśe ḣtayetu yunkan ceya wakeya kin el hi ke'. Tawicu t'a iyecel teḣi akipa śke'.

> As for the young man, he must have been staying nearby, instead of going away with the tribe, for in the evening, he came weeping to the tipi in which the young woman lay. He carried a sorrow as bitter as if he had lost his wife. (*Dakota Texts* 227)

A more literal translation suggests the value of *leyalaka*: "The young man, *however*, came from somewhere near the campsite and stayed there until evening; then, crying, he went to the burial tipi. It made him suffer as deeply as if his wife had died."

The predominance of *k'eyaś* over other forms of "but" also reveals the relatively quiet tone of stories expressing intensely dramatic emotions. Narrators tend to let the situation assume an effect appropriate to the values of the listeners rather than to push particular judgments or interpretations. "A Bad Deed" is intrinsically compelling because it concerns an intratribal murder and intertribal alliance, unusual events especially since the other tribe is the Crow. The narrator balances conflicting emotions in his characters and in his listeners by not pressing them. The man's emotion upon seeing the funeral scaffold and dead horse, while helping his former enemies steal horses must be overwhelmingly confused, but the narrator gives him only words of guidance for his new relatives, effectively leaving the shock and guilt of betrayal to the listeners' imaginations:

> Ho, letu *welo*. Letu ca he lecala s'e wati tka'. Na kaki ka wakeya kin hena hokśila wan wakte k'un he atkukupi ca ti *pelo*—eye. Holazata watohanyankel hel lecala wicaagnakapi wan eglepi ca wanyanke. He wana tunśkaku wan kikte k'un e-iteka ca slolye

nakunś śunkakan gluha iyayelaka ħpaye cin ikiyela śunkakan wan t'a ca yunke'.

"Now, this is the place. Here is where I lived only recently. And yonder live the fathers of him whom I killed," he said. Somewhat back of the camp circle, there was a new burial scaffold that had not been there before. He concluded that it was the grave of his victim, his nephew whom he had slain. He evidently took his horse with him, for near by lay a dead horse. (*Dakota Texts* 251)

The restrained formality of his words is conveyed by the enclitics *welo* and *pelo* at the end of phrases indicating the general location and the specific tipi of his wife's uncle, the father of the man he killed. Since *lo* punctuates male speech of distance and respect, the use of it in conjunction with his uncle's tipi creates a subtle irony. He now offers his enemies the respect he should have shown his nephew. Earlier in the narrative the Crow leader uses the same enclitics: "When used to close a sentence expressing a well-known fact or one previously not known to the hearer, it [lo] can be applied only by persons of authority" (Deloria, *Dakota Grammar* 110).

From the degradation of exile, the Lakota man's entry into a different tribe is foreshadowed by the style of the following exchange (*Dakota Texts* 250) even before the Crow leader makes his offers of marriage and fellowhood. The Lakota man might never have expected to engage in a courteous, dignified exchange marked by *lo*. The Crow leader tells him how they watched him as they lay ("unħpayapi *lo*") on top of a nearby cliff, all the while knowing ("slolunyapi *lo*") that he was the only man guarding the women. But because the leader had a special reason, he spared his life and arrived ("wahi *yelo*") to talk. Then in speech annotated by Deloria as "elegant and formal," he suggests that they smoke a pipe together as the ultimate symbol of good faith. The Lakota courteously agrees that they should smoke— "wicayake *lo*" 'you are right'—but insists that he speak first, "wowagla-kinkte *lo*." When he has finished, he adds that he would be pleased to hear ("nawaħunkte *lo*") the Crow's response.

He then recapitulates his plight. He travels as a fugitive—"napa omawani *yelo*"—taking his wives as well as his mother-in-law, who accompanies them ("u *welo*") because she has no husband. The reason for their exile is his murder of a fellow tribesman, "ti wicawakte *lo.*" After committing the crime they immediately fled ("naunpapi *lo*"), their escape being facilitated by a snow storm so that he is unsure whether they are being tracked ("otanunpapuni nacece *lo*"). Although he is still alive, he often wishes he was not ("tokel unt'apikte c'eyaś hecetu-unlapi *lo*"). Therefore he must refrain from smoking the pipe as if he were an honorable man ("ociciṗaġikte owakihiśni *lo*"), since the Lakota consider a murderer's hand to be bad ("sece unyawapi *lo*"). The speech ends with his willingness to die if the Crow wishes to kill him ("mayaktekta hantanhanś hecetu *welo*") and his wish that the Crow leader will take the women captive: "unśiwicala po. Ho henala *yelo*" 'Pity them. Now that is all' (*Dakota Texts* 249–50).

The Lakota man's honesty and eloquence are contained in sentences concentrating more *lo* endings than anywhere in the story. The endings lend manliness and dignity to the murderer's character. The narrator creates sympathy for a character otherwise unlikely to evoke it, because the violator of the most sacred Lakota law now demonstrates great respect for a fellow warrior and concern for preserving the lives of his relatives. Accordingly, the Crow leader answers in fluent Lakota, carefully using the language of respect for the outcast. He has made a decision in consultation with his warriors ("unkeyapikte *lo*"), based on the recent death of his wife ("makit'e *lo*"), and her resemblance to the Lakota man's younger wife. And he has made this visit ("wau *welo*") to say ("epinkte *lo*") the following: "Ito hecel iyonicipi kinhan iyuha Kangi wicaśata unglapi na heciyani iyanunpikte *lo*," 'If it is agreeable to you, you will all go home with us to Crow land, and you will stay and make your permanent home there' (*Dakota Texts* 250).

The *lo* endings continue from this point on when the men address each other but are not so frequent and so concentrated as in this interchange, where a man who has lost his humanity by Plains standards, reenters the human race. Humanity defines itself in respectful expressions of kinship. The man who has so dramatically destroyed himself by breaking his kinship bonds now reestablishes them in speech sparing no detail of formal respect. The narrative frequency of *lo* implies that this time he will get it right.

Another aspect of the approval/disapproval feature of the Lakota language occurs in the frequent use of the dative particle *ci* (with one's sanction). In the last sentence quoted above the Crow leader invites the Dakota party to live among his people "iyonicipi" 'if it is pleasing to you,' although their approval is virtually a foregone conclusion. The *ci* adds a dimension of choice, or at least the dignity of its appearance to the proposal and shows sensitivity to their situation. The Lakota man had earlier used the dative to cushion his refusal to smoke with the Crow man: "He un le ocicipaġikta owakihiśni yelo," meaning not simply "that is why I cannot fill a pipe for you" (Deloria's translation) but "therefore I cannot, with your approval (and at your request) fill a pipe for you."

Just as the Crow man carefully validates the sanction of someone in a weaker position, so the girl in "The Lovers," returning to the world with a message that everyone will heed, tactfully puts her desire to inform her husband of matters beyond his knowledge in the form of a request. Seeing her brothers approaching, she speaks with controlled urgency: "Towaś ena inazin; wociciyakinkte" 'I have something to tell you before they get here' (*Dakota Texts* 229). The use of the dative allows the girl to demonstrate her message before she makes it explicit. Through her the narrator speaks of the marriage relationship as a sharing of the most profound experiences, making a husband or a wife the primary confidant, even before one's brothers or sisters. And although she feels a certain anxiety ("lila nihiciya") in establishing the bond to her husband as something special, among so many other vital kinship relations, she does not forget that the bond depends upon consistently mindful speech. She will eventually say that a long and full life together requires "ohinni unśiunkicilakte" 'constant kindness,' and so before they meet the brothers she says not simply, "stop, I want to talk to you," but "stop, with your permission, I want to talk to you."

A skilled narrator can also employ the dative ironically. One example occurs at the end of "Incest," when the greedy woman bites off more *wasna* (pemmican) than she can chew. It expands in her mouth until she almost chokes to death before the onlookers take a knife and cut it out—"ikicicu," i.e. they took it out for her, on her behalf, with her sanction. Although the woman had selfishly complained of unjust distribution, the dative accentuates the priority of kindness over justice when the recipient is a relative, even an undeserving one.

The particles cited here imply that although human beings cannot control their fate, they can maintain their spiritual integrity in all situations. The language supports the people's ability to love themselves regardless of circumstances. It is what you feel and think in spoken or unspoken words that matters, not what may befall or enrich you. The following list of causative verbs serves to illustrate the importance of *ci*. In Lakota, actions and events often require predications that include the relationships and feelings attached to them:

sapmakiya	he causes mine to be black without my sanction
sapmakiyewaya	I am the unintentional cause of his causing mine to be black without my sanction
sapkiyemayakiya	you cause me to cause his to be black without his sanction
sapniciciyewakiya	I cause him to cause yours to be black with your sanction
ikiciyukcanmayakiya	you made me think about it for him
iniciyukcanmakiya	he made me think about it for you

(Deloria, *Dakota Grammar* 100)

In a culture and society that depended so absolutely on internal harmony, subtle speech meant plain survival.

7
Waterlily: The Novel as Guide to *Dakota Texts*

Dakota Texts is a literary adaptation of oral tradition rather than a verbatim record. It would be ranked as highly as work by any North American writer, Indian or non-Indian, if academic canonists were literate in Lakota. Even if more original language literature existed, Deloria's poetic concision and verbal subtlety would make her stories a magnet for literary critics. Her English language novel, *Waterlily*, is as notable for these qualities as for its recreation of *tiyośpaye* life in the late nineteenth century: the obtaining and preparation of food; the instruction of children, the manufacture of tools, containers, clothing, and other material objects; major ceremonies including the Ghost-keeping, Sun Dance, and *Hunka* rites; games and amusements.

The novel begins in midsummer when Plains people were frequently "on the move." Blue Bird, Waterlily's mother, leaves "the line of march" to give birth by herself. The endurance of suffering for *kitakuyepi oyas'in* (all one's relatives) is a primary Lakota virtue and is linked to the idea of withholding careless expression of any kind. As Blue Bird gives birth, she remembers her grandmother's words: "No woman cries out like a baby; people ridicule that. To carry a child is an awesome thing. If one is old enough to bear a child, one is old enough to endure in silence" (5).

Such cries would show ingratitude for the gift of a child and might be punished by its withdrawal. But Blue Bird's cultural lessons have helped her to perceive a wide range of experience as benelovent. Her child is not her possession, as her body is not hers to be hurt, but only to use as an instrument of vitalizing the larger life she shares. After ceremonially putting the placenta in a tree to protect it from predators, she senses her kinship with a unifying mystery focused in the waterlilies: "She glanced from one to another, and suddenly it was impossible to distinguish them from her baby's face" (6).

In naming her daughter, Blue Bird is born into an appreciative wonder for the larger movement of being. She then returns to the steadily progressing line, joining it in another place where she is as welcome as she had been with her immediate relatives. Deloria is writing of Lakota survival. Although Blue Bird's husband is "foolishly jealous," wanting to possess rather than create life, most Lakota make the life of their children the primary value: "With supreme effort she retained the composure and the placidity conventional to women, for even lingering pain was itself a pleasure. Her return to the group attracted no special attention. After all, young women with babies in their arms were the rule rather than the exception" (6).

As the story unfolds, Deloria finds ingenious ways to repeat variations on the keynote themes of establishing respect and the proper forms of expression between fellow beings. Near the beginning of chapter 2 Blue Bird remembers how she and her grandmother and younger brother gathered beans from the cache of some field mice. Blue Bird had understood the necessity of leaving a return gift for the mice but had not learned to treat her younger brother as a gift. She calls him "silly" for not remembering that "mice have to have something to live on too" (9). While her ecology is correct, she has forgotten something just as essential: "That was no way for a girl to speak to a brother, and few adults would fail to correct such a slip. Blue Bird's mother said gently but firmly, 'Daughter, one does not call one's brother silly'" (9). The extreme care for language is again in evidence, allowing fewer and fewer spontaneous slips into mockery or denigration as a person matures.

Frequently, the withholding of overt expression communicates supportive intent more effectively than words or explicit gestures. When Blue Bird returns to her own circle after Star Elk throws her away, she refrains from enthusiastic greetings: "You know what they say of one who does that, 'like a dog greeting familiars,' rushing at them too eagerly before sensing their mood and situation . . . and 'leaping up their frame' as an untrained puppy will, soiling the gown with its clumsy fat paws" (21). Adults continually taught and exemplified this reserve: "'That is not done, grandchild,' they said quietly, or 'Nobody does that,' meaning 'and neither ought you.' No cross words, no whipping . . . The very calmness of grandparents soothed a child and made him inclined to obey" (24). As children are spoken to, so they soon learn to speak. Kinship terms rather than names are the only form of address and reinforce the thoughtful attitudes associated with those terms.

Perhaps the most remarkable use of words in the novel comes from the revered storyteller, Woyaka, who was eagerly awaited throughout the winter as he traveled from camp circle to camp circle. By reciting winter counts, myths, legends, and true stories, he creates the tribe in words. His grandfather told him: "You owe it to our people . . . If you fail them, there might be nobody else to remind them of their tribal history" (51). Woyaka must therefore sacrifice ordinary comforts. When not performing he is almost taciturn, saving strength for his art like any serious artist: "His eyes were fierce and searching and he went about with a great preoccupation that everlastingly set him apart and made ordinary men uneasy in his company unless he was telling a story" (51). The people value his stories so highly that "he was showered with gifts" though "he had no desire for things" (52).

Woyaka's longest story tells how the people survived before they had horses through reciprocal kinship with the buffalo. Deloria again implies the people's ability to adapt to changing times as long as they remember to pray to the animal spirits. A vision seeker "was visited by the spirit of the buffalo, who promised to be his brother for all time. 'Call me when you are hungry,' he said, 'and I will come. Sing this song I am about to teach you, and then I shall know you.'" (54). The right kind of vocal expression assuages hunger, and therefore the buffalo dreamer ritually addresses the buffalo in a sacred language. The buffalo then enter the ceremonial circle to feed the people's understanding as well as their bodies: "A magnificent buffalo bull led them; with eyes aglare he approached, frightening the people. But they knew they must stand their ground . . . everyone must cooperate, for that was where the power finally lay" (55). This collective recognition must be fulfilled in overt expression. In ceremonies spirits enter the circle of prayer because the people ritually accept and then remove the barrier of fear: "[the buffalo] entered the circle . . . to the accompaniment of the continuous clatter, clatter, clatter of wood on wood, which the women and children made, striking their clubs in rhythm on the dog-travois poles. The singing of the holy man, the clatter, and the pace of the buffalo never slackened. Meantime each hunter picked out his animal and shot it from over the women's shoulders" (55).

When enough buffalo are killed, the song stops and the source of nourishment departs. The people are confident that ceremonial articulation will always make the animals their friends and the world their home. As long as their need has been satisfied, the memory of the song will suffice. And when hunger returns, the dreamer will sing. Although the buffalo no longer perpetuates the people's physical life, they still represent the ultimate source of generosity. Because their symbolic presence has not diminished, the episode's conclusion implies no regret: "And the children went home singing, 'While the buffalo live we shall not die!'" (57).

Deloria maintains this confidence in almost every episode. In another striking instance a huge snake coils itself around a small basket holding an infant. The snake dreamer arrives to sit quietly alone in the tipi until the snake leaves. Again, respect and assurance remove danger, much as these attitudes strengthen the people in every ordeal: "the [snake] glided past his friend and brother, so close that he all but brushed the toe of his moccasin, and still the man sat calm, with eyes closed, still smoking . . . 'I did not wish to embarrass my brother by looking at him as though to hurry him,' the quiet little snake dreamer said later" (68). The absence of speech is often eloquent in *Waterlily*. The snake dreamer is effective because he is silent, and so in varying degrees the Lakota kinship system values private experience as a source of individual strength. At the honoring of certain children in the *Hunka* ceremony, the onlookers learn to enjoy differences without envy. One child may have been selected because his parents "prayed for his recovery and promised to feast the people in his name if he should be spared . . . 'You are all one,' they were told. 'Be happy for each other.' " (76).

And they are taught to suffer with each other as well. A less prominent aspect of the Sun Dance strikingly represents the theme of personal sacrifice in the ceremony and the novel. Wives and girlfriends ritually slip small containers of water to the dancers during rest periods, as if they were secretly aiding captives. The sneaking dramatizes the subordination of self to the universal life that the Sun Dance renews. For this ritual reason and for the opportunity to secretly express her feelings for a young man she barely knows, Waterlily gives Lowanla water and escapes before he sees her face.

Despite this strongly felt commitment, Waterlily first becomes the wife of another man, because her family desperately needs horses to give away in the ceremony of "keeping" her grandmother's ghost. Although she has misgivings, the marriage offer of two good horses determines her choice, giving her individual character and upbringing. Waterlily sacrifices personal autonomy for her family's honor and to enable *Wanaǧi Gluhapi*, a ceremony that helps the whole *tiyoṡpaye* accept mortality. Years later, after the death of Sacred Horse, the husband she had come to love, she marries Lowanla. Although mutual attraction undoubtedly exists, the marriage answers another paramount concern. Lowanla is a cousin of Sacred Horse and therefore automatically one of several fathers to her children: "While kinship law did not demand that a widow marry a brother or cousin of her husband, it was always desirable for the child's sake, that he might have for a father one who was his father already" (220).

After they have been married for a time, Lowanla passionately hopes that Waterlily was the girl who gave him water. Part of her wishes to romantically confess, but social protectiveness prevails: "If she, a well-brought-up girl, could do that for me, then why not for other men? Were there other men? Who were they?' In time a curtain of distrust would separate them, and that was no way for husband and wife to spend their life together" (227). Waterlily's final silence warns that words can be dangerous. Whether sounded or held back the voice should be used as the buffalo dreamer used his—without regard for self.

For most readers whose first language is English, *Waterlily* is a good introduction and supplement to *Dakota Texts.* Numerous parallels may be drawn, and the following list, limited to the stories discussed in this study, only begins to suggest the usefulness of *Waterlily* in the general study of the Lakota oral tradition:

1)   Blue Bird's first husband, Star Elk, is "foolishly jealous," an infantile, selfish emotion that the tribe cannot afford. It keeps both men and women from contributing to the tribe's sustenance—Star Elk spies on his wife all day instead of hunting (*Waterlily* 15)—and it potentially endangers innocent bystanders with violence in small communities dependent on cooperation. Jealousy is a major theme of several stories in *Dakota Texts*: "The Elk Man" (159–62), "A Bad Deed" (246–53), "A Woman Kills Her Daughter" (166–71), "The Feather Man" (142–45), and "A Woman Joins Her Lover in Death" (261–62).

2)   While the jealous husband in the Lakota scheme of things is bad because he is selfish, the ideal husband is concerned to protect rather than possess his wife and everyone else in the tribe. A special ritualized expression of esteem and reassurance occurs in *Waterlily* when the heroine, early in her marriage, feels homesick: "Waterlily instantly recalled that Rainbow used to dress Blue Bird's hair just like that. It seemed very long ago and remote, that childhood life of hers when they had sat so. It was a mark of tender affection and the only bit of demonstrativeness between husband and wife that any outsider was permitted to see, for such things as kissing or embracing, even in fun, were definitely not done in public" (*Waterlily* 173). This extended description of the custom helps us to understand the emotional impact of the Feather man's braiding the hair of the girl who had foolishly eloped, been disgraced (scalped), and then had run away. By braiding her hair, the Feather man shows more than forgiveness of mistakes; rather, he will treat her as if they had never happened (*Dakota Texts* 143).

3)   While the Feather man is the perfect male adult, Waterlily's mother teaches the feminine ideal: "When you marry, my daughter, remember that your children are more important than you. Always

the new life comes first. Your duty to your children must be in accordance to this rule" (*Waterlily* 180). Against this tribal rule the title character of "A Woman Kills Her Daughter" becomes especially outrageous. Accompanying her obvious lack of maternal feeling is her unnatural regressiveness. When she tells her daughter she wants to swing, the daughter identifies her desire as "childish," reflecting the larger thematic emphasis (*Dakota Texts* 167). In *Waterlily* the message is explicit: "Accept your new life as a mature woman, even while you are gentle and yielding. Do not behave in a childish manner toward your husband. You are his helpmeet, not his baby. Be grown up" (180).

4)   Just as a mother must be maternal, so a sister has a special relation to her brother, one of particularly intense respect and devotion to his honor. In *Waterlily* the heroine knows that wives never confide anything negative about their husbands to their sisters-in-law, since it was their kinship duty to defend him in "all phases of his life" (*Waterlily* 180). Knowing the special nature of the brother-sister relation adds a sharper, grimmer dimension to the dishonoring by seduction intended by the Deer woman sister in "Incest" (*Dakota Texts* 176–78).

5)   While "Incest" presents the ultimate misdirection of female sexuality, other stories warn girls of elopement and of the consequences of not being cautious during courtship. In *Waterlily* several passages correspond to the lesson of the Double-face stories. Blue Bird's inexperience leads to the disastrous acceptance of Star Elk's suit. Even after telling her what a sad choice she has made, Blue Bird's grandmother can only reiterate the general cultural importance of keeping one's promise: "Ah, if only you had told me he was courting you so I could have warned you, grandchild. Since you have promised already, there is nothing I can do. Once she gives it, an honorable Dakota woman does not break her word to a man. Those who make false promises are ever after derided. To give your word is to give yourself" (*Waterlily* 12).

6)   The Double-face stories also emphasize a girl's need for pro-

tection by male relatives other than a husband. In "Double-Face Tricks the Girl" (*Dakota Texts* 46–50) the heroine survives with the help of a "little brother," her pet beaver, while in "Double-Face Steals a Virgin" (*Dakota Texts* 51–64), the fugitive wife is adopted as a daughter by the mysterious tall man of the iron tipi who kills the Double-face and saves her life. A passage in *Waterlily* makes the plight of both girls sharply apparent: "To be cast out from one's relatives was literally to be lost. To return to them was to rediscover one's rightful haven. It was to such a haven that Blue Bird finally came back. It was where she belonged, and where her child belonged. It was important for her daughter to grow up with backing, in informal association with the girls—her cousins and sisters—and in a respect relationship with her brothers and male cousins, who stand back of her, ready if she should need help" (20–21).

7) Although girls could make mistakes in courtship, the mistakes were not always permanent in their effects. The Double-face and other stories in *Dakota Texts* prepare young listeners for an existence in which adversity can generally be overcome by resourcefulness. The society did not forbid girls from running away from abusive husbands and did not even insist that girls remain with men to whom they had been married in the most honorable way: "It was true that the rejection of a husband in a purchase marriage was not unheard of. To be sure, it was not in the noblest tradition to repudiate a promise, but it was condoned under certain circumstances. If a girl had been persuaded to accept, against her inclinations, because someone in her family wanted the gift horse, and if, before the marriage was consummated, she ran away, unable to accept the man, then the marriage was annulled" (*Waterlily* 155).

8) Almost as difficult as marrying a man discovered to be different than he appeared in courtship was the fate of a girl who went to live with her husband's people. Relationships to in-laws were much more formal than to one's birth relatives, and a girl in her husband's camp always had to be on her best behavior and could rarely relax, joke, or confide intimately as she had spontaneously done while growing up with her daily companions. Waterlily begins to understand the

initial sadness of her marriage: "She needed family relatives such as Sacred Horse was enjoying in his own *tiyošpaye*. She needed an environment charged with parental affection, where she could indulge her moods and could be herself without constraint. Parents, uncles, aunts, and grandparents humored you, even spoiled you a little. Before them you could be outspoken, impudent, and perhaps say or do silly things, with the assurance that they would understand. Waterlily needed her menfolk, too, her brothers and cousins ready at all times to protect her and give her social backing. Without them, a woman felt insecure against—she did not know what. But she felt as if here she stood vulnerable and alone" (*Waterlily* 175–76).

In *Waterlily* an explanation appropriate to a novel fills in the unspoken connotations of the young wife's trials in "The Feather Man" (*Dakota Texts* 142–45). Not only does she live in a community where nobody knows her, she must also suffer the resentful malice of an older co-wife. Her final victory is given special meaning by the people's cheering. It is their way of accepting her as a member of the community (*Dakota Texts* 144–45).

9)   The young woman in "The Feather Man"(*Dakota Texts* 142–45) learns an important kinship lesson from a mouse who assures her victory in the earth-bean contest because she has approached him as a daughter. The custom of leaving a gift for the mice before taking some of the earth-beans they have gathered is explained in *Waterlily* to Blue Bird and her brother by their grandmother: "Blue Bird went with her grandmother to open the cache and they found an abundance of beans, unusually large and meaty. They would cook up rich and sweet, the old woman said. She found more caches and went to work at once, happily drawing out handfuls of the black, earth-caked store and piling it on her blanket, spread out to receive it. For each handful she religiously returned a handful of green corn that had been parboiled and then sundried, a treat for the mice indeed" (9). The passage from *Waterlily* not only makes the girl's exchange with her mouse grandfather culturally meaningful, it makes the technique of storytelling more apparent. In the story, the fantasy of reciprocation is enacted and so described more fully, while the novel complements the emotional relation with a description of physical details. Since

description is not usually included in oral narration, the novel gives us the physical feel of a situation the original listeners would know from experience.

The story, on the other hand, gives a deeper emotional feel for the relationship than the novel does. While gathering earth beans is vividly real in *Waterlily*, the feelings reinforced by the girl's spiritual relatives come to life in the oral narrative. Just when the girl most needs help in her desperate contest with the older wife, the mouse-man, whom she addressed earlier as grandfather, formally announces her need to the mouse camp: "Ho, wana mitakoza tiyole u welo! Inaḣni po!—eya śke'. He un oksaṅtanhan omnica waśteśte tanktanka ece ahitoksupi canke kin glicu na tiyata glihunni" '"Now, my grand-child comes for food. Make haste!" From all quarters, the mice brought fine, large earth-beans, and piled them before her. So she took them home' (*Dakota Texts* 144). In both *Waterlily* and "The Feather Man" the respectful relation to the mice strengthens the people's relation to each other. The girl who honors the mice will honor and feed her own people. In *Waterlily* the lesson in consistency of respect has to be taught when, as mentioned earler, Blue Bird is reproved by her grandmother for calling her younger brother "silly," because he has not yet heard that earth-beans have to be shared with their givers.

10)   Perhaps the most unusual relationship described in *Dakota Texts* and *Waterlily* concerns the making of relatives by enemies. Among the nineteenth-century Lakota the hardest and therefore the most admired response to the murder of a relative was for the family of the victim to adopt the murderer as a kinsman. In *Waterlily* the ceremony of adoption is described and then followed by the reflection of an elder named Yankton: "The spokesman said, offering him the pipe of peace, 'Smoke, with these your new kinsmen seated here. For they have chosen to take you to themselves in place of one who is not here' . . . As he said these words, tears began to course down the slayer's cheeks. You see, he had been neatly trapped by loving kinship. And you may be sure that he proved himself an even better kinsman than many who had right of birth, because the price of his redemption had come so high" (*Waterlily* 193). While no story in *Dakota Texts*

tells of such an adoption within the tribe, the adoption of the murderer by the Crow war chief in "A Bad Deed" (246–53) has much the same effect. The adoption interrupts a series of intertribal murders extending back through many decades. The narrator of "A Bad Deed" may have used the adopting-a-murderer tradition to promote intertribal unity.

8
Reading Oral Narratives:
Hymes to Jahner

FOR MANY READERS the method employed in this book will be familiar—explication supported by references to the ethnography and to narrative conventions in the stories. In the context of scholarship on American Indian oral narratives, however, some of the procedures may raise questions. Few writers have discussed oral narratives using original language texts. Those who have are highly regarded and have helped to direct all work in the field. Of Dell Hymes's many essays the last chapter of *"In vain I tried to tell you,"* "Reading Clackamas Texts" (342–81), reprinted in Kroeber's *Traditional American Indian Literatures* (117–59), is probably the most well known. It is also thematically related to the stories discussed here.

Hymes demonstrates how a prefix determines the meaning of major characters and events in a series of stories concerning a Grizzly Bear ogress. When *a-* precedes the ogress's name in the Clackamas Chinook language, she is not yet directly involved with human beings. When she threatens, pursues, or harms people, on the other hand, her name begins with *wa-*. Hymes shows how the Clackamas narrator uses *wa-* and *a-* to indicate the bear's state of mind even when her actions are not overt (just as I have attempted to show how psychological subtleties are expressed by particles, conjunctions, and quotatives in Deloria's texts). For attentiveness of this sort all scholars in the field must acknowledge their debt to Hymes.

The strictly symmetrical structures that Hymes builds from such particles, however, do not seem to be present in Lakota stories. Perhaps Ella Deloria's skepticism toward J. R. Walker's construct of Lakota theology might also be applied to Hymes's conceptions of the stories he treats:

> If an investigator were to find those versions in the way Walker
> has them, and especially that scheme of fours, the Gods arranged
> in classes and hierarchies, which I personally still strongly feel to
> be the work of a systematic European mind, I should be more
> interested and surprised. (letter to Boas, 12 May 1939)

While Walker's scheme is one of fours, Hymes has one of threes and fives—a large five-part structure of scenes, composed of stanzas, composed of verses, composed of lines, all expressing actions occurring in "the threefold sequence of onset, ongoing, and outcome" (*"In vain . . ."* 353). Hymes illuminates the use of verbal conventions in support of these structures, and when rare discrepancies arise, he recommends persisting until the "loose ends" either disappear or, by their exceptionality, confirm the pattern: "One may have blocked out this-this-that, that-thus-thus, but be forced to reconsider by failure of fit. Confidence comes from experience of fit being there to find and of coming to experience pattern without conscious analysis" (*"In vain . . ."* 354).

Dennis Tedlock has expressed skepticism toward a method that discovers perfect symmetry in an improvised art:

> The problem is that when the object of the analyst [Hymes] is to
> divide verses internally so that their lines will add up to a pattern
> number, and when there is no metrical scheme (in the strict
> sense), line-making is wide open to gerrymandering, however
> clear the larger units—verses and stanzas—may sometimes be.
> (*On the Translation of Style* 57)

The pattern number Tedlock refers to is five in Clackamas culture, and while Hymes goes to great lengths to structure a story in patterns of fives, he does not tell us in any detail what five meant outside of the stories to the narrators and listeners.

But Hymes cannot be blamed for the omission of all such matters, since his retranscriptions are based on texts that Melville Jacobs believed to be ethnographically insufficient. Although Jacobs argued that oral literature could best be understood in "interpreted and annotated presentations," revealing "probable audience and community responses," he laments that his own "advent" was too late to learn enough about the people. By 1929 when Jacobs obtained his stories from Victoria Howard, the "content, form, and functions" of Clackamas narrative were "in a late stage of deterioration" (*Content and Style* 2–3). Hymes goes far beyond Jacobs in deducing Clackamas genres but is less intent on reading the stories for their sociocultural heritage, understandably, perhaps, considering the "feeble light" (Jacobs 3) of Clackamas ethnography.

If Jacobs regretted that the Clackamas culture had largely disappeared by 1929, how much more hampered must Hymes have been in collecting Chinookan stories in the 1950s. Nevertheless, Hymes was able to further illuminate the purpose of a traditional narrative performance. By adding a song to one story, Hymes's informant, Hiram Smith, confirmed the idea that myths were told only in winter, because their purpose was to bring the spring (*"In vain . . ."* 21, 124, 133, 242). In extending Jacobs's rule that oral literature must be "written out in terms of the total literary event" (*Content and Style* 2), Hymes connects winter as the time of telling with the spiritual purpose of specific story structures and verbal formulas:

> Why should people say certain things when the first salmon and swallows come? Because in the myth Coyote had said that they should. Why should one believe Coyote said such things? Believe the myth? Because what he, what the myth, said the swallows would do (come with the first salmon) and the people would do when they came, observably is the case. Within the circle of the traditional culture, before the coming of the whites, there is nothing promised that is not performed. (*"In vain . . ."* 305–6)

Since Hymes does not work with a living culture, he cannot be expected to provide the abundance of contextual detail offered by Ella Deloria, who generates as well as preserves her own traditions. Even where Deloria did not herself directly receive information from scholarly informants, she was able to draw on a vast body of earlier ethnography. George Bushotter, in Deloria's revised transcription and translation, presents the occasion and purpose of myth-telling with an immediacy that Hymes's hypotheses cannot evoke. The following passage describes an "ideal" or typical narrative event that reversed an earlier ideal. The narrator is an "anti-natural" or *heyoka* (see Black Elk, *The Sixth Grandfather* 232–35) whose unfinished story goes on to tell how Iktomi tricked some pheasants into dancing with their eyes shut by arousing their curiosity about his "songs." The trickster then clubs all but one to death, only to lose his already roasted dinner to an even trickier wolf (see appendix 1):

Whenever someone is now requested to tell myths or old stories, before he actually begins, he plays tricks on his listeners, if he wishes. In that case, he says a few opening words of the tale, and then, he says, "That is the end of the story."

Or he will dally for a while, making them suffer, so slow is he and so eager they. It is said that this way was first made by an Anti-natural, and that is why it is in order to play tricks or fool the listeners before actually telling a tale.

And it is said that this way of relating myths started this way: They kept asking one another to tell a story, but some were bashful, and refused, saying of this one and that, "Why, that one is better; he knows many tales." This kept on and all the time over in an obscure corner there sat a man who was an anti-natural, and he thought to himself: "Why is it, of all the men present, they avoid asking me to tell a myth?"

After thinking this a while, he suddenly said, "Come ye, friends, I (since everyone else fails you) I will now tell a myth." So because the desire to hear tales was very strong among them, they settled back quiet, and looking with concentration at him, they sat with ears open to him. So he pushed himself to the fore and began:

"Well, it so happened that Ikto was now going into yonder direction, carrying a load of songs on his back." Altogether they gave the usual reply at the pause. "Yes," they said.

With a great hum of voices they said it, but then he said this. "And behold, he saw the white dung of a wolf, and he died, they say!" With that he retired to the background with a very

solemn face. So they all exclaimed, "O, shucks!" they said; "And
we thought he was going to tell a real story decently!"
    And it is said that the custom of fooling round at the start
and deceiving the hearers started in that way. (Bushotter 1: 1–2)

By tying the narrated origin of a performance convention to a
particular tale, Bushotter suggests that the audience should read a
speaker's motive more alertly than did the pheasants. Like Iktomi the
narrator communicates in opposites. He begins the story's lesson before the story proper by awakening the interpretive faculties of the
listeners. His diffidence about speaking corresponds to Iktomi's reluc-
tance to sing, but both reluctant performers mean to take hold of
their audience—Iktomi, to provide (temporarily) for his dinner, and
the narrator, to shape (permanently) the consciousness of the tribe.
    Because Hymes lacks a body of source materials comparable to
Deloria's, many of his cultural allusions seem superficial. When Grizzly
Woman picks berries with some women she will eventually kill, Hymes
comments that it is "grimly grotesque" for her to be their "sing-along
leader," since women loved picking berries together (*"In vain . . ."*
370). Then, to make the scene both familiar and horrifying, Hymes
compares her to a "mass murderer" under "cover." Though this makes
the incident cross-culturally vivid, some readers may want to know
more about berry-picking as a ritual of food gathering. Such concerns
are generally subordinate in Hymes's work to the analytic praise of
aesthetic virtue.
    He is concerned, of course, to contradict the primitive stereo-
type, but in so doing he has superimposed a decidedly Western concept
of "art." When he describes a passage, he attends to its "music,"
implying that this is also the narrator's purposed effect. Hymes often
appreciates his texts in such phrases as "there is diminution in the
expressive weight of the passage" (*"In vain . . ."* 373), and he develops
his sense of structural units musicologically:

The relations of verses to each other in such a sequence is
analogous to the use of bar lines in musical scores. The bar lines
define a relation of equivalence. One bar may include a single
note . . . another bar may include sixteen sixteenth notes. The
underlying equivalence allows the composer or narrator to gain
effects . . . ("Bungling Host" 185)

Another dominant characteristic of Hymes's criticism is quan-
tification. He offers tabulations, such as the number of times Grizzly
Woman is named with *wa-*, or with *a-*, with no prefix, or not named
at all. Using five texts, Hymes determines that prefix alternation
occurs more often in some stories than in others (*"In vain . . ."* 379).
In the same way, I have mentioned that *śke'* and *ke'* alternate as
quotative endings in some stories, while *śke'* is used more consistently
in others. However, I do not think that even Deloria's sixty-four texts
show a "semantic pattern" of the sort Hymes often draws. Rather,
the Deloria texts reveal a range of conventions available to narrators
to use variably in individual tellings.

Narrative events develop as they are told rather than conforming
to a preset structure of form or theme. Both form and theme are drawn
and recombined from existing sets in the whole "mythbody." For the
benefit of their adolescent or preadolescent listeners, Lakota storytellers might draw on a number of motifs: Double-face elopement,
Deer woman sexual obsession, Elk Man, or incest. The stories that
emerge in new combinations of character, action, and symbol refer
the listeners to experiences they may have had, might anticipate, or
might avoid. But when Hymes interprets the central meaning of the
Grizzly Woman story that he has already analyzed in great detail, both
linguistically and structurally, his brief thematic comments do not
seem to be in the least culture-specific:

> Danger and death are rather closely associated with long pointed
> things. Safety, on the other hand, is mediated by things that are
> long but not so pointed, paddles. The safest paddles of all are
> those that are not intact, but have holes (presumably from use),
> those of an elder sister. All this strongly suggests an opposition in
> terms of phallic symbolism. The opposition seems to express a
> contrast between the danger of sex outside, away, as against the
> safety of sex that is more domestic, more muted. Arrow-spears
> versus paddles, as it were. (*"In vain . . ."* 381)

Hymes's interpretation is not doctrinally Freudian, but his sexual
symbolism is implicitly expressed as universal. This is interesting in
that Hymes goes to great lengths to differentiate the inductively recognized structures of Chinookan mythology from the "universalistic

proposals of Levi-Strauss, Greimas, or others" (*"In vain . . ."* 308). He defines good philological practice as sentence by sentence close-reading, "using cumulatively all there is to use" (*"In vain . . ."* 275). But in Hymes's case the texts alone provide the resource, so that the scholar's job is to eschew "shortcuts," whether structuralist or psychoanalytic, by selecting from many texts those that best represent the genre.

Nevertheless, Hymes's conclusive portrait of Grizzly Woman is authentically Chinookan only if we assume contemporary concepts of psychological gender to be universal. When he says that Grizzly Woman is aggressive *and* masculine, it is because she throws mucus at her victims. The mucus must be semen because the nose and the penis are "longitudinal" (*"In vain . . ."* 381). That physical fact helps to establish that the similarly shaped canoe paddles used by the women to escape are phallic. Hymes finds that the women have enough masculine energy to survive but not too much to cause an identity crisis, because the paddles have holes in them: "The integration or unity of the two genders is the means of safety" (*"In vain . . ."* 381). Even though the paddles have holes, the women masterfully "insert" them into the water. He concludes that in a story told by a woman and understood to be part of a tradition of women's stories, the Clackamas people put a high priority on women integrating their male and female sides.

Hymes's symbolism might well be applied to the Lakota stories discussed here, and it might also be applied to innumerable examples of the world's literature. "Double-Face Tricks the Girl," for example, portrays a girl able to concentrate in a dangerous situation and free herself from an abduction. Many Lakota stories concern the ability of women to escape and survive, but they do so on the basis of their culturally feminine virtues. When that female strength does not suffice, the heroines of the "Double-Face," "Feather Man," and "A Woman Kills Her Daughter" stories accept help from men. The ability to act effectively under pressure appears in both genders. Some of Deloria's stories concern women who kill Crow warriors or bears, as well as women who rescue husbands from captivity. A Freudian universe can encompass any fiction one encounters. In *Dakota Texts* Freudian symbols might include the crack into which the evil mother-in-law falls (her own lust), the rising tree on which the young man is glued (his repressed lust for his sister), the Elk man's flute (his potency), and the knife that kills the younger wife's lover (the protagonist's suppressed sadism, or homosexuality).

But such symbols do less to clarify a story's central message than attention to the cultural context of Deer woman, Elk man, male speed, female stillness, i.e. sexual psychology and aspects of physical sexuality considered important by the listeners. The girls of "Double-Face Tricks the Girl" and "Heart-Killer" carry pet beavers that eventually build bridges, enabling their return. The girl in "Double-Face Tricks the Girl" and the one in "Double-Face Steals a Virgin" (see Rice, *Lakota Storytelling* 67–83, and chapter 9) depend on adopted male relatives, a brother (the beaver) in the former, and a mysterious father in the latter, to bring them home. The young women in "The Feather Man" and "A Woman Kills Her Daughter" triumph over evil older women with the help of their husbands. White-Plume and Blood-Clot Boy (*Dakota Texts* 106–13, 113–20) in four demarcated episodes experience early triumphs, are humiliatingly immobilized by Iktomi, marry a mistreated girl, and use supernatural power to feed the people. Within such broad outlines of structure and character development the Lakota narrators had great latitude. It is unlikely that they built architectonic models of the sort Hymes ascribes to the Clackamas Chinook. Other stories are also in four basic parts. Previous discussion suggests the scope of variation within the elopement structure of courting, elopement, captivity, and return. As Hymes notes the importance of five for the Clackamas Chinook, so four is clearly the pattern number of Lakota culture (see Powers, *Sacred Language* 138–40 for the best discussion of its ramifications).

Eschewing such structural patterns, Dennis Tedlock transcribes, translates, and describes traditional Zuni performances that he has personally recorded. In contrast to Hymes's method of ending lines systematically after each predication, Tedlock believes pauses should occur "naturally" and irregularly as they do on his tapes. Pausing is the "hallmark" of the spoken word and "foremost among the paralinguistic devices that shape the Zuni narratives and distinguish them from prose" (*Spoken Word* 48). The pauses create tempo, many pauses slowing the pace while long lines seem fast. To indicate loudness

Tedlock uses capital letters and/or exclamation points. Softness and other changes of tone appear in parentheses like stage directions. Still one wonders if many readers come any closer to hearing a performance in Zuni by reading translated words set in Tedlockese. The reader can see that the material is something special, but beyond the denotative meanings that may require extra effort to grasp because of the original punctuation, the reader only receives the outline of a story and an impression of the ingenuity of its translator.

Still on occasion Tedlock offers striking examples of cultural analysis. In regard to a particular story, he recounts his education in Zuni sexuality. A young man, in the tale of "The Female Ahayuuta" (*Spoken Word* 287–301), presented with several prospective brides, presumes to make a choice by measuring their sexual areas (presumably pelvic but not more explicit) with a notched stick. Because of this childish disrespect for women, the war god, Ahayuuta, humiliates him by appearing in women's clothes, prosthetically measuring up, and "marrying" the young man. Having shamed him enough, the god delivers a "lecture on proper courtship and marriage" (*Spoken Word* 288).

Following his entertaining account of the performance, Tedlock makes himself the center of an illuminating exchange. As an ethnographer Tedlock asks the storyteller just how the bottle-necked gourd in the story was used to measure the girls' anatomy. At first the narrator tells Tedlock to look again at a similar gourd hanging on the wall. Asked again, he says with neither "smirk" nor "indignation" that the gourd measured the girls "across the hips." In retrospect Tedlock gets the picture. Measurement across the hips is like an American beauty contest, "a form of abuse of women's bodies in Zuni eyes." As for the actual procedure in the story, the Zuni talk around rather than directly of matters that are precious, valued, and guarded. By withholding speech the storyteller shows respect and appreciation for the female sexuality that the boy blockishly profaned. Perhaps the story, like the Lakota stories, teaches adolescents to know the psychological danger of sexuality. Men who "use" women insult the sacred power to give life. Tedlock's bottle-necked gourd tells us more about Zuni attitudes toward sexuality and toward human values than Hymes's canoe paddles. As a symbol the canoe paddles teach us to wrap a Western concept of gender in a Freudian package. Tedlock, on the other hand, tells us that a Zuni considers the feminine spirit to be something mysterious and precious, part of the collective life rather than the feminine side of an individual male (see Tedlock 293–94, as opposed to Hymes, "*In vain* . . ." 381).

More consistently than Tedlock, Barre Toelken interpretively places the stories he records and translates in their Navajo cultural setting. And Toelken's emphasis on texture rather than structure achieves relatively emic readings compared to those of Hymes. My discussions of *ške'* or *tkaš* or *lo* aspire to Toelken's definition of "linguistic features" that "evoke, suggest, and describe, or those which in any way qualify, modify, expand or focus the rational structure by reference to or suggestion of emotions, mores, traditional customs and associations, aesthetic sensitivities and preferences, and so on" ("Poetic Retranslation and the 'Pretty Languages'" 82).

These details of language help to build stories that are not meant to be *tour de force* demonstrations of technique but "dramatic presentations performed within certain cultural contexts for moral and philosophical reasons" ("Poetic Retranslation" 83). The narrator and his responsive audience fulfill expectations based on the story's genre, as in Hymes, but the characters assume importance "in the Navajo world view," and the performance has value to the extent that it causes "important ideas to come alive in exciting ways" ("Poetic Retranslation" 83). Like Hymes, Toelken emphasizes the culture's pattern number (4) in the structure of Navajo stories, but he adds that "the ritualism of four-ness in so many other areas of Navajo life now carries over to suggest an almost ceremonial significance for the actions of the characters in the tales" ("Poetic Retranslation" 86). Commonly he will connect details of the stories he treats to the customs and rituals they evoke. Stories often present extreme behavior, "obtrusiveness, intrusiveness, or gluttony" that must be cured, making the narrative another type of healing ceremony.

In writing his translations Toelken does not adopt special print devices to render the sound of the performance, partly because Navajo is a tonal language unlike Zuni. He arranges the story in lines that do not signal pauses but exist on the page to "keep track of . . . units of expression" in order to facilitate analysis. He explicitly rejects the idea that these units or "verses" (to use Hymes's term) have a "deeper structural" foundation. Instead he concentrates on such conventions as the Navajo quotative *jiní* (it is said) in his text. The quotative "is so frequently a mark of storytelling throughout Native America that many ethnographers simply didn't record it, or if they did record it in the source-language text, they did not bother to translate/transcribe it in the English text" (Wiget, "A Performance Analysis of a Hopi Coyote Story" 329). Toelken notes that *jiní* is used thirty-four times in a short story, and that in his first analysis of the story he missed its importance because he did not hear *jiní* in its contracted form of *jn.* The contraction is analogous to the Lakota *ke'* in place of *śke'* or *keyapi'.* As in the case of the Lakota quotatives *jiní* and *jn* occurred most heaviliy in sections of the story where description is central, least heavily in dramatic dialogue. In Deloria's "The Lovers," discussed in chapter 5, the quotative is dropped within the girl's directions for her ritual but reappears following each interruption of direct speech by the narrator:

> Miye etkiya lila wicayaka ca atanin ye. He unhca ca le wagli ye, unk'unkta ca un. Ho tka ohinni unśiunkicilakte. Hecel unk'un hantanhanś ecela oihanke kin ekta sakip unkihunnikte. Tipi wanzi cokap iticagapi na hel unkiśnala yamnica unyankinkte. Icitopaca kinhan hinhanna-eciyatanhan oyate kin wowicawakiyakinkte. Ca hecel tiblo owicakiyaka. Towaś tuweni omayutankteśni ye,—eya *ke'.*

> It is very evident that you are sincere towards me. That is why I have returned, that I may be your wife; but we must always live in mutual kindness. If we do, then we shall reach the end together. They must erect a tipi inside the camp circle, and there for four days you and I will live alone together. On the fourth day, in the morning, I will have something to tell the people. That is what I want you to tell my elder brothers. For a while, I want nobody to touch me," she said [it is said]. (*Dakota Texts* 230)

Since Deloria always omits the quotative from her translation, I have completed unit 19 with a bracketed quotative.

But while Toelken observes that the quotative is frequent and that it is an "apologetic device"—it validates the speaker by acknowledging the tradition—he apparently does not think that the quotative affects meaning or feeling in the ways *ske'* and *ke'* appear to me to function in the Lakota stories. Similarly, Toelken points out that an intensifier, *haahgooshíí,* expresses urgency, acceleration, or stress, but he does not explain the term's function in specific parts of "The Pretty Languages." Instead he admits that the term "begs for comment but defies full analysis." He can note the location of its use but wonders, "are these key elements of cultural reference being foregrounded for some special reason?" ("Pretty Languages" 109). Or are they simply devices of "pacing, intonations, ritual inferences, and so on?" His suggestions encourage close attention to quotatives and other "surface" details in subsequent studies of tribal narrative.

Techniques, Toelken concludes, must be compared in numbers of taped, orally delivered stories. While I cannot follow his further advice to consider other stories by the same narrator, since Deloria does not identify the narrators of *Dakota Texts,* I can compare the uses of *ske',* *keyapi',* and *ke'* in different stories. As we have seen, the Lakota tradition allowed considerable variation, so that a single narrator might use several styles or sets of conventions. In addition to details of language Toelken gives us tribal *topoi,* like those of the Elk man and the Deer Woman in Lakota stories. Thematic messages are attached to situations arousing specific intellectual expectations: "These concerns do not simply float up out of an uncomplicated plot structure; rather, they cluster in tableau scenes in which particular actors are shown in particular actions in particular places" ("Pretty Languages" 94).

Elaine Jahner, a scholar of Lakota oral literature, has described thematic conventions in specific stories more thoroughly than Hymes, Tedlock, or Toelken. My own critical approach would use some of her methods even if her subject were not Lakota oral narratives in general and, in an important article, an Ella Deloria story in particular. For Jahner the Lakota world view is the basis of stylistic connotations in both text and performance. In her article, "Cognitive Style and Oral Literature," Jahner defines themes in Deloria's "Blood-Clot Boy" by analyzing specific uses of Lakota words both linguistically and culturally, as Deloria does in her annotations.

To describe a story's structure and texture, as they adhere to an educative purpose, Jahner does not rely on a recasting of Deloria's prose into verse to provide a convenient model for analysis. Instead she simply quotes Deloria's prose translation of "Blood-Clot Boy" and then goes on to discuss specific Lakota words as they create theme and feeling. Most readers will benefit by getting the gist of the story first in readable prose before the analysis begins. Those who read Lakota can consult the Deloria text. The majority of readers, those without Lakota, will be able to understand her descriptions of the untranslatable effects of Lakota words and stylistic elements.

"Blood-Clot Boy" (*Dakota Texts* 113–20; appendix 1) is composed of motifs that recur in many tales. Jahner traces the pattern from the culture hero's initial outcast state, to his achievement of supernatural powers, to his dangerous journey to the west, to his attainment of marriage and mature responsibility in his own camp circle. Having established this structure, she then shows how details of language instruct listeners in prevailing Lakota values. The narrator (and Deloria) almost immediately put the listeners in the place of the rabbit whose skill as a hunter is appropriated by the greedy, brutal bear. The bear comes from somewhere "tokiyatanhan," like the Double-face monster discussed in chapter 4, and perhaps like the white man, and is therefore not related by blood or inclination to the rabbit. The narrator locates the listeners in the rabbit's place by referring to the bear's arrival with the word, "hi," meaning "a place not one's own, the fact mentioned at that place." This serves to remind the listeners "that the tale is about maintenance of their own social group" (Jahner, "Cognitive Style in Oral Literature" 45).

Having established the fictional home as the story's empathic point of view, the narrator uses more loaded words, carefully selected by Jahner: "To be driven from one's rightful place within the group was to lose one's social identity. Bear occupies Rabbit's place (*tohe*), a word that can mean office or social position as well as camp site" ("Cognitive Style" 45). This sort of linguistic annotation describes both the story's meaning and its socially directed purpose. The narrator always wants the story to be about his listeners. The story's aesthetic qualities are side effects only. The same is true of most adult Lakota work from quilling moccasins to counting coups. The ideal purpose always serves the health and intelligence of others rather than the independent fulfillment of a job well done. As Jahner describes the work of hunting buffalo, the hero produces while the villain takes, and a single word precisely points the lesson: "Rabbit performs brilliantly only to have Bear move again into his space. After the buffalo are dead, Bear 'rushes up' ('hiyu'). The basic meaning of 'hiyu' is 'to come toward,' but it also can mean 'to come out of.' Both Bear and Rabbit come out into the space of the hunt; one to produce, one to take away what is produced" ("Cognitive Style" 46).

The rabbit, as we have seen, however, is able to save the blood clot, a potential for renewed life always imminent in Lakota experience. Jahner knows the importance of the sweat lodge in turning fear into confidence, but she also reveals the similarity of the story's verbal and moral sophistication by analyzing the Lakota word: "Rabbit builds a sweatbath for the blood clot, 'inikaġa.' The Lakota term means literally 'to make life.' The morpheme 'ni' means life, and the sweatbath is a ritual place for the purifying and intensification of the life force" ("Cognitive Style" 46).

The subsequent emergence of Blood-Clot Boy's power to maintain the camp circle could be said to occur in the act of telling the story. "Blood-Clot Boy" begins in despair and indefiniteness and ends in the confident possession of the means of life. The movements of the main characters are conveyed in verbs that reinforce the story's thematic direction. When the bear is killed, the rabbit returns to his home, but Jahner adds that he doesn't just travel, since *ku* means to return to a place previously lived in. Thus the verb connotes the restoration of what has been lost. Correspondingly, when Blood-Clot Boy begins his journey, he is said to "icimani" 'to go somewhere purposely,' not simply to roam like Iktomi, whose devices he must learn to avoid. It is not an easy lesson, however. Anyone can have lapses, and Ikto leaves the hero stuck to a tree for a long interval. In the context of the whole tale's lesson in living purposefully for the people, Jahner notes that Blood-Clot Boy's resumed movement is expressed in verbs prefixed with locatives, suggesting goal directed activity. In the end his coming home to the rabbit takes the verb "aku," meaning that "he comes back here bringing something (someone) with him."

In this study, I have tried to follow some of Jahner's leads. The references to verbs of movement in "Blood-Clot Boy" (see also "Stone Boy: Persistent Hero" 174–75, and *Lakota Myth* 48–49) are vivified by her reference to a salient fact of nineteenth-century Lakota life. The Lakota lived as seminomads, having separate winter and summer locations, following the game, and periodically moving their camps within general areas. They did not wander but lived in "constant interaction between concepts of movement and concepts of rest" ("Cognitive Style" 36). In life as in the oral tradition no event or story finalizes movement. An end is always "a concrete realization of power that in turn gives rise to the need for further movement." The conclusion of any one story always necessitates new ones in the oral tradition, as in any other event crucial to the life of the people from the Sun Dance to hunting, to rituals of puberty, and death. In one well-known instance, the Lakota often killed the favorite horse of a dead man so that the man could continue to travel in the next world. Elsewhere Jahner shows that the Lakota considered home "a particular state of mind or well being" rather than a place where movement stops ("Stone Boy: Persistent Hero" 175). Homecoming as plot resolution never equals literary closure in the Western sense.

The end of a story may therefore be thought of as a pause. Usually several stories were included in any storytelling session, but more importantly, major elements of theme and character, like the constant elements of human nature, will certainly return in new combinations in an unending series of "narrative events." Like Tedlock, Jahner stresses the stylistic value of pausing, and foreshadows the discussions here on the significance of the quotatives *ške'* and *keyapi'*: "*Ške'* occurs much more frequently at particularly suspenseful points in the narrative, as though the narrator were keeping the audience on tenterhooks" (*Lakota Myth* 35). Unlike Deloria, Jahner includes the quotative each time it appears in her translation of a Lakota language manuscript of George Sword's "Stone Boy." She also calls attention to structural divisions formed by the initial particle, "yunkan," 'then' and acknowledges Hymes's dictum that "the recurrent initial elements represent the regulatory principle itself" (*Lakota Myth* 35).

But Jahner does not versify in a Hymesean structure of acts, scenes, stanzas, verses, and lines. And of course she is translating a manuscript, not trying to transfer an oral performance to print *à la* Tedlock. Instead her method resembles that of Ella Deloria, except that while Deloria writes prose in numbered units, Jahner makes every sentence, or group of sentences ending in *śke'* (her translation is 'so they tell') into a separate English paragraph. She does not reproduce the Lakota manuscript, printing only her English version. Following each pause, "so they tell" is placed beneath the preceding line in parentheses. Whenever "yunkan" 'then' occurs, it is placed on a separate line immediately before the unit it introduces:

Then
    The woman said more yet, she added this
(So they tell)
    "Hakela's hair is too, too awful but I'll put it there at the end," she said.
(So they tell)
    Then from that great big bag she took heads. That's what she took. She roasted them and ate them. So Hakela almost died of fright.
(So they tell) (*Lakota Myth* 91)

Jahner's method strikes a sure balance between excessive structuring and popularization, between Hymes and the Erdoes-Ortiz collection he castigates in "Anthologies and Narrators." Her style is close enough to English storytelling prose that it allows readers to have the feel of fiction rather than formula. And by placing "then" and "so they tell" on separate lines, Jahner indicates pauses as they occur in Lakota without creating the histrionic look and feel of blank verse. Her phrasing sometimes has elements of Lakota-English, the English idioms of bilingual speakers that Anthony Mattina has called "Red English" ("North American Indian Mythography: Editing Texts" 139–43). But Jahner evokes a "Lakota accent" with subtlety. As she points out, Ella Deloria considered George Sword to have adopted elements of the oral tradition into "the beginnings of fiction," written for the first time in the Lakota language (letter to Boas, 24 February 1938; qtd. intro. Walker, *Lakota Myth* 23). Unlike Mattina's transcription of English speech, Jahner's translation adds a colloquial echo to a text originally written in polished Lakota. As any translator must, she walks a fine line between making the English story sound awkwardly foreign and retaining a semblance of its Lakota flavor. I have heard enough Lakota speakers, fluent in both languages, to appreciate some of Jahner's literary rather than literal renditions of Lakota-English. Phrases that have a Lakota accent appear in my italics. I have quoted representative rather than comprehensive instances:

> There was a young woman, a most beautiful woman. The front part of her hair was bound and she had a great big bag. *Like that* she came and stood. *Hakela* saw her and he said, "*Brothers*, a young woman is there; she has arrived and she is standing: the front part of her hair is bound and she has a bag," *That's what he said.* (*Lakota Myth* 90)

> Then from that great big bag she took heads. *That's what she took.* She roasted them and ate them. So *Hakela* almost died of fright.
> (So they tell)
> *That's what he saw.*

These few phrases can be heard in reservation speech, especially from those whose first language is Lakota, although the basic rhythm influences everyone. Some common speech rhythms are perfectly reproduced in the following prose:

> "Our oldest brother says we have no elder sister so you can be our sister." So the woman said, "Yes," and she settled down in their home.
> (So they tell)
> They gave her food but she didn't eat. She just sat there.
> (So they tell)
> The young men thought she would eat but they bothered her and made her bashful and so they called her and said this,
> (So they tell)
> The oldest one, that one, said this,
> (So they tell)
> "Younger brothers, we'll go for a walk. *Hakela* will stay here with our sister and we'll bring wood," he said and they started walking. So *Hakela* stayed with the woman. (*Lakota Myth* 90)

The prose commas and periods express the actual sound better than lines that might suggest a more stilted, staccato quality. People really do talk in short phrases, but to mark them with line endings would falsely imply that this speech is halting and awkward. The rhythm of—"They gave her food but she didn't eat. *She just sat there*"—has an intensity in speech that is appropriate to an outrageous violation of hospitality. That short phrase has an edge, remaining sharp in prose because the pause is not thickened by a line break.

Other qualities of Sword's written Lakota are less recognizable in current Lakota-English, but Jahner is wise to translate them because they retain important thematic aspects of the story. When the monstrous sister arrives, she "hinazin" 'came and stood.' Jahner explains that *hi*, as mentioned in regard to "Blood-Clot Boy," connotes a purposeful arrival at a place that is not the home of the traveler:

> The Lakota version of the Stone Boy story, then, does not have the sense of some straggler coming haphazardly upon the tipi. Rather, it conveys the idea of someone deliberately deciding to join the group. The woman comes to the boundary of the brothers' organized living, the tipi. That is as far as her own powers permit her to go without some response from the brothers. Then she must stand. The next move is theirs. (*Lakota Myth* 50)

"Hi" is repeated to ironically introduce a woman who will try to cannibalize her adopted brothers, as she properly waits for an invitation to kinship. Then when the oldest brother asks her in, Sword and Jahner identify her in a phrase that sounds redundant but that is almost always repeated until the characters of a story have been well established:

> And the oldest brother, *that very one*, said this, they say.
> (So they tell)
> "Invite her into the tipi. We have no woman who can be a sister, so she can be our elder sister," he said. (*Lakota Myth* 90)

The frequency of phrasing with "ca" or "canke" 'so' may also sound overly repetitive but is a characteristic of Lakota narrative like "yunkan" 'then' and "śke'" 'so they tell.' So is the frequent use of a quotative to refer to words spoken by a character, "he or she said," usually in close proximity to the quotative referring to the narrative tradition:

> The young men thought she would eat but they bothered
> her and made her bashful and so they called her and said this,
> (So they tell)
> The oldest one, that one, said this,
> (So they tell)
> "Younger brothers, we'll go for a walk. *Hakela* will stay here
> with our sister and we'll bring wood," he said and they started
> walking. So *Hakela* stayed with the woman.
> Then
> The woman said this,
> (So they tell)
> "My brother, go hunt a little in the woods," she said.
> (*Lakota Myth* 90)

Another characteristic of dialogue is that approval or disapproval is often stated starkly without explanation: "Our oldest brother says we have no elder sister so you can be our sister." So the woman said, "Yes," and she settled down in their home. (*Lakota Myth* 90). Sometimes strong assent is not articulated at all but demonstrated in immediate action: "'Mother, make some arrows. I'll go seek my uncles,' he said. So his mother made him arrows, they say. So they started to look for his uncles, they say" (*Lakota Myth* 95). The unquestioning response indicates the mother's respect for her son (see also "Incest" *Dakota Texts* 176–77, where the father does not question the strange request for objects used by his son to identify the temptress.)

Jahner also retains the exact repetition used to describe Stone Boy's gathering of power as he travels to recover his lost uncles:

> "Stone Boy, my grandson, is going to compete so I'll give
> you one of my powers," she said, and gave him a large hawk
> feather, they say. From there he kept going.
> Then
> Again, he is going along and sees a little tipi.
> Then
> That old woman says, "Stone Boy, my grandson, you will
> compete so I will give you my power," she said, and she gave him
> the feather of a kingfisher, they say.

From there he went on.
Then
    Again as he was going, he came to a little tipi.
Then
    "Stone Boy, grandson, you will compete so I will give you
one of my powers." So he went over there. (*Lakota Myth* 95–96)

The translated repetition of key words and phrases like "compete"
and "little tipi" and "he went on from there" helps to convey both
duration and endurance, the ordeal and the virtue as verbal experience
rather than simply meaning and goal.

While repetition conveys length and persistence, short, abrupt
phrasing often conveys lightning-bolt strength. When Stone Boy kills
the female ogre who has turned his uncles to bones, his accuracy and
force is suggested in another convention of culture hero narrative:
"He took his arrow and shot her in the neck. So she died" (*Lakota
Myth* 97). When he meets a buffalo bull eager for revenge against
him for killing his four granddaughters, Stone Boy talks just long
enough to elicit the buffalos' plan of attack, and again with a sudden,
lethal force that is expressed but not described, he defines himself:

    So Stone Boy said, "Grandfather, this is who I am," and he
shot him.
(So they tell)
    The buffalo died.
(So they tell)
    Just like that Stone Boy killed four buffalo, one by one.
(So they tell) (*Lakota Myth* 98)

Four shots do it; so do eleven English words, with no adjectives
necessary to indicate what kind of man can concentrate power so
skillfully. The brevity implies more about Stone Boy's knock-out force
than elaborate phrasing possibly could.

9
Explicating Lakota Prose:
"Double-Face Steals a Virgin"

ELLA DELORIA'S PROSE translations exclude some of the Lakota idioms Jahner retains. But Jahner does not give us a transcribed Lakota version of "Stone Boy" from the original manuscript by George Sword. Had she done so, one might assume that it would have looked like her English version—brief paragraphs framed by a preceding *yunkan* (then) and a conclusive *ške'* (so they tell). This is an effective scheme, but Deloria's transcript still reads well, especially in comparison to the au courant verse dramas of Hymes and Tedlock.

Several purposes may be served at this point by discussing an additional story, "Double-Face Steals a Virgin" (*Dakota Texts* 51–64). First of all it is another Double-face elopement story like "Double-Face Tricks the Girl" (*Dakota Texts* 46–50), discussed in chapter 4, and can therefore give some sense of how an individual story lives within a mythbody of conventions; at the same time it is an individual work of art. "Double-Face Steals a Virgin" is more thematically and stylistically complex than most of Deloria's narratives. It maintains the cautionary message of many stories directed toward young women (see Hymes, *"In vain . . ."* 133) and may have been told primarily by grandmothers, although we have only an internal hint rather than conclusive evidence of that. Just as a grandmother initiates the girl's escape from the monster's camp, so the narrator, as literal or symbolic grandmother, takes the listeners far enough away from certainty to scare them a little and then brings them home. A home for women is defined by the proximity of brothers and fathers. The story warns girls against committing their vulnerability to the sole protection of a husband, until the husband has demonstrated his identity.

"Double-Face Steals a Virgin" has a clear four-part structure, probably because four is the "pattern number" of Lakota culture. The rhythms of Lakota speech are preserved by the commas, periods, and dashes of English usage and an orthography that retains the accents of spoken Lakota. Deloria includes spoken pauses, marked by *śke'*, and uses dashes for unspoken pauses especially when following a quote: "Ca iyonicipi hantanhanś mihakaṗ hiyu wo,—eya śke'" 'So, if you are willing, follow me away' (*Dakota Texts* 52, 61).

Part 1 describes the girl's character and reputation, her being swept away by Double-face, her shock upon recognizing him, and the imminent possibility of being his dinner. Part 2 includes her killing the grandmother, the "dead" grandmother's delaying action, and the girl's terrified flight from the monster. Part 3 carries her to shelter with the tall man and his animal companions who kill Double-face. And part 4 brings her from the near death-dealing effect of Double-face's burning corpse, through her accidental cure, to her homecoming escorted by her adopted brothers.

The story's texture is more complicated than its episodic organization, and Jahner's suggestion concerning the Lakota concept of home in relation to verbs of coming and going may be usefully applied. (For the following discussion note that Deloria numbers units of thought and action to facilitate reference to the literal and free translation. These units include usually one but sometimes two or three predications. Their length cannot be systematized, but they are divided on the basis of actions or separate thoughts on the literal plot level.) Words of spatial relation function as psychological metaphors. "Kakiya" 'from far off' is used twice in close proximity (units 4 and 5) to describe the initial approach of the Double-face, as if to suggest the range of the girl's eventual journey from innocence to experience. Many verbs of movement extend the sense of home from immediate relatives, taken for granted, to another place that becomes "home" when she establishes kinship with its inhabitants. As Jahner points out: narrators and audiences in prereservation times were accustomed to the idea of fleeing various kinds of situations in order to find (or regain) a particular state of mind or well-being that, to them, meant *home* ("Stone Boy" 175).

Both of the Double-face stories discussed here define a young girl's home as a place where she can rely on male relatives for protection. Some girls married men who abused them so that the tipis they shared with their husbands were not "home." Several stories, including those about Double-face and the Feather man, concern girls who run away from relationships that diametrically reverse those of their childhoods (see also "She Who Dwells in the Rocks," *Dakota Texts* 238–45). As the narrator situates the listeners empathically in "Blood-Clot Boy," according to Jahner, so the narrator of "Double-Face Steals a Virgin" has the monster close the distance from "k̇akiya" 'far off' to "hi" 'here,' i.e. "arrival at a place, the fact being mentioned at that place" (unit 7, "hihunnikte" 'he had almost arrived here').

Almost immediately the monster speaks to convince the girl that "home" lies with him: "*Ungnikta* ca *cihiyowahi* yelo. Ca iyonicipi hantanhanś mihakaṗ *hiyu wo*" 'I have come to take you with me. So if you are willing, follow me away' (*Dakota Texts* 52, 61). "Ungnikta" means "you and I" (dual, not simply plural) will go to *our* home, while "hiyu wo" is a command telling her to "come out" of a place, not necessarily "home," as he begins to take her away in his opening words. In addition "cihiyowahi" 'I have come to take you with me' intensifies the monster's flattery of the girl by a verbal doubling of his singlemindedness: *wahi* (I arrived here), combined with another verb, typically expresses purpose as in *wahikte* (I arrived here to kill). But here purpose is additionally expressed by *hiyu* (to set out after something purposefully)—*ci-hiyo-wahi*. Perhaps the monster's speech is being satirized as redundantly flattering to accentuate her virtuous naïveté. A more experienced girl might immediately recognize his heavy-handed line, as in the courtship speech quoted from Bushotter in chapter 3.

Her sudden acceptance of his suit might also suggest that he has supernatural power, accounting for her immediate sexual attraction. The verbs of motion imply a psychological movement as well: "Heceglaḣcin eyin na *kigla* yunkan hecena ihakaṗ *iyaya*" 'That is all he said, and then he left; and at once the girl went after him' (*Dakota*

Texts 52, 61). He moves in the direction of *his* home—*kigla,* she follows—*iyaya,* meaning to set out *from* her home. Unlike "Double-Face Tricks the Girl," where the girl meets Double-face at night outside her tipi after a throat-clearing signal, this girl no sooner takes a step in his direction than she finds herself in a headlong rush from all she has known and become: "Yunkan hanhepi ataya kici *gla* hin na wana lila tehanl *glapi*" 'And then they traveled all night together, and for a long time they traveled' (*Dakota Texts* 52, my translation). The twice repeated use of *gla* (to be going back to where one belongs) indicates that the girl anticipates arrival at a new home, while it ironically foreshadows the danger risked by elopement. Pathetically, the girl herself uses the verb *gla* immediately before being answered roughly, an experience that would be entirely foreign to her in her own *tiyośpaye:* "Yu, eceś iwaśtela s'e *gla* na lila niluzan ca hehanyan owakihiśni *ye*" 'Ah, please, let us not go so fast. I cannot keep up the pace, you are so fleet-footed' (*Dakota Texts* 52, 61).

The man's flat refusal is the first indication that *gla* (to go back home) is not the right verb for her to use, especially because she has been deferential in praising his speed and has emphasized her own weakness with the particle "ye," thus creating within her sheltered sense of proper relationships the expectation of compassion and mutual respect. But rather than softening his language to justify her duress he simply scoffs, "hoħ!" at her request. As the man's brutality begins to emerge, the narrator metaphorically begins the process of the girl's realization: "Hoħ, inila keś inaħni ye, anpawi kin *hinapinkta* ca skaya u kin hehanl *unkihunnikte lo*" 'The idea! Stop talking and hurry; I want to reach home when the sun, about to rise, sends a white light in the sky' (*Dakota Texts* 52, 61). Double-face refers to the dawn as about to "hinapinkta" 'come out,' just as his identity begins to be apparent, while the verb of arrival now implies the idea that "home" for him is far from what it should be for anyone else, "unkihunnikte lo" 'we will arrive *there*' (*ki* implying still far from where they are).

The metaphor of light coming out is next used at the moment she discovers that the Double-face is not the man she thought she risked all for: "na wi kin hinapinkta ca skaya u kin walehanl koślalaka k'un he ayuta yunkan hanhepi kici *glicu* k'un he eśni śke'" 'and as the sun, about to rise, sent on whiteness ahead, she looked at the young man, and lo, he was not the one she started with' (*Dakota Texts* 52, 61). "Glicu" 'to start back to where one belongs' accentuates the dawning shock of being a captive rather than a wife. After berating her for being too proud to accept other suitors, the Double-face beats her with a wild rose branch, as they walk, treating her like a resistant captive or an unfaithful wife (see Bushotter 68: 1–2, 206: 1, and Deloria, *Camp Circle Society* 185–86).

After their arrival, the girl and the listeners witness a domestic scene that further suggests how carefully girls must choose a husband. Feasting upon the previous women he has "married," the Double-face reveals his insatiable appetites for sex, food, and elaborate clothing. He hunts to provide women for food rather than food for women. Like other men, he enjoys soup, but his bowl conceals marital en-slavement: "Ho, unci, ake omani-mninkta ca le wikoskalaka wan ehake-awagli kin le pa-kaksin na ake lecehcin ceh-ozula walolopya migle yo" 'Grandmother, I am going away again, so I want you to behead the last girl I brought home, and have another meal like this ready for me' (*Dakota Texts* 54, 62).

After he is satisfied, he dons his best outfit, presumably made by his grandmother and wives, in order to seduce more women. Bringing home wives as food suggests exploiting women for sex and work. Double-face repeatedly uses verbs of setting out from and returning to *his* home when he instructs his grandmother to prepare more "food," but when she offers to sacrifice herself for the girls, she tells them to run for *their* homes as fast as they can, "lila kiglapi." Now home is obviously no longer with an abusive husband but a place where girls are respected, where they contribute work but do not have to sacrifice their whole lives for a husband, as the grandmother sacrifices hers for them. Variations on the verb, *gla,* are repeated four more times, giving momentum to the return journey that forms part 2 of the four-part structure.

Once the girl has escaped, the narrator places the audience with her, so that when Double-face returns to *his* home he has "kihunni" 'arrived over there' in every sense. As before, when the grandmother respectfully ladled soup full of human meat, her post-death exchange with him reveals the hypocrisy of warriors who pursue enemies on behalf of the people, while they themselves are really enemies of the people. It is comical that he uses his grandmother's death to fire his "revenge": "Waȟteśni śicapi kin unci miktepi na toki yapikta ca!" 'The wretched beings! Having killed my grandmother, where do they think to escape?' (*Dakota Texts* 56, 62). After all, he has just threatened to eat up his grandmother if she does not prepare his dinner quickly: "Hecena canzeki na—Wan, Unci, inaȟiniciśi yelo. Na inayaȟniśni hantanhanś tepiciyinkte lo—eya" 'He got angry right away. "Grandmother, I am telling you to make haste. If you don't, I'll eat you up!" he said' (*Dakota Texts* 56, 62).

In the first part of the story the girl goes *out* of her own camp and enters *into* the monster's. In the second part she goes *out* of the monster's camp and *into* a "home," albeit not that of her birth. As the sun "hinapa" 'rose' when she realized the danger of elopement (*Dakota Texts* 52, 61), so now the man of the iron tipi "hinapa" 'comes out' to reveal where safety lies (*Dakota Texts* 57, 63). First he makes her review the whole list of male protectors, evoking her independent faculties of patience and concentration in the process. Only then does he add himself to the survival quotient: "Eca takumayayinkta he?—eya śke'. Canke—Hingnaciyinkte,—eya yunkan cinśni.—Hiya, takumayayinkta huwo?—eya canke wowahicun tonakeca kin iyuha cazeyata śke'. Ohanketa,—Ateciyinkte,—eya yunkan—Ha o, cunkś, mni kin ali hiyu wo,—eya ke'" '"What will you be to me?" he asked. "I will be your wife," she said, but that did not suit him. "No, try something else," he said, so she named over the entire list of kinships between men and women. At last—"You shall be a father to me," she said, and then he was pleased. "Very well; come over, walking on the water," he said' (*Dakota Texts* 57, 63).

Although the girl finds a temporary refuge in the iron tipi, the narrator does not immediately place the listeners in it at this time. The girl comes across the water to "ihunni" 'arrive there.' When he tells the girl to go inside, he says, "tima ilaninkte" 'you will go in there,' even though she is to tell the bull, bear, cat, and snake that "her father" has sent her. When he himself comes back in, however, the word is "glicu" 'to start coming back to where one belongs.' Only when the Double-face arrives as an immediate threat to the girl and her new family does the narrator draw everyone, including the listeners, into a definition of home as a place people defend from a common enemy. The monster "hihunni" 'arrives here' and bangs so hard on the tipi door that it comes loose. This is analogous to the psychological effects on women who have been terrorized by physical force. The girl in this story has acquired a father and brothers, the best deterrent in Lakota society to the serious (though uncommon) problem of wife abuse.

The initial conflict is a verbal standoff. The Double-face claims the girl as rightfully his—"hiyumiciciya yo" 'send out mine to me,' but the father doubles his claim by referring to her as "micunkśi" 'my daughter' and then using a verb specifying her as his own, "imaya-hihaha ye" 'you are insulting my own,' followed by the particle "ye" for emphasis. He then adds a subtle insult to counter the Double-face's calling him a "wicaśa śica" 'bad man' when he says "gla yo," meaning not simply 'go home,' but 'go home for your own good,' when used as an imperative.

When the battle occurs, the man is not too proud to rely on his companions to deliver the coup de grace once he has felled the monster with his spear. Kinship defeats egotism. But even after the girl appears to be safe from prideful abuse, her own greed still threatens. She forgets her father's admonition to ignore the valuable objects that fly out of Double-face's burning corpse. The fine handled awl that buries itself under her arm, causing a near fatal infection, represents another form of monstrosity. To fix the mind on personal possessions permits poisoning by the same spirit that makes a man regard his female relatives as ornaments or tools.

In the larger perspective women who elope may become wives in name only, dooming themselves to become objects of gratification (food) and dehumanized servants (the awl). And women who do not elope may still be servants of their appetites, in this case greed, if they do not honor their relatives first and foremost. Still, even if they do some of these things by mistake through inexperience, they will be given second and third chances. Unlike the Double-face, the man of the iron tipi does not force the girl to abandon her own *tiyośpaye*. Soon she "very much" wants to return home, "lila tiyata cin." "Lila" 'very' accentuates the importance of home, though "tohantuka" 'she stayed for a while' shows respect for her host. In his final instructions, the man tells the bear and the cat to bring her within sight of her camp before returning to their home: "Tiotaninyan eihpeyapi na glicu po" 'Escort her to a point within sight of her home, and then return' (*Dakota Texts* 60, 64).

Since the story is told primarily for girls like the one in the story, "home" from the speaker's point of view is most frequently the girl's original home, but because the bear and the cat are models of male kinship, their return is also to a home situated with the speaker. Both "homes" should be together in the minds of the listeners though the homes are geographically separate within the story: "Gla" 'to return home' is used to describe both the girl's approach to her own camp and her escorts' return to theirs, universalizing the verb's application to all listeners:

> Ho, canke mato na igmu kici winyan k'un wana *aglapi* na tiotaninyan inazinpi na hetanhan winyan k'un isnala *glahin* na tiwegna *kigla* canke hehanl kawingapi na is eya tiyatakiya *kiglapi* ske'.

> So the three started forth, the girl, escorted by the bear and the lynx; and when they were within sight of camp, they paused; and the girl alone went on while they stood watching her. When she entered the tribal circle, they turned about and left for their home. (*Dakota Texts* 60, 64)

Although the four forms of *gla* at the end, "aglapi," "glahin," "kigla," and "kiglapi" might be said to represent the "pattern number," stylistic devices augment meaning without conforming to formal structures. In the companion story, "Double-Face Tricks the Girl" (*Dakota Texts* 46–50, see chapter 4) *ske'* is used four times at the beginning, four times at the end, and twice when the girl realizes her husband is a Double-face. Otherwise *ke'* is used throughout. In the longer "Double-Face Steals a Virgin," however, *ske'* is used irregularly and much more often than *ke'*. In fact the narrator creates intensity with softness, since *ke'* is the relative exception in sequences marked by the repeated use of *ske'*.

Deloria marks the end of the first two units (each including more than one predication) with *ske'* but switches to *keyapi'* to set off the arrival of the Double-face: "hcehanl itokagatanhan koskalaka wan u *keyapi'* " 'and during that time, a new young man approached from the south' (*Dakota Texts* 51, 60). Although the shortened form *ke'* is used many times in the story, the complete word *keyapi'* is used only once to dramatize the villain's entrance. Thereafter, *śke'* is used seven times until the narrator substitutes *ke'* at another descent, immediately preceding the girl's polite request for Double-face to pity her fatigue: "Yu, eceś iwaśtela s'e gla na lila niluzahan ca hehanyan owakihiśni ye" 'Ah, please, let us not go so fast. I cannot keep up the pace, you are so fleet-footed' (*Dakota Texts* 52, 61). The monster's retaining a semblance of his chivalric facade may be suggested by the *eya ke'* indicating a somewhat gentler tone than *śke'* for his telling her he must arrive before daylight, nevertheless *śke'* is the next quotative used, probably because it serves as an exclamation point to her shocked recognition that the Double-face is not the man with whom she agreed to elope. As the storyteller escalates the fears and increasingly real danger, *śke'* is used to describe the monster's appearance and his whipping her with a wild rose branch while *ke'* twice follows "eya" 'he said,' first after Double-face lectures her on pride, and again after he orders her into the tipi. In this instance *śke'* follows strong images of action, while *ke'* follows his commands.

Throughout the rest of the story *śke'* is used fifty-five times, while *ke'* is used five times. This probably reflects the story's extremes of anxiety and action. The narrator's relatively infrequent use of *ke'* is therefore a means of heightening dramatic effect because it interrupts an aural expectation based on *śke'*. Using *ke'* also makes the succeeding *śke'* stronger than it would have been in an unbroken series of *śke'* endings.

For the failure of the bear to heal the girl's spiritual infection, the narrator uses *ke'*: "na mato kin pikiyeśi k'eyaś ituya hnahna ohitiya śkan nanś iyakcuni *ke'* " 'He tried, grunting officiously, but in vain' (*Dakota Texts* 59, 64). This is the first *ke'* after fifteen *śke'* endings; its softness suits the mood of disappointment and heightens the surprise, since the bear spirit was traditionally revered for healing (see Walker, *Lakota Belief and Ritual* 157–59). But when the next section describes the impotence of two of the remaining power animals—the buffalo and the cat—the failure bcomes serious and *śke'* appears: "Canke hehanl igmu-tanka k'un he iyute c'eyaś iś eyaś okihiśni yunkan hehanl tatanka kin iyutin na ake okihiśni *śke'*.'" 'Then the lynx made a try, but he too failed. Then the buffalo-bull attempted to doctor her; he also failed.' (*Dakota Texts* 59, 64).

The snake is given a complete sentence for his try, but his inadequacy is emotional as well as medical when the buffalo steps on him, and he bites the girl. For his unheroic behavior the sentence appropriately descends to *ke'*: "ĥcehanl tatanka k'un opta iyayin na zuzeca kin sinte ali canke canze-hingnin na winyan k'un wanunyaĥtaka *ke'* " 'But at that moment, the bull awkwardly stepped on his tail. This angered him so that he bit the girl accidentally' (*Dakota Texts* 59–60, 64). But the softness of *ke'* for the failure prepares for the good news of the girl's "accidental" recovery:

> Yunkan a kin lila po hihuyin na naĥleca yunkan etanhan tun-
> aopeya tahinśpa k'un he nasluta canke winyan kin akiśni *śke'*.

> The armpit began to swell horribly, and then broke and from it there came the awl, along with pus, so the young woman recovered. (*Dakota Texts* 60, 64)

Śke' is the only quotative used from here to the end, perhaps because the narrator has only good news to report, and because *śke'* often signals conclusion. If the story were structured according to a pattern number, perhaps *śke'* would appear exactly four times at the end, as it happens to in "Double-Face Tricks the Girl." While all the stories in *Dakota Texts* can best be understood in terms of narrative conventions, these conventions are never used identically. Each story deserves to be read as a unique achievement in the written art of Lakota narrative.

Appendix 1:
Translations from *Dakota Texts*

THE 1974 AMS PRESS REPRINT of *Dakota Texts* is an exact facsimile of Deloria's 1932 original: volume 14 of *Publications of the American Ethnological Society*, edited by Franz Boas. A 1978 Dakota Press paperback with introductory notes by Agnes Picotte and Paul N. Pavich includes only the translations.

"THE DEER WOMAN"
(1974:163–64; 1978:74–76)

Once a man was walking, away from camp, but as evening was now coming on, he turned homeward and was going through a wood when he met a woman. And it chanced to be a very beautiful woman whom he had been asking for, and offering presents; but he had been rejected repeatedly. And even the girl herself had not looked at him with favor. And here she was. But she turned out to be very agreeable, so he talked pleasantly with her. He thought it was plain that she was after all kindly disposed towards him, so he was happy as he talked, and all the more he wished to have her for his wife. She was wearing a beautiful robe, tan in color; and the man carried a thong-rope, coiled about his arm. So he took an end of his rope, and playfully, without her realizing it, ran it through some of the holes in the limbs of her robe, as he talked. Thus they stood when, of a sudden, a woman with a dog emerged from the wood and walked along towards them. The instant the dog saw this young woman, he barked and ran towards her, and she was frantic, and struggled to get away quickly. But now it was clear that she was not a woman but a deer, and in the joint of the foreleg the man's rope was twisted into a knot and held her fast. The man knew at once that he had been tricked, and in his anger, he drew his hatchet from his belt, and would have struck her on the head, but the deer threw herself here and there to avoid being hit so that he struck out wildly every way without hitting her. It was a female of the wood-deer known as the black-tail. At last she spoke again, as a woman. "That's enough; come on and let me go now. Wait and see, for I shall give you many powers." The man replied, "Doubtless you will be sincere in that too!" and he released her, so that she ran back toward the wood, like one flying. The young man became dizzy, and without knowing just how, he got home; and he vomited at intervals. Ever so often when the spell came over him more than usual, he would whistle like a deer, and make as if to run off, like a wild animal; so the people all felt badly, and were especially saddened when they recalled what a fine young member he used to be, in the tribe. At last they made a sweat-lodge for him, and purified him, and that seemed to help him; so then they exploded some gunpowder in his face and he really came to his right mind, it seemed. So he recovered. But as long as he lived, he alone, by some mysterious luck, always brought home the finest horses from war. The people explained it by saying that the deer-woman who promised him many powers in exchange for her release must have kept her word. That is all.

"DOUBLE-FACE TRICKS A GIRL"
(1974:46–50; 1978:19–20)

In a tribal camp there lived a girl who was very beautiful and greatly loved. She was kind and also virtuous so that all men coveted the right to marry her, but she was contrary-minded. Then one day a young man from somewhere else came to pay her court; he was very handsome. Whereas formerly she did not want such attention, now she was pleased, and promised to marry him. But she didn't confide in her parents that she agreed to go with him, and she got ready secretly, preparing pemmican and moccasins too, for the journey; carrying them in her belt she waited for him. In the twilight of evening, someone cleared his throat back of the tipi. That was the arrangement for a signal. "When I clear my throat behind the tipi, come out; for we shall go off then," he had said. She took her pet beaver and went outside and there stood the young man behind the tipi, his blanket pulled up over his head; so she went off with him. They travelled fast till they came to a deep river, and then the man said, "I will swim across; sit on my back." She didn't care to do that and immediately he became very angry, saying, "Do it, I tell you. If not, I'll throw you into the water!" Because she feared him greatly, she did as he said; especially since she couldn't swim. As she sat on his back while he swam along, she looked at the back of his head, and on that side, also, there was a face! This man was what is known as Double-face. Now she knew that this was not that handsome young man she loved; and she despised and loathed him. They stood on the farther shore, now, and walked from there to a large tipi in the wood, from which smoke was rising. Right away the man said, "I'm sleepy. So put me to sleep by hunting lice in my hair." She hated him so much that her whole body cringed at his nearness, but he lay down before her so she began to hunt his lice, and induced sleep to him. For lice, he used miniature hop-toads which jumped about in his hair. So she took each one she caught, and laying it between two flat stones beside her, she smashed it to death by striking the top stone on the lower one. She had him in such a deep sleep that he lay utterly unconscious; so she took some of his hair which was very long and tied it to one tipi-pole; then she took some more and tied it to the next pole, and thus she continued to do. She completed the circle about the tipi, so that the man lay in the centre of what appeared like a spider-web. Snatching up her pet, the woman proceeded to run away. All she did was to run and when she neared her home, there lay a deep lake across her direction so that she could not go on. She sat down and wept. Immediately, the little beaver ran about, cutting down trees with his teeth, and in no time at all he had a bridge finished so they crossed on it. As they stepped on the ground on the opposite side, someone came shouting from the rear and it was the Double-face who came along, angrily shaking his fist at them. He stopped at the shore, and then he too tried to walk on the bridge, but because it was very narrow he had to walk very slowly, picking his way with care; so the beaver meantime started to undo the bridge at his end. When the Double-face was halfway across, it broke down, dropping the man in the midst of the lake where he drowned. At once the young girl took her pet in her arms and ran hard all the way homeward and soon she entered the camp, to safety; so a great shout went up from the excited people. Her parents were very glad and this time the right young man for whom the Double-face substituted himself, was told he might marry the girl; so it happened. The little beaver was so well-loved and well-treated in that camp that he came finally to consider himself the most privileged citizen in the entire tribe. That is all.

"HEART-KILLER"
(1974:127–33; 1978:55–58)

Four young men lived together; and Hakela, the last-born, who stepped out to get firewood, came back in again and said, "There is a young woman standing outside. What shall we call her?" So his brothers said, "Let us call her our elder sister. Ask her in, Hakela," they said. Hakela asked her in and she replied, "Thank you, younger brother," and entered the tipi. From that day she lived there; a fine girl, as well as a beautiful one, industrious and skilled in the things women do. She made beautiful clothes for her brothers, and when they brought home meat, she took care of it all so that they were never without food. One day all her brothers went away and she was staying alone when she saw a very pretty feather blown along, so she tried to get it but it kept eluding her, leading her on and on, till she was in the dense woods. There near the water, was a hole to which the feather led her. Then certain somethings pulled her into the hole. They were beavers which lived there. So when her brothers got home, they went weeping through the woods looking for their sister, in vain. And then, the one next to the youngest who felt especially sad and walked along a stream hunting her, thought he saw something out of the corner of his eye, so he took a better look at it. And behold! there was his sister, lying face upward, and beavers were draining their hot fish on her face! For a long time they must have been doing this, for by now her face was a mass of sores. He hurried home and told the eldest brother who went angrily to the scene and said, "You worthless, no-account beings, can it be that out of your number, someone was kind to my sister? If so, say, 'I'." The room was filled with, "I, I, I" and when the noise subsided, a meek small voice said, "Of what good for them to say, 'I'? The one with the right to say it is I, is sitting in the corner;" and the girl said, "My elder brother, he is speaking the truth. When they drain their hot fish on my face, he always drops a small piece of food into my mouth; that is how I keep alive"—"Very well; come outside. You shall live," the elder brother said; so the little beaver went outdoors, and the man killed all the rest. Then he took his sister and the little beaver home, and everything went well again.

Once when Heart-killer, (that's what they say she was called), made a fire away from home and was tanning hides, her beaver-pet was picking chips for her fire. After a time, Hakela came out, and said, "Elder sister, come home now; it is time to eat." So they started for their tipi, but Beaver stayed behind and walked about, singing something; so they listened and heard, "My elder brothers, the best of our family, they have annihilated; and only I, with my inferior hide, am left. I wear red leaves for mittens!"—"Hey, come along, will you? You too must take food. What do you think you are doing?" said Hakela to him, and he called back that he was singing a death-song.

Once more the woman was tanning hides when two women came from somewhere and said, "Heart-killer, come with us. We are going to marry B. lec'e', and you must marry Teal-duck." So she said, "Why? I'm perfectly happy and well off at home, why should I leave my brothers and go away?" They kept teasing her. Then, after a while, seeming to give up, they walked away; but at a distance they turned and called back, "Well, then, just for that, we will take this along," and they showed her her beaver-pet. So she ran after them, begging it back, but they carried it away; she followed them little by little, until they were too far away for her to find her way home; then they surrendered her pet to her. They were now stopping beside a deep stream. And across the river was a tribal camp. So, "We have come to marry B.*lec'e'*, and this one has come to marry Teal-duck!" they called; and, almost at once, a white boat started over. As it neared them, a man, spitting out white beads, came; so they saw him. "There, now, the one coming is Teal-duck; you shall marry him," they said, so Heart-killer was very unhappy and wept as she stood, but there being no way out, like lying down to die, she entered and went off with him. Just then a blue boat started coming, and the man in it was spitting out blue beads. The two women entered his boat and went off with him. As a matter of fact, it was B.*lec'e'* who brought the white boat and Teal-duck the blue one; but they, in ignorance, went with him. It was evening, and a man came and said, "B.*lec'e'* is to dance; so you are to come," and Teal-duck tried to confuse the matter as if not hearing, and said, "Yes, yes, I am to dance." When the man left, Teal-duck told his wives, "Don't come. Whoever looks on, gets a sty in the eye; therefore nobody ever looks on." He feared they might recognize him. But after he had gone they followed him there and saw him lying on the ground, and B.*lec'e'* dancing on his back. They returned, very angry, and one made a bag of flying ants, and one a bag of wasps, and those two bags they laid on either side of Teal-duck's sleeping place as if they themselves were sleeping there; and ran away. Some time in the night, Teal-duck returned and, "Ouch, ouch, I've worn myself out dancing," he said as he crawled into bed. Just then, one pricked him. So, "Little jealous ones, lie still, will you?" But, just then, the other stung him. So, "Well, well! This one is certainly stinging me!" so saying, he turned over, but that moment, like a great roaring they all came at him; so. "*Yah! Yah!*" he cried, and ran to the deserted places, weeping. There came an Iya to him, "Why are you crying?" he asked; and he lied to him, "B.*lec'e'* has stolen my wife," he said. "Well, then, go home and bring me a white knife whetted until it is very keen." So off Teal-duck went, and soon returned with the knife, whetted until it was flexible from thinness. It was night; so Heart-killer and her husband lay sleeping when all at once she felt something wet, and it wakened her. "Get up, something around here is wet," she said, but she could not rouse her husband; and there he lay, his head severed from his body, swimming in blood. This she was not aware of at first. Immediately she jumped up, weeping; and the next day, he was laid away and the people moved to another campground; but she stayed behind, weeping. As she wept, she heard a voice; and as she listened, she happened to see Iya come up over a distant hill, and run toward her. So she ran with her little beaver, from the Iya. They came to the deep stream already mentioned, and paused there while Beaver hurriedly built a bridge over which they crossed to safety. At once he proceeded to undo it, so they came on and that night they saw Iya up in the moon which was sailing high in the sky, and in his hand he held the head of B. lec'e'. The reason was that he had no way of crossing the stream. At once Heart-killer and her beaver travelled homeward; and after a long time they arrived at her brothers' home, where they were very happy to see her. From that time, she never went anywhere again but lived with her brothers. The young men kept closer watch of their sister now; so that never again so terrible a thing could come to her. That is all.

"THE FEATHER MAN"
(1974:142–45; 1978:63–65)

In a tribal camp lived an only daughter who was greatly loved by her parents, and one day a man came from somewhere and wanted very much to marry her. So they asked around to know who he was, but nobody knew about him. Even so, the girl was very deeply in love with him, and had promised to marry him, and had agreed to run off with him during the night. She lay ready, listening for him, so the instant he came, she went outside and started off with him secretly. And he took her to a house of wood; but as they entered the room, she looked at the man and knew that it was not the handsome youth to whom she had promised herself. This was another man, and he had some beautiful girls imprisoned there. On one side of the room were some girls with their legs missing; and on the other side, girls with their hair and scalp all removed. He said to her, "Choose which side you wish to join." So she said, "Those which have no hair I wish to join." So he told her to sit on that side. Then he made a sweat-bath and said, "The newcomer is to hand me my stones." So when she leaned over, head foremost, to push the stones into the sweat-lodge, he reached out and caught hold of her hair, pulling off her entire scalp. Immediately the woman ran crying round and round over the meadow; and she saw a beautiful feather in the grass. As she stooped to get it, it blew off, so she caught up with it and tried again to pick it up. And someone said, "Then you will drop blood on me!" It was a Feather-man who spoke, and now he took her home with him. They came to a stream and he said, "Now, dive in here and stay in as long as you can hold your breath." She did so, and on emerging, she saw that her hair had grown somewhat. Again she dived in and stayed a long time, and this time her hair had reached her waistline, so the man dressed it, becomingly for her, and they went on from there. "That will do. Now, I must tell you that I am married, but to a terrible woman. Therefore, first of all, I want you to go to yonder bend in the river, and run about crying, as though in distress. And when a man comes to you, say to him, 'Grandfather, two days from now, I shall come here, expecting food. Tell the people!' Those are the mice-people and you shall appeal to them for earth-beans. And tomorrow, she will come to ask you to play on a swing with her. The woman I am married to, will say this. In that case, take the swing that is painted brown," he said. So the woman followed the instructions. And the next morning the bad woman stood outside her door and said, "*Ma!* Come out and let us swing." So she went out but as they were starting, the Feather-man interfered, and a beautiful feather fluttered in the wind before them. The woman took time out to run after the feather, and meantime she called, "The swing colored brown is mine!" But the young woman, not heeding the feather, ran on and reached the swings, and sat down in the brown one. Swinging herself several times, she jumped back down and started homeward; and soon arrived. Sometime after that, the other one came panting in and the people jeered at her. Next morning she came again and said, "Let us go to find earth-beans." So she came out, and ran crying towards the bend in the river. And that Mouse-man whom she addressed earlier as grandfather, started to announce around the camp, "Now my grandchild comes for food. Make haste!" From all quarters, the mice brought fine large earth-beans, and piled them before her. So she took them home; and a long while afterwards, the other woman came home, all covered with sweat from her efforts, and the people laughed at her. Again next morning she stood outside and said, "Come on out, let us go digging." So she went out and took a badger that her husband had brought to her. Going to the hillside, she lay down with it and threw a blanket over herself and it; and the badger dug with a humming sound, so she followed in the tunnel it thus made; and came out on the other end; and still the other woman was not in sight. So the people laughed at her. "She is always doing that; don't let her escape," they said. So the young woman took a club and stood ready. So first a bear cub came out, but she killed it with a blow; and then, after that, the woman, its mother, as it were, came out, so she killed her also. And from then on, everything went well for them. That is all.

"A WOMAN KILLS HER DAUGHTER"
(1974:166–71; 1978:76–79)

A woman had two children, a boy and a young woman. And a young man came from somewhere and married the girl, so the four lived together. As they lived there, in the same tipi, the woman became enamoured of her son-in-law and because she wanted him for herself she planned to kill her daughter. She was on the constant lookout for a good way to do away with her. Whenever the son-in-law was in the tipi, she became very silly in her actions, and hardly knew what to do with herself, and couldn't sit quiet. One day when the man was away, she said to her daughter, "Let us go swinging," so the girl replied, "How silly! We are not children!" and she laughed. But she said again, "Daughter, I am always unhappy, and I really wish to swing, just to amuse myself a little." So then the girl consented and together they went to the water. It was deep and along its edge stood a tree with a large branch arching over the stream. And on it were two swings already tied. So she caused her daughter to take the one farther over the water, and took the outside one for herself; and now they swung themselves and at once the girl's rope broke, landing her in the deep stream where she was drowned. It came out later that the crafty woman had previously set those swings and had hacked the rope in one of them so that it would break at once; for what was there about it to make it strong? Immediately she who was so eager to swing, ran home; and as there was nobody around, she hurriedly dressed herself in her daughter's clothes;, and because there was great resemblance between them, she applied her face paint just like her daughter's. She was sitting in her daughter's place, and was busy at some task when her son-in-law returned. Just then the baby began to cry; so the man said, "What is the need of allowing him to cry? Why don't you nurse him?" And with that he glanced at her and at once knew it was not his wife who was sitting there. "Where has my wife gone?" he thought, and a great sense of worry came over him. But of course he could not question her, because she was his mother-in-law. And she said, "I have nursed him, and still he cries; what next can I do?" and then, addressing her boy, though it was her own son, she said, "My younger brother, carry your nephew on your back; I must cook some food, yet he detains me." So the boy took the baby on his back, and walked along the bank, crying. "Elder sister, come back to us! My nephew is crying," he was wailing, when his sister appeared, visible from the waistline up. She lay on the shore and said, "Bring him here, little brother, that I may nurse him. Mother has done a dreadful thing to me and now it is too late for any hope. Who is that man anyway? If she wants him so, how much better, had she told me; gladly I would have turned him over to her! but alas, I am now a fish from my waist down." At this, the little brother cried harder than ever. The baby, now satisfied, was asleep. "Now, brother, stand here with your back to me; I want to help you to take him on your back," she said; so he turned and stood with his back to her while she placed the infant there and arranged the blanket about him. Then, the moment she finished, the boy turned about quickly; but already his sister had disappeared; and all he saw was the tail of a fish as it vanished under the water. The next day, when the child cried and the woman could not quiet him, she caused the boy to take him out again. So he walked along the bank, singing, "Elder sister, my little nephew is crying!" And she called out, "Bring him here, little brother!" And she lay on the shore and fed him and when he slept, the boy took him home. And then the woman who was in love with her son-in-law, went off somewhere, so the man questioned his young brother-in-law like this, "Brother-in-law, where has your sister gone?" So the boy told him how his mother had cut into a rope and then made a swing and caused her to fall into the water. And also how once in a while his sister would come to the shore to feed the baby. So the man said, "The next time your little nephew cries, take him and say what it is that brings your sister to the shore." So when the child began to whimper again, he took him along the bank and called to his sister. Meantime the man had transformed himself into a tree stump, and stood near by; so when the wife came and lay exposed, only as far as her waist, out of the water, and took her baby in her arms, she suddenly saw it there. "Little brother, that tree stump was never there before, was it?" she asked, and he said "*Hoh*! Of course, sister, that has always been there; you just never noticed it before!" She said, "All right, then," and proceeded to feed her baby, and as she replaced him on the boy's back, and arranged the blanket about him, the man rushed forward and with a single stroke, he severed her body from the fish. The body curved and jumped like a fish, but they managed to get it home where they made a sweat-bath and restored the young wife to her former self. Next day, the man was going to hunt; so he said to her, "I shall bring meat and pile it in a heap beyond the hill; and when I call for assistance, bring your mother with you." Accordingly in due time, he called out, "Come and meet me!" So she said, "Mother, that one wishes someone to meet him and help carry the meat; let us go!" And the mother agreed all too eagerly; so they went. They divided the meat and each one took a pack on her back. When they were starting home the man said to his wife, whispering in her ear, secretly, "Stay near me all the time," so she said she would. "And when I make a mark on the ground, step over it quickly." So the woman kept closely behind her husband. He was carrying a staff in his hand. With it he suddenly made a mark on the ground and started forward quickly, so his wife followed directly behind, and jumped over the line. Then the crafty older woman came along, and as she was about to step over the line, the ground separated right over the line, so she disappeared into the abyss, as if someone had dropped her down. At once the ground came together once more. So from that time on, that old woman who was in love with her own son-in-law, was never seen again by anyone; neither she nor the pack of meat she carried. That is all.

"THE ELK MAN"
(1974:159–62; 1978:72–74)

Originally, they say, this legend belonged to the Pawnee but it is not known just when it came to the Dakota. However, the Dakota now own it also.

Among the people, there was a man who could attract any woman. Women who held themselves dear and lived as if unattainable, easily fell where he was concerned, and those very ones would one day find themselves disgraced by having gone off with him. For this reason, he was greatly dreaded. At last the chiefs met in council and discussed possible ways of getting rid of him. The best plan seemed to be to find the brother of this man, a self-respecting member of the tribe, and talk with him. "Come, now, it is becoming a source of worry to the whole tribe that your brother is spoiling everything, and you must grant us your permission to do away with him. Later we will give you horses, a home and a beautiful woman for a wife," they said to him. "How could I? Were not we two nursed at the same breast? How then could I sell my own?" thus he mused many days with a sad heart. Even so, he grew weary of their repeated asking, and at last he was tempted by their offers; so, without more delay, he assented. And then they said, "Let us kill him at the next *hàka'*-game, now that at last the brother is willing." And the object of these designs knew what was about to take place. When the date drew near for the next *hàka'*-game, he outdid even himself, by eloping with all the remaining women with good reputations; and ruined their names. Then one day he sharpened a knife to a keen thin blade, and took it to his youngest sister-in-law and said to her, "Now, sister-in-law, they are planning to kill me at the next *hàka'*-game. So be on hand, and the instant I am killed, rush up, stopping for nothing, and say, 'This one used to abuse me too!' and cut off my head, and sever my right arm at the shoulder-joint. Then run with the head and arm to the thick wood and leave them there," he said. The day came for the *hàka'*-game, and the young girl, though she dreaded to carry out the order, still felt she should, since he had asked her. She therefore concealed the knife under her blanket and went to the game, pretending to be a spectator of it. And now, her brother-in-law, handsomely appareled, came to look on, but as soon as he stopped, someone shot him from behind so that he died. Then his sister-in-law ran and exclaiming, "This one used to abuse me too!" she cut off his head and arm. She ran with them to the thick wood, while the people dug a hole into which they threw the body, and made a fire over it. Then they declared the country polluted, and moved away. It was now evening, and the tribe was making camp. But the brother who sold his own, not having received any of the favors promised him, went and pitched his tipi, pitifully, at the end of the camp. And then, that evening, someone approached along the way the tribe had come. Ever so often he would say, "U + !" A long elk-call. He came to the brother's tipi and was the one they had killed and cut up that morning; and yet he entered, whole and well. Not at all angry, he said to his brother, "Now where are the horses, tipi and woman that they have given you? Wasn't that why you sold me?" he said. And the elder brother wept and said, "Alas, my younger brother, they gave me nothing!"— "In that case, go to the council tent and say, 'My brother sends me to claim the things you promised me!' and see if they don't give them to you," he said. So he went to the council tent and said what his brother had advised. But they answered, "*Hoh!* How could he, when we have just killed and burned him up?" He answered, "My brother sits in my tipi, at this instant. Come and see for yourselves." So they went to his tipi and were awe-struck to see him sitting there. Immediately they became very agreeable, because of their fear, and proceeded to give all the fine things they had promised to the brother and then had withheld from him; and they said no more about the matter. But things grew even worse after that. He fascinated all the women so much that there was not a good woman left in that tribe. And then it was clear that the young man was really an elk, and so it was beyond their power to subdue him by killing him; neither could they put a stop to his attraction for women. They finally gave in and said no more. That is all.

"A Bad Deed"
(1974:246–53; 1978:122–26)

This is the tale of a tragic deed that was committed within the Dakota tribal circle. There was a Dakota woman who had two daughters with whom she lived. A young man came and married both the sisters, so his tipi was placed inside the circle, where he lived as a son-in-law. Immediately behind his tipi, the three uncles of the sister, lived side by side, in the tribal ring of dwellings. They all lived in harmony together there. Now, this young man who married the sisters, went every evening to the council tent which stood in the centre of the circle and returned at a very late hour. It happened that one day the elder of his wives talked thus to her husband, "When you are away at the council tent someone comes in and lies with my younger sister, on the opposite side of the tipi. And when it is almost time for your return, a young man goes out." And the husband said, "I will go to the council tipi again tonight. But I will return early. When I get to the doorway, I will stop and clear my throat. When I do so you must answer me by clearing your throat also, if he is inside again. That shall be the sign." So the two of them had an understanding of what to do. According to the plan, he went as usual to the council tent, but returned soon after, and, stopping outside, he cleared his throat. And his elder wife cleared her throat also. Thus he knew that a man was with his younger wife. He took his knife out of its scabbard, and stood in readiness as a young man rushed out from the tipi. As he came past, the husband caught hold of him and at once dug his knife into his rival's abdomen, tearing a great gash across it. Straightaway the intestines dropped out, unwinding themselves, and the wounded man died instantly. The angry husband picked up the body of the dead man and threw it against the side of his tipi, letting it slide down to the ground. Then he withdrew to one side. His two wives burst into tears, but he took out his arrows and said, "No. Don't you dare to weep! On your account, I have done horribly for myself, and if you start to weep, I will kill you both!" As he stood watching them every instant, his wives did not dare to cry; his mother-in-law did not weep either. The slain man was one whose father was dead, and whose grandfather kept him as his own son. And the grandfather was the eldest of the wives' three uncles! Secretly, unknown to the family, for nobody knew how long, those two had been intimate— the boy and his young aunt. It was he whom his uncle now had killed in the dark, by ripping his body open with a knife. When this became plain, an unspeakable horror fell upon them all. Straightaway, that

very night, the man and his two wives and his mother-in-law fled
from the tribe. Planning to get away when the camp was asleep, they
quietly prepared in the dark, and, when nobody knew about it, they
left. For two whole days, aimlessly; not knowing to whom to fly for
safety, the fugitives travelled, and the second evening saw them at
last making camp. The man shot a buffalo so at least they had plenty
of meat. At least, though they were sorrowful, they were not starving.
While they were in flight, a snow storm was raging, making it difficult
if not altogether impossible, for anyone to follow them. Therefore
they had no fear from that quarter. They made their third camp now.
In a protected spot, in a bend of the wood where it was pleasant,
they placed their tent; and while the women prepared supper at home,
the husband went out and cut green tree bark for the horses. This he
fed to them. Now the sun had set, and the wives had supper ready;
so the man went inside and sat down; and when they placed his food
before him, he ate. As he sat there, he heard someone stamping his
feet, as people do to get rid of the snow on their moccasins before
entering a tipi. At once, instinctively he reached for his gun. A man
entered. Then more followed him, one after the other until they filled
the opposite half of the tipi, where they sat down. "Well, how good
this is! Come, (to his wives), put on plenty of food to cook that our
guests may eat!" he said. So his two wives hurried about preparing
supper for the visitors. Soon it was ready and placed before them—
plenty of excellent food it was. An entire warparty had walked in on
them. They were Crows, and there were five of them. When they
finished their supper, the war leader began to speak. "When you first
began to make camp, and when you stood in the bend of the wood
to cut green bark for the horses, we were watching you from the end
of yonder cliff. We know you are the only man in this camp and that
there are three women. If I had wanted to, we could have killed you
then, and these women we would have taken captive. But I had a
special reason for coming here this way instead." Thus the war lord
spoke. Then he added, "When man meets man, when they visit one
another, they fill the pipe for a smoke together!" And the Dakota
replied, "You are right. But first won't you hear my story? When I
finish it, then I shall be glad to hear what you have to say about it.
I have done a tragic deed, and therefore, with these two women, I

roam about, a fugitive. The two women are my wives, and the third is their mother whom her daughters keep with them because she has no husband, and that is why she is here with them. I have committed murder. There was a boy, he was a nephew to these women. But alas, one of them was secretly intimate with him and so I killed him. I killed him first, and afterwards I knew it was he! Immediately, while the tribe slept, we broke camp and stole away. A great blizzard came up meantime so we do not know whether they are trying to follow us. It is impossible for me to remain in the tribe, so I must roam about in this way, I have decided; and if death overtakes us out here, what of that? I think to myself. That is why I can not fill a pipe for you. Among us Dakota, a murderer's hand is bad. So won't you just blend the tobacco yourself and smoke, my friend? And then, if you kill me, that will be well. But grant me this, that you spare these women. Take them home with you and be kind to them. That is all," he said. And the war leader conferred with his comrades in the Crow tongue and then, turning to the Dakota once more, this is what he told him, "Now, this is what we have to say about your story. Recently, only six days ago, in truth, my wife died. And when I first laid eyes on this young woman who is your younger wife, I saw a great resemblance to my wife in her appearance. Because a great sorrow came over me when I saw her, this is what I want to say to you. If it is agreeable to you, you will all go home with us to Crow-land, and you will stay and make your permanent home there." The Dakota laid this invitation before his two wives who found it agreeable to accept. So he told the war chief that his wives were both glad to go and that they said, "Even if we die there, it will be well." The war chief was very happy that his plan was to be accepted. "We will rest here four days," he said, "during which time, a sweat-lodge will be prepared for you and you shall be purified. Then, you shall discard the clothing you now wear and put something different, something unpolluted, on your body. And after that, you shall take us to the Dakota camp where we will steal some horses. When we return here, then we shall go on to Crow-land." When the murderer had been cleansed and new clothing put on him, they went forth until they neared the Dakota camp. Here the women with the baggage were left in care of one Crow, and the rest went on. This place where the women waited was just near enough to the camp so that the warriors could reach it without too much trouble, and yet it was sufficiently remote, for safety. "Now, this is the place. Here is where I lived only recently. And yonder live the fathers of him whom I killed," he said. Somewhat back of the camp-circle, there was a new burial scaffold that had not been there before. He concluded that it was the grave of his victim, his nephew whom he had slain. He evidently took his horse with him, for near- by, there lay a dead horse. By this time, they were convinced that he was telling them the truth in all respects. Now, "There and there and there they possess swift running horses," he told the Crows. So they distributed themselves about, in such a manner that they might attack the herds of the various families he had pointed out, at about the same time. And they succeeded in bringing away many beautiful horses. They fled with their stolen horses to the place where the women waited. There they stopped to eat hurriedly, and then, chang- ing their footwear, they went on at the same rate until they came to the camp site from which they had started together. From there they began their flight homeward in earnest and kept going until they reached the land of the Crow Indians. The war leader told his people in careful detail how it came about that he brought these Dakota home; and they realized the situation. "Nobody is to regard them as captives in any sense, and nobody is to do them any harm," he told the people. Accordingly, the people treated them with the highest deference and respect; and that Dakota, who had married sisters so that they bore the *t'e'ya* relation to each other, took his younger wife, and gave her to the war chief to be his wife. It was the woman whom the war chief had admired, seeing a close resemblance between her and the wife he had just lost. It was because of this likeness that he refrained from killing the Dakota family in the first place. Thus it happened that the young woman who by her folly had brought disaster on her husband and sister and mother, was now the very means whereby their lives were spared. The war leader took the Dakota into relationship, and they accepted each other as friends in the kinship sense. So the families of the two men lived together in a happy group and were as closely related as if they were natural relatives. And that was how, after a time, the children, and the children's children, though they were Dakota, grew up as Crow Indians; and there they multiplied, and there they died. From the very beginnings of people, the Dakota had always kept their tribal unity, and they had lived in a group. To be sure, now and again someone from an enemy tribe came in and made his home there and adopted the Dakota as his own people. But never, till now, did any Dakota separate himself from other Dakota to adopt another tribe and feel content to live and die there. After this, however, it happened that some Dakota did, at one time or another, live abroad. This story they say comes from very far back in the history of the people.

"INCEST"
(1974:175–80; 1978:81–84)

There was a tribal camp. And in it lived a young man who was the only son of his parents, and was greatly loved; so they had him live by himself in a special tipi in the manner of a boy-beloved. He had two younger sisters who lived with their parents. The entire tribe loved this young man, and the plan was to make him a chief some day. And it happened that one night as he lay sleeping, a woman entered his tipi and lay down beside his bed. This she did to tempt him. But of course it was dark, so he could not tell what woman it was. In the morning he did not tell his father; he simply said, "Father, this evening I want you to set a dish of red face paint near my bed."— "What does he mean?" the father thought, but was reluctant to ask him. The next night, the woman entered again and bothered him, so he secretly dipped his hand in the paint and applied it over her dress as thoroughly as he could. The next morning he said, "Father, I wish all the women in the camp to engage in a shinny game."— "What does my son mean?" he thought, but he was reluctant to ask him; so he went without a word to the council tent where he told the boy-beloved's wish. Immediately a shinny game was arranged for the women. But he could not tell whether the woman who visited him nightly was in the game or not; because she could change her clothing for other before taking part. Again she came, (the next night), so this time he covered her entire face with the paint, and sent her out. Next day he ordered another shinny game, and it was arranged through the council tent. In time, all the women assembled in the centre of the enclosure, and now they ran. Out of all the players there was one who unbraided her hair and left it hanging loosely about her face. As she played, with her face thus hidden, he studied her to make sure, and it shocked him to realize that she was the elder of his own two younger sisters! Her face was as if dipped in blood. That is why she hid it as she played. It came over him then that one of his own sisters was tempting him, and he was filled with anger and shame. As he was retiring he said, "Father, get an iron rod and heat it thoroughly, and wait near the tipi. When I clear my throat, slide it in to me." Why he should request this was not at all clear, but the father did what his son commanded. And now, once again the woman entered and came and lay down beside his bed. But that instant, he cleared his throat, and his father, who sat immediately outside the tipi, slid the heated iron in to him, under the base of the tipi. With the iron he branded the woman's face all over, and then sent her out. Now that he was aware that this was his own sister he was very much ashamed, and angry. After she left he slept, and on waking, he felt something move under him, so he looked down and saw that he was standing attached, as if glued, to a tree which was rapidly growing taller; of course, since he was part of the tree, he was rising higher all the time, too. Until now he was rising out of the tipi through the smoke-vent. So the people below took down the tipi in haste. Then the tree grew even faster, elevating the young man higher and higher. The people were frightened by the miracle, and because of fear they moved away and disappeared from the scene. Only the good little sister of the young man stayed at the base of the tree and wept. It did not disturb her that the people had left her behind, and as she stood weeping, suddenly, from the wood near by, the wicked sister looked out, and called tauntingly, "There's someone loves her brother very much; but I have caused him to grow onto the tree!" And the young man called down to his good sister, "Reply this to her, little sister, 'There is someone who tempted her own brother, but he caused her face to be branded with a hot iron!'" So the girl called back as her brother had taught her, and straightaway the one in the wood called back, "O, that's the thing I resent!" and a deer ran back into the wood amid rustling leaves. From then on, the girl who was very weary, slept, until a man came from somewhere, and said, "Young girl, roast this for your brother," and he threw her a piece of deer meat. So she rose and cooked it and tossed it up to her brother, though by now he stood very high. Her brother ate it. Then the man said to her, "Now, I have something for you to decide. If it pleases you that we two shall live together, I can cause your brother to come down." So she told her brother what the man had said to her; and the brother said, "Do it, sister; I want to come down; I am so thirsty." So the girl consented to become the wife of the stranger, and he said, "In that case, lie down under here." She did so, and he covered her with a blanket, and pegged down the four corners so securely that she was imprisoned underneath. Thus it was that she did not see how her husband worked his magic, and was unable to tell it. He was actually a Thunder man, though they did not know at first. For the Thunder man opened his eyes, (lightning), and repeatedly he roared (thunder), and the tree was split in two, and fell broken to the ground so that the young man stepped off. Then the man took out the tipi-base pegs and removed the blanket, and helped the girl to her feet. So she greeted her brother. Because he was thunder he killed many buffaloes, and with his bare hands he ground the meat and bones, and made a cake of pemmican which he handed to his brother-in-law. "Now, go to your tribe, and invite them back to this camp-site they have abandoned," he said. So he went to his people and called them together. Then he gave everyone a piece of the pemmican, in very small amounts. He was distributing it in that manner when a very greedy woman who was in the company complained at the smallness of her share, and threw it all into her mouth at once. Then she chewed; but it gradually increased in amount until finally her mouth could not hold it all; and she was choking on it. So they took a knife, and cut out piece by piece until she was relieved. Despite the smallness of the cake, the quantity continued to increase, until they were able to fill many containers with it. Then the young man invited the people to their old campground. So they followed him back, and on their arrival, they found at each individual site, great quantities of meat, jerked, and drying on poles. "That is our campsite!" was heard on all sides as families identified their places and proceeded to set up their homes again; and they were very well provisioned. From then on, that people never knew want, they say. Then the Thunder man told his wife this, "Now, young girl, you whose love for your brother was so big that you consented to be my wife for his sake, I am going home. It is enough, for I have now given you aid." And so he went away, somewhere, wherever it is that the thunders abide. That is all.

"A Woman Joins Her Lover in Death"
(1974:261–62; 1978:131)

There was a big hill, a butte, where years ago a war-party was held at bay till all the members died; and none escaped, they say. And it was there that the people stopped, on a journey, and stood looking for a suitable place to make camp, when this, which I am about to relate, took place. At the foot of that butte, there was already a camp; and this group came to it and stopped, when a woman, her shawl pulled up over her head, started to sing. "There was a man I love, alas. Can it be that I shall see him again, my own?" With such words she stood on the hilltop, singing. As the tribe fixed their attention singly on her, she started taking dancing steps backwards, and allowed herself to fall headlong over the cliff, landing all bruised and broken, among the rocks below. She was dead. So they took up her body and carried it to her tipi, but her husband, evidently jealous, did not so much as weep a tear; but said, instead, "No, do not bring her here. Take her back, she has announced that she loved him; so let her rot with him!" so they could not enter her tipi with her body. Instead they took it back and left it where she fell. And they came away. So there, with him, who from all appearances was her lover, she mingled her bones, and they together in time became as dust, just as she desired in her song. Then a crier went around announcing the removal of the camp. It was according to the magistrates' decision. They said, "There is no other way; we cannot stay here. We must move from this spot where such a foul deed has taken place." So, in spite of the fact that the camp had just been made, they all packed in haste and moved away that same evening.

"The Lovers"
(1974:224–32; 1978:110–14)

The Dakota learned this story from the Cheyenne tribe among whom it is said to have happened, and they relate it frequently.

The whole tribe was living in one place when the crier went out from the council tent, making this official announcement as he rode along, "Hear ye, and take warning! The magistrates have decreed it. From this place, the tribe is to separate into two groups. Tomorrow, you are to break up the camp and go away from each other in two directions. All summer long, the time is to be spent by both groups in hunting and the chase; and then, in the fall, you are to meet here again. From here, a suitable place for winter quarters will be found." Now it happened that there was a certain young man and a certain young woman who were greatly affected by this news. This young man had been courting the girl, until, by this time, there was a great love between them. And it happened that the tribe's separating into two groups made it necessary for them also to part. One of them, the woman, belonged in the section that was going towards the Rocky Mountains. As for the young man, he must go towards the Missouri, for his people belonged in the group assigned to hunt in that direction. Now the people were slowly moving away in two great paths, in opposite directions; but the young man sat on the edge of a bluff near by, holding his horses by a rope; and dreaded to leave with his people. He had two horses. One which he rode and one which he led, as a spare one, by a rope. As he sat there, he felt as though he must die of grief.

The people going towards the Rockies had, somewhere among them, a young girl who also was very heavy of heart. That evening when this group stopped for the night and camp was being made, the girl became very ill. So her parents brought in the most skilful of medicine men who took turns doctoring her; but she seemed to grow worse; until it was evident, after two days' march, that she was about to die. Meantime the young man, her young man, must have joined this group without her knowledge, for he was coming with the crowd, not able to withstand the pull to join this rather than his own section of the tribe, now well on towards the Missouri. They say he said, "I wish I could see that young woman," and the reply was, "Why, say! This is the one who, they tell, is very ill because she can not see you!"—"Well, in that case, won't you please speak for me. I want the chance to see her," he said. In due time, he came to the tipi where she was and was politely ushered inside. When he entered, the sick girl looked at him and said, "Come over here." So he went to the place of honor of the tipi where she was lying, and sat down beside her. She took his hand in hers and said, "If you came long before this, why didn't you come directly to me? I am sick because of you, and I could have been well long ago. But now, I am on the way to die. Take this, instead of me, and remember me some days." Saying that, she gave him a very beautiful pair of moccasins which she herself had embroidered with porcupine quills. And the young man, caring nothing for the others who sat in the tipi looking at him, broke down and wept. He came away from there, and that evening the news went about that the young woman had died, and then it was that he came face to face with a great sorrow. He roamed about over the hills and did not return to the camp. After two days, the young woman's body was laid away in a tipi, and from there the tribe moved on to another camp ground. But the mother and the father remained behind and spent the time weeping over their loss. When the sun was low, the man said to his wife, "Come, now, it is enough. Let us start out along the trail towards the new camp," and so the woman was just getting to her feet, when they heard someone weeping. It proved to be the dead girl's two brothers who had returned to conduct their father and mother to the new camp, which they reached by sundown. As for the young man, he must have been staying near by, instead of going with the tribe, for in the evening he came weeping to the tipi in which the young woman lay. He carried a sorrow as bitter as if he had lost his wife.

He found that the door had been securely fastened and laced, but he worked at it, untying it wherever it was tied, until at last he entered the tipi, thinking thus to himself, "I shall spend at least one night here with her and when morning comes, then I will leave and go on to the camp." He ceased weeping, and sat quietly under the scaffold which held the body of his love. Suddenly, the woman who was lying above him said, "Make a fire, and undo my wrappings!" and the young man fainted from fright. After a time, regaining consciousness, he uttered some bear-cries to make himself brave. And again the woman said, "Make a fire, and take me down. I have come back to life, and I lie here living," and once again, as completely as before, the young man fainted away from fright. After a while, he felt as though whistles (as of steam) charged out of his ears, and then he came to his senses once more. "Is what you just said the truth?" he asked and she said, "I say I have returned to life. Make a fire and take me down." So he went from one tipi site to another, feeling about for wood, and gathered and brought it in. He built a fire and when it was large enough to warm the place he unwrapped the covers from her. Over everything, a smoked tipi had been wrapped. This he removed and made a sort of partition wall, or screen, reaching to the ground. Then he made a bed of the several fur robes he found, and then, taking the girl in his arms, he laid her down on the bed. When she was lying there, she said, "Get my bag and open it. You will find in it several packages of medicine (grass-root). Find one that has a blue cover and give me some of the contents." He did as she had instructed him. She ate it, and gave a great deep sigh and then said, "Now, have no fear of me. I am really alive. Now, get the bag I used for a pillow. In it you will find a cake of pemmican." He found it as she had said. He gave her to eat and ate some himself. And stayed with her till morning. Then he went out and made a travois, using a single pole on each side. He placed her thereon, and started towards the tribal camp, on the trail they had made in moving. When they had travelled a long time, two men came in sight. As the young man walked, he tried to recognize them, and saw at last that they were the girl's brothers coming back again. "Both my brothers-in-law are coming back this way, weeping for you," he told the girl, and at once she became very much agitated, and said, "Stop a little while. I have something to tell you before they get here. It is very evident that you are sincere towards me. That is why I have returned, that I may be your wife; but we must always live in mutual kindness. If we do, then we shall reach the end together. They must erect a tipi inside the camp circle, and there for four days you and I will live alone together. On the fourth day, in the morning, I will have something to tell the people. That is what I want you to tell my elder brothers. For a while, I want nobody to touch me," she said. When the brothers were a short distance off, the young man went forward to meet them, and said, "My brothers-in-law, it is your younger sister that has come back to life, and I am bringing her with me. But first she wants me to tell you something." So saying, he gave the instructions she had just spoken. Both the elder brothers, very greatly amazed, said, "We will go back to camp and tell what we know," and turning about, they hurried away. On arriving there, they related everything and the whole tribe was thrown into awe and fear over it. They set about at once to build the tipi and make the arrangements exactly as the young woman had specified, and soon everything was in readiness for the marriage. When the young lovers arrived, it was understood that nobody should touch the girl even to greet or help her, except her own husband, and so the people, even the girl's close relations, stood afar off, watching. The mother and father were too astounded to realize what had happened for some time. Four whole days the young couple lived there alone together, and people bringing them food left it outside the door and nobody entered. After four days, the young woman said, "Now, will you ask my father and mother and my elder brothers all to come here?" So the husband went outside and said to his brothers-in-law, "Brothers-in-law, you and your father and your mother are all to come in now. It is your sister's wish." In due time they all entered the bride's tipi and with great happiness they met the girl. These people were filled with joy over the fact that a dead person should have taken up life again and come back to them. And this was the way the young woman talked to them: "Now, it is a proven fact that this young man's love for me is genuine. He showed it in the days when I was still alive; and at my death, too, he showed it. His sorrow over my going was sincere, and for that reason I have been instructed to return that I may marry him. But there is one rule that we must observe. It is this: Neither of us must ever scold or be unkind to the other. If we show only kindness to each other all our lives, then at the end we shall arrive full of years, together. And if we do so, then we shall have built a great lesson for the tribe, so that hereafter, when men and women take each other in marriage, they will be kind to each other." Now, that was the lesson which the young woman brought back with her from spiritland and gave to the people. And so, from then on, whenever two people lived together in kindness towards each other and made their marriage a peaceful one, then it was said they were to live to a ripe old age together.

"BLOOD-CLOT BOY"
(1974:113–20; 1978:47–51)

A rabbit lived happily until a bear and his young came and took possession of his home, driving him out. So he was obliged to dwell in a makeshift hut near by. And each morning the bear stood outside his door and said, "You Rabbit with the ragged muzzle, come out. Your Buffalo-surround is full." Then Rabbit came out with his magic arrow and, with one shot, sent it piercing through each buffalo in turn till all were killed. Then the bear would rush up with his young, and take all the meat home. They never gave the rabbit any meat, and the result was that he was now very thin. Once again they were cutting up the meat; so he came and stood to one side, but before he even asked for a piece, they ordered him off, so he turned to leave. Somewhat removed from the scene was a blood-clot on the ground. So, as he went over it, he pretended to stumble, and picked it up, thrusting it under his belt. And the bear called out, "Hey, there, you worthless wretch, you aren't taking anything, are you?" So the rabbit answered, "No, I only stagger because I am weak from hunger." Then he came home. Immediately he made a sweat-bath over the blood-clot. He was busy pouring water over the hot stones when someone within heaved a deep sigh, and then said, "Whoever you are who are thus kind, open the door for me." So he opened the door, and a young man (red from the heat), stepped outside. Rabbit was very happy. "Oh, would that my grandson had such and such things," he would say, and instantly they would appear, so that all in the same day, he had everything desirable. Everything he wished for was his. But Rabbit couldn't offer him food, for he had none. Then Blood-Clot Boy said, "Grandfather, how is it that you starve while a rich man lives near by?" So Rabbit related everything to him. "Alas, grandson, what do you mean? Why, the fact is that it is I who shoot all the game, and then they when I am through, the bear comes with his young and they take the meat all away. They always call me by saying, 'Say, you Rabbit with the ragged muzzle, come out; your surround is full.' So I come out, and do the shooting for them." On hearing this, Blood-Clot Boy was very angry. He took a piece of ash and burned it here and there, and made a club, and sat ready with it. As usual, the bear stood outside very early in the morning and, "Hey, you Rabbit with the ragged muzzle, come on out; your surround is full," he said, so he answered as his grandson had taught him, "*Hoh!* Get out, what are you talking about? I suppose you'll be claiming all the meat again!" And he didn't come out. The angry bear came in, thinking to force him out, but Blood-Clot Boy was ready for him, and killed him with one blow of his club. Then he sent his grandfather to the bear's wife, telling him what to say. He said, "Bear sends for extra help." And the wife called out, "Is that so? How many is he carrying?"—"He is carrying two buffaloes."—"That's funny. I never knew him to carry so few!" So the rabbit tried again. "He is carrying three buffaloes," he said. "How funny. He used to carry more than that," she said. So Rabbit said, "He is carrying four buffaloes." And this time the wife said, "Is that so? Well, wait, then." And she started to come out of the tipi but Blood-Clot Boy was ready for her and the moment her head appeared, he struck her with a resounding blow and killed her. Then he entered the bear's home, and found all the bear children sitting in a circle, eating their meal. So he said to them, "Now, if anyone here has been kind to my grandfather, let him say, I," and they all yelled, "I." And then one said, "Do you think that, simply by saying the word 'I,' they will be spared. He who was kind to your grandfather sits over here!" he said. And in the corner they saw him sitting, the very youngest little bear wearing his very brown coat. The rabbit spoke up, "Grandson, he speaks true. Ever so often he dragged a piece of meat over to me, and pushed it with his snout into my hut." So Blood-Clot Boy said, "In that case, step outside; you shall live." After he had gone out, the boy killed all the other cubs. The rabbit now moved into his old home and as he still had his magic arrow, he provided meat in abundance so that the three, including the little bear, lived without want.

And then one day Blood-Clot Boy declared his plans. "Grandfather, in what direction do the people live?" he asked; so he told him they lived in the west. Then he said he planned to go there on a visit. The rabbit advised against it vigorously. "No, grandson, I dread it for you. Something very deceptive lives on the way." But that made him all the more eager to be off, and he started. He hadn't gone far before he saw a man shooting at something. "Ah! This must be what grandfather warned me of as not to be trusted," he thought, and tried to go around him, but he called, "My younger brother, come over here and shoot this for me before you go."—"Impossible! I am on a rush trip, I haven't time to loiter and shoot your game for you!" he said. But he begged so earnestly that he persuaded the boy to turn and come back to him. The boy sent an arrow which pierced the bird; and then he started to go on. But he called again, "That's a fine arrow, younger brother; who would discard it this way?" He shouted back, "Well then, take it and own it," and would go on, but, "My younger brother, please climb the tree and get it for me," he pleaded; so, as the best way to get rid of him, the boy came and prepared to climb the tree. But the man said again, "My younger brother, you better take off your clothes. They are very beautiful; it would be a pity to tear them on the branches." With that he persuaded the boy further, until he removed all his clothes and started to climb the tree in his naked state. He got the arrow and was coming down when he heard the one below saying something under his breath. "Are you saying something?" he called out. "I just said, 'Hurry down, brother!'" he answered. So, "Oh, all right!" he called and continued down. Then, just as he was about to step on the ground, the man called in a great voice, "Stick to the tree!" And at once Blood-Clot Boy became glued to the tree. It was Ikto who had thus deceived him, and now he hurriedly dressed himself in the boy's finery and flung his old garments at him saying, "There, Blood-Clot Boy, put those on!" Then he went towards the village. In that village was a young woman, the eldest child of her parents, and greatly loved by them. "She-dwells-within-the-Circle" was what her name meant [*C'oka'p T'i'wị*]. He was going to her. As soon as he entered the tribal camp, the cry went up, "Blood-Clot Boy comes on a journey, and *C'oka'p T'i'wị* is the one he comes for!" The parents immediately gave their daughter to him and placed their tipi within the circle. So Ikto, all in a day, settled into the role of the son-in-law. The next morning he proceeded to demonstrate his supernatural powers. "Let all the young men remove the hair from a buffalo-hide and scatter it about in the bend of the river, beyond the hill." It was done accordingly. Next day he told them to send scouts to see the result. They went; but came back to report that nothing had happened. Now *C'oka'p T'i'wị* had a young sister who stayed around her tipi. She didn't like her around, and ordered her off each time, saying, "Go on away! I don't want her to even look upon my husband!" Finally the girl went crying into the woods and gathered firewood. There she came upon a youth, very handsome, stuck fast to a tree. He said to her, "Young girl, if you have pity, free me from this tree. Ikto has dealt thus badly with me and gone into camp leaving me to my fate." So the girl took her ax and peeled the man off from the tree; and then, sharing her blanket with him, she took him home. And then he said, "Now, go to the one who is living inside the circle and bring my clothes to me; Ikto has worn them long enough." So the girl stood at the door of her sister's tipi and said, "Ikto, you have worn certain clothes long enough; I have come after them for their owner." But her sister said, "Go away. I don't want you to look upon my husband!" But all the while Ikto repeated without a pause, "Hand them out, hand them out." At last then, the young woman realized that Ikto himself had duped her; so she began to cry. Now Blood-Clot Boy put on his own clothes and sat looking very handsome, and said, "Let all the young men remove the hair from a buffalo-hide and scatter it about in the bend of the river beyond the hill." They did so; and the next morning when they went to see, the bend was packed with buffalo, so the people had a real killing, for this young man had true supernatural power. That evening everyone took part of his killing to the council tent where men sat about and feasted and talked; and they say all Ikto took was a shoulder-piece, it was all he managed to secure (from some hunter). Soon after, Blood-Clot Boy announced that he was going home, taking with him the girl who saved him. So they made preparations. And the once-proud elder sister who had been so mean to her younger sister, now rejected Ikto and went following the girl and her young husband. They in turn ordered her back, but she did not have any ears. And so they came on until they neared Blood-Clot Boy's home. The little bear who was sitting on a hilltop saw them. He had been sitting there alone, viewing the country round about. He started up, evidently having seen them, and disappeared downhill in the other direction. Breathlessly he arrived home and said, "Grandson is now returning; but he brings a woman home." Immediately the rabbit, very happy, ran hopping out to meet them; and taking his grandson on his back, he carried him the remainder of the way. The little bear also came to meet them, and he took the daughter-in-law on his back; but she was so heavy (for him) that he could not lift her entirely off the ground; so her feet dragged on behind. As for the proud elder sister, nobody took any notice of her, so she came along behind them, and lived with them there. They kept her to take the ashes out for them. That is all.

"IKTOMI TRICKS THE PHEASANTS"
(1974:19–25; 1978:9–11)

Iktomi was walking at random along a creek and he heard dancing, so he stopped to listen. He finally located the source of the sound; so he went towards it and stood within sight of the place; and saw that those were all pheasants who were dancing and having a jolly time. Immediately he withdrew into the wood and wrapped some red grass about a piece of wood; this he put on his back, and then walked past without paying the slightest attention to the dancers. "Hey, there goes Ikto. Let's call him over," they said. "Ikto!" they called but he continued as if he hadn't heard; so they called repeatedly until he stopped; and then they asked, "What's that you carry on your back?"— "These? Why they are just some silly little songs. There is to be a dance farther up, and I've been sent for. That's why I am in a rush; now what are they after?" he added. "O, elder brother, come over here and sing us one tiny little song; just one," they said and again he said, "Indeed not! I've just told you I'm in a hurry. What's the idea?" and he walked on. But they were very insistent, so he relented. "Very well, then," he said, undoing his package and bringing out a single song. "Now, this song has its special regulation; will you heed it?"—"Surely," they said. "All right, then. While I am singing it, nobody is to open his eyes," Ikto told them; and they said that would be all right with them. So he got out his drum and began beating it as he sang; so the birds danced, making a rhythmic noise with their feet. It was a good sight to watch them dancing; females included. This is what he said,
"Dance with your eyes closed.
Whoever opens his eye shall get a sty,

Dance with your eyes closed."

They danced with their eyes closed and meantime Ikto was selecting those with the fattest breasts, and killing them in turn. One
happened to look, after a while, and seeing many dead, called out,
"Fly for your lives! Ikto will kill you all off!" and with that, he flew
out of the place; so the rest followed him. Iktomi laughed as he picked
up his prey, and, tying the birds into a bunch, he said to himself,
"On those rare times when I am faring poorly, that's the trick I work!"
and he began looking for a pleasant spot; yonder in the woods was a
lovely place where the grass was soft and thick; he built a fire there.
Then he set some of the pheasants up on spits to cook, and some he
covered with ashes to roast; but while he sat there waiting, two trees
in contact overhead kept making a loud squeaking noise each time
there was a gust of wind. So he called up, "Little brothers, please
don't do that. Why, you will injure each other that way!" But the
noise persisted. At last Ikto climbed up one of the trees, planning to
hold the two apart, but just when he put his hand between the trees
there was a calm, and he couldn't pull his hand out. "Little brothers,
little brothers, let me go, please. I am cooking something in ashes
and I need to go and attend to it." But his hand continued to be
pinned there. At that moment, a wolf was going by, in the distance,
on his own business; and Ikto called to him, "Hey! I, a chieftain, am
cooking meat on spits here. Get out; I won't have you eating it up
for me!"—"The idiot might just happen to be talking sense," the wolf
thought; so he turned and came over to find out; there, sure enough,
was some meat on spits, just about done, so he sat down and ate it
all up and then started to go. From overhead Ikto called again, "At
least I hope you have left for me what is cooking in the ashes," he
said; so again the wolf thought he might just be talking sense and
came back to the fire; and sure enough, there were some birds cooking
in the ashes. So he brushed them off, and took them and feasted
again. He finished and was going off when at last the wind came up
again and the trees separated so that Ikto took his hand away and
came down, only to find all his food gone. Thus it happened that he
didn't eat after all; and he was going away very hungry; when, as he
walked along, he came upon the wolf who had taken all his cooking.

He was lying dead directly in his path, so Ikto stopped to scold at the dead animal. "There you are; and that's just what you get. Everybody dies like this who tries to pull something on me!" With that, he lifted the wolf to his shoulder and walked along with him. Puzzling as to the best way to handle that body, he walked till he found another pleasant spot in the wood. There he built a fire and sat beside it to think. "I believe I will use at least a piece of this hide as a head-kerchief; and some of it I shall use for a blanket-robe; a piece will make me some leggings, and—aw shucks, what shall I do with it anyway?" he was saying, and at last he took it in his arms impatiently and said, "It has been done; even very fine things are sometimes discarded!" So he hurled the body into the fire. Now, the wolf wasn't really dead, it appeared, for he sprang up, scattering live coals about, and ran away; so that Ikto was himself so frightened that he repeatedly grasped and let go of himself. From there who knows whither Ikto went? That is all.

"DOUBLE-FACE STEALS A VIRGIN"
(1974:51–64; 1978:20–24)

In a tribal camp there lived a young girl that nobody could get. Very beautiful and skilled in woman's arts. Every man wanted her and from all sides they courted her but they could not succeed. Then on a certain night, as usual, many came to see her; while one tried to persuade her, the others lay about on the ground waiting their turn; and during that time, a new young man approached from the south. While he was still far off, fragrant odors came from him, so this young woman's head was turned his way, and seemed to remain so, and she could not stand still. She paid no further attention to the one with her, watching only the one coming. As he neared the place, he seemed all covered with porcupine work, and his beautiful long hair he wore hanging loose. When he had nearly arrived, the young man who had been talking to the girl, withdrew, so he advanced and went past and around her and then stopped, facing her. And he said, "Young woman, you alone I can love, and that is why I have come from so far away. I have come to take you with me. So if you are willing, follow me away," he said. That was all he said, and then he left; and at once the girl went after him; so the suitors all stood up and looked now and then at her, going away; and after a time they scattered to their homes. All night they travelled, the man and girl, and after a long time, she said, "Ah, please, let us not go so fast. I can not keep up the pace, you are so fleet-footed." And he answered, "The idea! Stop talking and hurry; I want to reach home when the sun, about to rise, sends a white light in the sky. That is why I am in a hurry." So she tried to brace herself again and again to the effort, as she followed, and now as the dawn broke, all yellow, and the sun, about to rise, sent on whiteness ahead, she looked at the young man and lo, he was not the one she started with. The embroidered clothing and decorations were gone, and the man, though facing forward, had also a face in the back, and appeared to be walking backwards. The Double-face! "*Yah!*" she cried, and stopped. " '*Yah,*' did you say? You have spurned the advances of all the fine young men of the tribe who wished to marry you; and have insulted them in doing so. Woman is made to marry and have a home, why should you consider yourself an exception?" he said. He turned and came to her then, and caused her to walk in front of him while he whipped her with rosebush stalks with every step, along a creek; thus they travelled till they reached a tipi in the wood from which smoke was rising. It was a smoke-tanned tipi; so they stopped outside the door, and the man said, "Now, go in," so she entered, and saw two young women sitting at the honor-place. Their faces and hands were covered with sores. "Sit down with them; they too have been haughty like you, and I have brought them here." So she did as he told her. A fire was going in the centre, and a kettle was on it, bubbling over with loud sounds. And from it, a human hand rose to the surface. Near the door sat an old woman, to whom the Double-face said, "Grandmother, this must be about done; serve me some that I may eat with the young women." She served a big dish full, soup and all. She set it before the Double-face who devoured it, and drank the soup with the meat. Finishing, he offered the rest to the two young women. When they refused it, he struck them across the face with the thorny rosebush stalks so then they ate the meat and soup. Then, when the Double-face finished eating he carefully dressed, and again donned the beautiful things he wore when he tricked the girl. He said, "Grandmother, I am going away again, so I want you to behead the last girl I brought home, and have another meal like this ready for me. And be sure that you cut off a foot, and unwind the intestines, and stretch them along the path I return by; and tie the foot to the end of the intestines. Those first I shall eat as I return. Now, grandmother, do exactly as I say. I am going now," and off he went. So the old woman said to the young women, "Grandchildren, many times before this, he has brought beautiful girls home and killed and eaten them. Undoubtedly, he is going to do the same to you. But you are young. Take me, instead, and do to me as he instructed me to do to you, and run away." Then she said, "You know the place in the wood where I always cut firewood. Leave my small ax and my head and right arm there and the three of you run away," she said. So the virgin stood up and executed the order, killing the pitiful old woman; and then she unwound her intestines, and laid them along the path and then tied the old woman's foot to one end. Then they ran away. Not sure where to go, they still ran hard. All day till sundown. Again all night, and now dawn was coming; and again all that day they ran. Then they travelled all night, and morning came. They had been going three days when Double-face got home. Taking up the intestine down the path, he continued to eat it as he approached the tipi. He came to the foot at the end, and said, "How her feet resemble grandmother's! I think I'll keep that for a souvenir," he said and tucked it away. Somebody was chopping wood in the forest, so he called to her. "Grandmother, come home and serve me this; I am hungry," he said. The answer came back, "Grandson, wait till I finish the little I still have to do." He got angry right away. "Grandmother, I am telling you to make haste. If you don't, I'll eat you up!" he said, and the answer was, "Wait, grandson, it is very little that is left." But without more talking, the Double-face ran toward the woods, and saw, instead of his grandmother, her ax and head and right arm at the foot of a tree. "The wretched beings! Having killed my grandmother, where do they think to escape?" he said, and running home he took up a big knife and started after them. When he was just about to overtake them, the two whom he had first taken home, could no longer go on, so they hid in a clump of bushes; and the last one kept going on. The Double-face was such a good runner though, that he found them. But he decided that he didn't care about them, so he continued on his way to bring back the other girl. She looked back and saw Double-face only a short distance behind her, running hard and calling to her, "Worthless one, the world is only so large," as he flashed a knife at her till she ran crying. She came to a lake and stopped at the shore, because it was a very wide lake; and in the centre she saw a house of iron. A man, very tall, came out of the house, so the woman in her panic cried out to him, "Man, come, please; there is something about to kill me!"— "All right; but first, what will you be to me?" he asked. "I will be your wife," she said, but that did not suit him. "No, try something else," he said, so she named over the entire list of kinships between men and women. At last—"You shall be a father to me," she said, and then he was pleased. "Very well; come over, walking on the water," he said. She did so, and as she reached the iron house, the Double-face arrived on the shore she had just left, and having no way to go on, he ran back and forth along the edge. "Be careful about entering, my daughter. I have four animals. On either side of the entrance, lie a big-cat and a bear. And in the centre of the room a snake lies coiled; in the honor-place lies a buffalo-bull. So as you enter, say, 'My father told me to enter,'" he told her. "And sit down in the space back of the snake and this side of the bull," so she did that. Then, "No matter how fearful you are, don't touch me!" he said. He too now entered. And closed the iron door. Then the Double-face, having gotten over somehow, arrived at the door, and knocked. "Bad man, send my woman out to me," he said. "No; go away; you insult my daughter," he said, and immediately the man became very angry. He took his great knife and banged it so hard on the door that he knocked the lock loose. So the ironhouse dweller said, "Lynx, bear, lie ready," he said and hurled his spear at the Double-face. It happened that he struck him full in the chest and the spear stood impaled in his flesh; so the lynx and bear jumped on him and killed him quickly. The man now dragged the Double-face to a smooth ground and bade his daughter gather much dry wood and build a fire and stand by to watch it burn the body. "When choice articles, as are dear to women, spring out of the fire, don't touch one of them," he said. "If by chance you took even one, then you would bring disaster on yourself," he said. She did as her father had instructed and stood by while the Double-face's body burned; and all manner of desirable things jumped out, scissors and other things that women own. But when an awl, the kind used for sewing moccasins, came out and fell upright into the ground, before her, she was tempted. Contrary to her father's warning, she took it and hid it under her blanket, tucking it under her arm. At once it began to work its way into her flesh, in her armpit. She kept it a secret until it was undermining her health, and she feared she might die; then, risking all, she told it. "Father, though you told me not to take anything, I took an awl; and from it I am about to die," she said. "Very well, my daughter; that man was bent on destroying you but you have foolishly assisted him indeed," he said, and ordered the bear to doctor her. He tried, grunting officiously, but in vain. Then the lynx made a try, but he too failed. Then the buffalo-bull attempted to doctor her; he also failed. Only the snake was left; so he lay down in a straight line, and put his mouth to the wound to suck it out. But at that moment, the bull awkwardly stepped on his tail. This angered him so that he bit the girl accidentally. The armpit began to swell horribly, and then broke, and from there came the awl, along with pus; so the young woman recovered. Her father then said, "Daughter, when you want to go home, though you are welcome here as long as you like, tell me," so after a time, she longed for home, and told her father so. He therefore detailed the bear and the lynx to see her home. "Escort her to a point within sight of her home, and then return," he told them. So the three started forth, the girl, escorted by the bear and the lynx; and when they were within sight of the camp, they paused; and the girl alone went on while they stood watching her. When she entered the tribal circle, they turned about and left for their home. That is all.

Appendix 2: Lakota Language Study

ELLA DELORIA'S *Dakota Grammar* (1941) and Eugene Buechel's *A Grammar of Lakota* (1939) are still indispensable guides to the study of the Lakota language. The Buechel *Grammar* is organized to correspond with English grammar and may therefore be easier for beginners whose first language is English. Many of the examples, however, are drawn from the Bible or Catholic practice and custom, in accordance with Buechel's vocation as a priest. Deloria's *Grammar*, co-authored with Franz Boas, presents the structure of the language as intrinsic to itself and related languages rather than English. It is somewhat harder to adjust to the overall scheme, but the examples are culturally inclusive, many of them coming from *Dakota Texts*, and the subtleties of the language are more thoroughly explained.

Deloria and Buechel used different orthographies. Although the Buechel orthography is presently more favored on the Lakota reservations, the use of both orthographies is still practiced. The following books can be ordered from the book stores of Oglala Lakota College, Kyle, South Dakota 57752 and Sinte Gleśka College, Mission, South Dakota 57570:

TEXTBOOKS

Hairy Shirt, Leroy et al. *Lakota Woonśpe Wowapi*. Aberdeen, South Dakota: North Plains Press, 1973. (Buechel orthography).

Mathieu, David J., Bertha Chasing Hawk, and Elgin Badwound. *Lakota Language.* 2 vols. Spearfish, South Dakota: Center of Indian Studies, Black Hills State College, 1978. (Buechel orthography).

Picotte, Agnes. *An Introduction to Basic Dakota, Lakota, and Nakota.* Chamberlain, South Dakota: Dakota Indian Foundation, 1987. (Deloria orthography).

Taylor, Alan. *Beginning Lakhota.* 2 vols. Boulder: Univ. of Colorado Lakhota Project, 1976. (modified Deloria orthography). (accompanying audiocassettes).

DICTIONARIES

Buechel, Eugene, S.J. *A Dictionary of the Teton Dakota Sioux Language.* Pine Ridge, South Dakota: Red Cloud Lakota Language and Cultural Center, 1970.

Karol, Joseph S. *Everyday Lakota: An English-Sioux Dictionary for Beginners.* St. Francis, South Dakota: The Rosebud Educational Society, 1974. Accompanying audiocassette, *An Oral Introduction to the Study of the Lakota Language.*

BILINGUAL BOOKS

Around Him, John and Albert White Hat, Sr. *Lakota Ceremonial Songs.* Pierre, South Dakota: State Publishing, 1983.

Black Bear, Sr., Ben and R. D. Theisz. *Songs and Dances of the Lakota.* Aberdeen, South Dakota: North Plains Press, 1976.

Orthographic Note

SINCE LITERATURE is always heard even when read silently, Deloria's transposition of oral art to the page includes the sounds of spoken Lakota in a visually systematic way. However, Deloria's orthography is harder to write, type, and print than Buechel's orthography. Since the latter is currently favored in schools and colleges, I have quoted Deloria's texts in a combination of the two styles. I have retained most of Deloria's spellings to refer readers back to the original text, e.g. *nazį* (to stand) rather than *najin,* the Buechel spelling. But for the sounds of Lakota consonants that do not correspond to English consonants, I have used diacritics directly over the letter rather than in the intervening spaces used by Deloria.

In this book the following practice is observed:
When ħ is gutteralized, it has a dot above it.
When ġ is gutteralized, it has a dot above it.
When k̇ sounds like g in give, it has a dot above it.
When ṗ sounds like b in bill, it has a dot above it.
When ṫ sounds like d in day, it has a dot above it.
When ś sounds like sh in ship, it has an acute accent mark.
Nasalized ŋ or ͅ is simply written as n.
The letter c sounds like ch in chair.
The letter z sounds like Russian zh, except for the following words (quoted here) where it sounds like English z: *canze*

(angry), *holozata* (back of), *maza* (iron), *okiciyuze* (marriage),
and *pazuntapi* (laced).

Several finer distinctions, particularly the gutteralized k, p, and
t are not marked here, but their use is often interchanged with medial
pronunciations, closer to English, in different regions and speakers,
sometimes in the same speaker. Unmarked consonants have English
or near English sounds, while vowels are consistently European rather
than variably English.

Works Cited

Andersen, David M. "Isaac Bashevis Singer: Conversations in California." *Modern Fiction Studies* 16.4 (1971): 423–39.

Ambrose, Stephen E. *Crazy Horse and Custer.* New York: Doubleday, 1975.

Around Him, John and Albert White Hat, Sr. *Lakota Ceremonial Songs.* Pierre: State Publishing, 1983.

Beckwith, Martha Warren. "Mythology of the Oglala Dakota." *Journal of American Folklore* 43 (1930): 339–439.

Black Elk. *The Sixth Grandfather.* Ed. Raymond J. DeMallie. Lincoln: U of Nebraska P, 1984.

Blocker, Joel and Richard Elman. "An Interview with Isaac Bashevis Singer." *Critical Views of Isaac Bashevis Singer.* Ed. Irving Malin. New York: New York UP, 1969.

Breger, Marshall and Bob Barnhart. "A Conversation with Isaac Bashevis Singer." *Critical Views of Isaac Bashevis Singer.* Ed. Irving Malin. New York: UP, 1969.

Buchen, Irving. *Isaac Bashevis Singer and the Eternal Past.* New York: New York UP, 1968.

Buechel, Eugene, S.J. *A Dictionary of the Teton Dakota Sioux Language.* Pine Ridge, South Dakota: Red Cloud Lakota Language and Cultural Center, 1970.

———. *A Grammar of Lakota.* Rosebud, South Dakota: Rosebud Educational Society, 1939.

———. *Lakota Tales and Texts.* Ed. Paul Manhart, S.J. Red Cloud Lakota Language and Cultural Center, 1978.

Bushotter, George. *Teton Myths.* Ed. and trans. Ella Deloria. ca. 1937; MS 30 (X8c.3), Boas Collection. Philadelphia: American Philosophical Society.

Catches, Pete, Sr. Interview about Bear Butte and The Black Hills. Audiotape. Kyle, South Dakota: Oglala Lakota College Archives.

Carr, Pat and Willard Gingerich. "The Vagina Dentata Motif in Nahuatl and Pueblo Mythic Narratives: A Comparative Study." *Smoothing the Ground: Essays on Native American Oral Literature.* Ed. Brian Swann. Berkeley: U of California P, 1983. 187–203.

Clifford, James. "Introduction: Partial Truths." *Writing Culture: The Poetics and Politics of Ethnography.* Eds. James Clifford and George E. Marcus. Berkeley: U of California P, 1986. 1–26.

Deloria, Ella. *Camp Circle Society.* Unpublished manuscript. Pierre: South Dakota State Archives.

———. Correspondence with Franz Boas (1927–1934). MS 31, Boas Collection. Philadelphia: American Philosophical Society.

———. *Dakota Autobiographies.* ca. 1937; MS 30 (X8a.4), Boas Collection. Philadelphia: American Philosophical Society.

———. *Dakota Commentary on Walker's Texts.* 1937; MS 30 (X8a.5), Boas Collection. Philadelphia: American Philosophical Society.

———. *Dakota Informal Texts and Conversations.* ca. 1937; MS 30 (X8a.10), Boas Collection. Philadelphia: American Philosophical Society.

———. *Dakota Grammar.* 1941. Vermillion, South Dakota: Dakota Press, 1982.

———. *Dakota Play on Words.* MS 30 (X8a.12), Boas Collection. Philadelphia: American Philosophical Society.

———. *Dakota Tales in Colloquial Style.* 1937; MS 30 (X8a.16), Boas Collection. Philadelphia: American Philosophical Society.

———. *Dakota Texts.* 1932. New York: AMS Press, 1974.

———. *Dakota Texts.* Vermillion, South Dakota: Dakota Press, 1978.

———. *Dakota Texts from the Minnesota Manuscript.* 1941; MS 30 (X8a.17), Boas Collection. Philadelphia: American Philosophical Society.

———. *Speaking of Indians.* Vermillion, South Dakota: State Publishing, 1983.

———. *Teton Myths* (the George Bushotter collection). MS 30 (X8c.3), Boas Collection. Philadelphia: American Philosophical Society.

———. *Waterlily.* Lincoln: U of Nebraska P, 1988.

Densmore, Frances. *Teton Sioux Music.* 1918. New York: Da Capo, 1972.

Dorsey, George A. and Alfred L. Kroeber. *Traditions of the Arapaho.* Chicago: Field Columbian Museum, 1903.

Erdoes, Richard and Mary Crow Dog. *Lakota Woman.* La Vergne, Tennessee: Grove Weidenfeld, 1990.

Erdoes, Richard and John (Fire) Lame Deer. *Lame Deer: Seeker of Visions.* New York: Pocket Books, 1972.

Erdoes, Richard and Alfonso Ortiz, eds. *American Indian Myths and Legends.* New York: Pantheon, 1984.

Evers, Larry. "I'isau and the Birds." Videocassette. *Words & Place: Native Literature from the American Southwest.* New York: Clearwater, 1976.

Fletcher, Alice C. "The Elk Mystery or Festival. Ogallala Sioux." *Reports of the Peabody Museum* 3 (1887): 276–88.

———. Interviewed by Ed McGaa (8–30–67). Tape and Transcript no. 453. Vermillion, South Dakota: U of South Dakota, Oral History Center.

Grinnell, George Bird. *Blackfoot Lodge Tales: The Story of a Prairie People.* Lincoln: U of Nebraska P, 1962.

Hassrick, Royal B. *The Sioux: Life and Customs of a Warrior Society.* Norman: U of Oklahoma P, 1964.

Hymes, Dell. "Anthologies and Narrators." *Recovering the Word: Essays on Native American Literature.* Eds. Brian Swann and Arnold Krupat. Berkeley: U of California P, 1987. 113–28.

———. "Grizzly Woman Began to Kill People." *Traditional American Indian Literatures: Texts and Interpretations.* Ed. Karl Kroeber. Lincoln: U of Nebraska P, 1981.

———. *"In vain I tried to tell you."* Philadelphia: U of Pennsylvania P, 1981.

———. "Victoria Howard's 'Gitskux and His Older Brother': A Clackamas Chinook Myth." *Smoothing the Ground: Essays on Native American Oral Literature.* Ed. Brian Swann. Berkeley: U of California P, 1983. 129–70.

Jacobs, Melville. *The Content and Style of an Oral Literature: Clackamas Chinook Myths and Tales.* Chicago: U of Chicago P, 1959.

Jahner, Elaine. "Cognitive Style in Oral Literature." *Language and Style* 15 (1982): 32–51.

———. "Stone Boy: Persistent Hero." *Smoothing the Ground: Essays on Native American Oral Literature.* Ed. Brian Swann. Berkeley: U of California P, 1983. 171–86.

Krupat, Arnold. "Identity and Difference in the Criticism of Native American Literature." *Diacritics* 13 (1983): 2–13.

———. "Post-Structuralism and Oral Literature." *Recovering the Word: Essays on Native American Literature.* Eds. Brian Swann and Arnold Krupat. Berkeley: U of California P, 1987. 113–28.

———. *The Voice in the Margin: Native American Literature and the Canon.* Berkeley: U of California P, 1989.

Locke, Kevin. *Lakota Wiikijo Olowan.* 2 audiocassettes. Pipestone, Minnesota: Featherstone, FS-4001-C and FS-4004.

Lowie, Robert H. *Crow Texts.* Berkeley: U of California P, 1960.

Mails, Thomas E. *Fools Crow.* New York: Avon, 1979.

Mattina, Anthony. "North American Indian Mythography: Editing Texts for the Printed Page." *Recovering the Word: Essays on Native American Literature.* Eds. Brian Swann and Arnold Krupat. Berkeley: U of California P, 1987. 129–50.

Murray, Janette K. "Ella Deloria: A Biographical Sketch and Literary Analysis." Diss. U of North Dakota, 1974.

Nurge, Ethel, ed. *The Modern Sioux: Social Systems and Reservation Culture.* Lincoln: U of Nebraska P, 1970.

Olden, Sarah Emilia. *The People of Tipi Sapa.* Milwaukee: Morehouse, 1918.

Picotte, Agnes. *An Introduction to Basic Dakota, Lakota, and Nakota.* Chamberlain, South Dakota: Dakota Indian Foundation, 1987.

Powers, Marla N. *Oglala Women: Myth, Ritual, and Reality.* Chicago: U of Chicago P, 1986.

Powers, William K. *Oglala Religion.* Lincoln: U of Nebraska P, 1975.

———. *Sacred Language: The Nature of Supernatural Discourse in Lakota.* Norman: U of Oklahoma P, 1986.

Rice, Julian. *Lakota Storytelling: Black Elk, Ella Deloria, and Frank Fools Crow.* New York: Peter Lang, 1989.

Shakespeare, William. *The Complete Works.* Ed. Hardin Craig. Glenview, IL: Scott, Foresman, 1961.

Silko, Leslie. *Ceremony.* New York: Penguin, 1986.

Tedlock, Dennis. *The Spoken Word and the Work of Interpretation.* Philadelphia: U of Pennsylvania P, 1983.

Toelken, Barre and Tacheeni Scott. "Poetic Retranslation and the 'Pretty Languages' of Yellowman." *Traditional American Indian Literatures: Texts and Interpretations.* Ed. Karl Kroeber. Lincoln: U of Nebraska P, 1981.

Visions 1992: Oglala Lakota College. Published objectives. Kyle, South Dakota: Oglala Lakota College, 1987.

Walker, James R. *Lakota Belief and Ritual.* Eds. Raymond J. DeMallie and Elaine A. Jahner. Lincoln: U of Nebraska P, 1980.

———. *Lakota Myth.* Ed. Elaine A. Jahner. Lincoln: U of Nebraska P, 1983.

———. *Lakota Society.* Ed. Raymond J. DeMallie. Lincoln: U of Nebraska P, 1982.

Welch, James. *Fools Crow.* New York: Penguin, 1986.

Wiget, Andrew. "Telling the Tale: A Performance Analysis of a Hopi Coyote Story." *Recovering the Word: Essays on Native American Literature.* Eds. Brian Swann and Arnold Krupat. Berkeley: U of California P, 1987. 297–338.

Wissler, Clark. "Some Dakota Myths." *Journal of American Folklore* 20 (1907): 121–31, 195–206.

———. "The Whirlwind and the Elk in the Mythology of the Dakota." *Journal of American Folklore* 18 (1905): 257–68.

Index